C000245155

Boxwallah

Boxwallah

An epistolary journey from
Liverpool to India and back
between 1941 and 1945

TJS WILKINSON

Boxwallah

First Published in 2019 by FastPrint Publishing Peterborough, England.

Copyright © TJS Wilkinson, 2019

The moral right of TJS Wilkinson to be identified as the author of this work has been asserted by him in accordance with the Copyright, Designs and Patents Act 1988 and any subsequent amendments thereto.

All rights reserved. No part of this book may be reproduced in any form by photocopying or any electronic or mechanical means, including information storage or retrieval systems, without permission in writing from both the copyright owner and the publisher of the book.

Printed and bound in England by www.printondemand-worldwide.com

www.fast-print.net/bookshop

'History frightens me. It reminds me
Of me and you
And everyone else.'

Norman MacCaig:
Backward Look

'...in talking about the past we lie with
every breath we draw.'

William Maxwell:
So Long, See You Tomorrow

'TO SEEK THYSELF, SEARCH
FIRST FOR YOUR FATHER.'

Anon

My Mother.

My Father

How well do <u>you</u> know your parents?

The author's mother and father were married in 1941 and almost immediately his father was posted to the North-West Frontier of India with the Royal Engineers, not to return until 1945. During that time husband and wife wrote an almost daily correspondence, a fascinating collection of letters which demands to be read. As the months pass the strain of separation begins to take its toll, particularly on Stanley, isolated in an intriguing but alien land.

Years later (he and his brother never having had access to these exchanges) Tim decides to read these letters to his parents as ill health begins to dog their old age, but by doing this he unwittingly revives the tempests of the past.

But this book isn't simply a private family saga: in his narrative Tim Wilkinson investigates whether any of us really know our parents. This book has a universal appeal because it's a journey of discovery we all might benefit from, a search for one's parents shaped by their past.

PROLOGUE

If my memory serves me well, and of that I have some doubt, I only became interested in my parents' past when I was in my 40s and they were in their 70s. Visibly ailing, my father was losing weight rapidly, but refused to speak about his condition to anyone (although I did learn after his death that he had been making semi-secret visits to his doctor). My mother, as ever, kept a cheerful face on things, but even she seemed lost and vacant at times. In my limited way I pitied them.

And so I came up with a plan to cheer them up, to take their minds off whatever gloom was beginning to subsume them.

Ever since I was a child I had been fascinated by two containers which had followed the family from house to house; even now, as I write this, they reside in my own attic. One was a plain but attractive rosewood box (9 inches high, a foot wide and 7 inches deep) with a strong metal clasp; the other was a small, oblong, battered leather case, the kind carried around by travelling salesmen in the 30s and 40s. As a child I first came across them in our Liverpool home in the 50s, dumped in what was pretentiously

The battered attaché case containing my mother's letters.

The rosewood box containing my father's letters.

called 'the box room', a lumber room really used to store my father's architectural books, his 'Concrete Quarterly' periodicals and, hidden away behind all these, a battered copy of 'Lady Chatterley's Lover'. My brother and I were never allowed to investigate, or even mention, the box or the case.

At some point I became a keen philatelist, often taking solitary train trips to Exchange Station to visit McGoff's, the stamp shop in Moorfields, where I bought their £1 or £5 weight packets, a trove of unsorted stamps. Recognising this burgeoning interest, perhaps, my father told me one day that there were letters in the box room: letters 'Mummy and I wrote to each other in the war. I was in India, she was here in Liverpool. You can steam the stamps off if you want, but promise me not to read them'.

And so I set to, massing a range of exotically drab stamps from both India and Britain. One thing I did notice was that my father's letters were kept in the sturdy box, all chronologically arranged from the very first letter dated 26.7.41 (and mysteriously headed 'The Ship') up to the final telegram dated 24.5.45. The leather attaché case, the receptacle for my mother's letters, had no such order to it as if they had just been dumped there. There were hundreds of letters: they had written unstintingly to each other every two or three days over a period of almost four years. I remember once asking my mother about them and she simply said they were 'full of lovey-dovey stuff' hence of no interest to anyone, especially a young boy. Yet, this vast correspondence was moved from house to house guarding its secrets safely....until the containers were washed up, bobbing, on the shores of my curiosity.

My present idea, then, was to go through both sets of letters, perhaps making a précis of them. It would cheer my parents up if I read it out to them, I thought somewhat naively, would divert their minds from an uncertain future. At the back of my head, though, there was one niggling doubt: as an English teacher I frequently taught that wonderful short story 'Secrets' by Bernard Maclaverty. It describes how a young boy, despite dire warnings not to, steals and reads some private letters locked away in his great-aunt's bureau. Her secrets are out, and when she discovers the theft her reaction is crushing:

"'You are dirt", she hissed, "and always will be dirt. I shall remember this till the day I die"'.

I wanted my parents' approval for what I was embarking on, but was I opening a Pandora's Box?

Initially, there was plenty of resistance to what I was planning. I think my father sensed some kind of boyish mischief because my brother and I had spent lifetimes winding him up, trying to demolish his po-faced façade. My early attempts at coercion went something like this:

---These letters that are in the attic -- would you like me to go through them and make a summary?

--- Oh no, I don't think so.

--- But why are you keeping them? Who are they for? You haven't read them ever since they were put away, have you? Wouldn't you like to relive those days again?

---I think I'd like our memories to remain locked away.

This was an extraordinary thing for him to say, a man not known for his profundities. Constant badgering seemed to bear fruitless fruit, but one day I received a phone call summoning me to the house. As I entered the hall I could just make out the end of an argument.

--- Oh, Stan, what are you wearing a sports jacket on a day like this for?

The windows were wide open, mainly to let out the miasma of grilled kippers which were now my father's staple breakfast diet.

--- I'm happy. Leave me alone.

There he was, seated, buttoned up and secure. He looked frailer since I last saw him and, as a medieval commentator might have put it, clearly marked for death. Mother, in contrast, was summer-bloused, vital and kitcheny.

--- God, it stinks in here. Why do you eat those things?

--- The doctor said I should eat more fish, to build me up.

A whole school of kippers wouldn't make a ha'porth of difference, I thought.

--- Why did you phone?

--- I want to show you something. Let's sit down at the dining-room table. He took a small notebook out of the sideboard drawer, the sort a stenographer of old might have used.

--- Since you're so keen to go through our letters I thought I'd show you this. It's a diary I kept during my journey from Glasgow to Bombay in 1941.

--- Wow!

I took it with great care and leafed through its neatly written pages.

--- This is amazing! But where's it been hiding? I've never seen it before.

--- I keep it in my study, he said, proprietorially.

---Why haven't Peter and I seen it?

--- I didn't think you'd be interested.

True enough, I thought. In my defective (or selective) memory I couldn't remember Peter or myself ever asking him about his life in India, nor did he volunteer

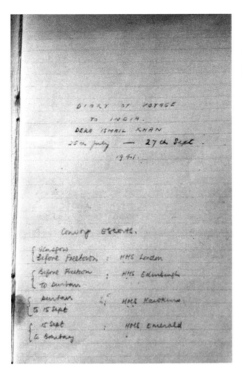

The title page of the diary of my father's voyage to India.

any information. There were photo albums full of sepia studies of exotically dressed tribesmen, or distant views of what might have been the Himalayas; some were of him in uniform. But few photographs were labelled, few explanations forthcoming. He had also brought back some souvenirs: a native table-cloth, garishly coloured and spotted with circular glass 'mirrors' the size of 5p coins; a tribesman's costume, along with a leather shoulder holster; a vicious-looking kukri, daggers...and two clay-coloured Tibetan Mani stones. These were often placed alongside rivers or roads as offerings to the local gods, and on them were endlessly carved the mantra 'Om mani padme hum': 'the jewel in the lotus'. My father once joked (a rare thing) that the family of whoever stole these wayside stones would be cursed forever. But these objects were mostly just **there** as part of the household. Look around your

The two Mani Stones

parents' house: would you honestly be interested enough to ask where they got that ornament from? That vase?

--- Of course I'm interested. Does that mean I've been given the go-ahead?

Mother suddenly got up.

--- Where are you going, Phyl?

--- I must feed the birds.

--- What, now? We're talking.

--- I can hear. I'm only in the kitchen.

Suddenly I had an idea.

--- Can I read your first ever letter? Now?

--- Oh, go on then. Come and sit down, Phyl.

Suddenly he seemed enthusiastically proud. I rushed upstairs and found the letter easily. The envelope was postmarked 'Glasgow 5-pm 27 JLY 1941'.

--- It's simply headed 'The Ship'.

--- Yes, it was the Cameronia belonging to the Anchor Line. We were one of four troopships. The censor wouldn't have allowed us to name the ship in any correspondence.

--- I see. *My dearest darling Phyl....* [I began]

Here are just a few lines before I leave – I am not sure whether it will get ashore or not but I am writing nevertheless because it relieves my mind and concentrates my thoughts on you in a more concrete form.

The train left Halifax last night at 10pm and toured all round England during the night. Eventually it reached Glasgow at 10am. The boat is quite nice and the officers have been placed in beautiful 1st class cabins. In my cabin there are three other officers as well as myself. Oh gosh I would give anything in the world to exchange all this for the company of my own darling – nay [nay!] I would exchange every man aboard for your presence. Oh my love it would have been magnificent if you could have travelled with me – but cheer up, when the War is over we shall accompany each other to all parts of the world. Yes Phyl we must protect ourselves in every way possible in order to enjoy OUR future happiness. I know that I am going to take every available precaution and safety device [?!] in order to give you this happiness which you deserve.

My dear be good, be careful and keep out of danger. Don't stay in Liverpool because I am sure that when the Germans are being defeated they will bomb our cities and ports with tremendous vigour. You will be doing me a duty – a loving duty if you live in the country in safety.

I am glad you knelt down and prayed in Halifax because I believe in prayer and I know that God answers. Pray to Him Phyl for your protection and I shall do the same for you. Periodically call at the bank and see how the money stands in the account and if you want to adopt an orphan child [what???] *to give you an interest and happiness, you have my consent. While I have breath in my body I vow to God and you that you will always receive my loyal and true love, affection and devotion.*

> *'May God bless you and keep you.*
> *May God lighten His face to shine*
> *upon you and protect you always'.*

I am Phyl

Your most loving hubby

Stan

There was a long, awkward silence. As I was reading it out I felt my excitement ebbing away with every well honed syllable, with every precisely constructed sentence. 'Hubby' was the only warm word in the letter. Mother was gazing out of the window, Father was staring at his hands. What was I supposed to say? That if every letter was like this (formal, stuffy, creepily religious) I might as well stop right here and now. And what was that Brontean guff about an orphan child?

--- Well, that's an enticing start, I lied. I can't wait to read more.

--- Take them home with you then. See how you get on.

--- Thanks.

I tried to be as sincere as possible and I **was** genuinely excited: the brief flick through the ship's diary allowed me to glimpse another side to him, a sort of freed-up, unbuttoned persona. But why such a formal tone? Was that how they wrote then? And it was almost as if he was talking to a retarded child. Mother then interrupted my thoughts.

--- I've made a quiche. Would you like some? We could have it in the garden.

And I had an idea.

--- OK, but let me read out **your** first letter. It seems unfair just to read out father's.

--- Whatever you want. Tea or coffee? You look for the letter and I'll get the lunch ready.

I went off and rummaged in the leather case eventually finding what I wanted. The letter was addressed to 2nd Lieutenant Stanley Wilkinson and postmarked 'Reading 5pm 16 SEP 1941'.

--- Mother, this is postmarked Reading. Why was that?

--- I went to live with the Meadowcrofts in Reading for a year.

--- Who were they?

--- They were my best friends at the time. Well, George was. He used to be a work colleague before the war.

I was the first to finish lunch, and while I read out the letter my parents were tucking in to her delicious walnut tart.

--- 'The letter is headed '249 Whitley Wood Road, Reading, Berkshire.'

My own darling

At last I can write to you after all this time waiting and waiting [it was better already!]. *I have received seven letters so far from you, but two came this morning giving me permission to write.*

After you had left Halifax that terrible Friday night I went straight to bed, got up early and came away Saturday morning. I came (as you know) back to Liverpool. I pondered and pondered where I should go to live. At last I sat down and wrote to Reading. I received a letter back saying that if I could wait 2 weeks they [the Meadowcrofts] would willingly come for me in the car. So you see darling I stuck to the promise I gave you. It was a magnificent car journey through Oxford and Kenilworth. Well! Here I am and here I will stay.

It is a beautiful place – quite safe – they have never heard the siren more than a couple of times. Our house is up on a hill in the country. I have a lovely view from my bedroom window across fells and forests...and the air is so pure and fresh! Mr and Mrs Meadowcroft are both most kind to me and I am waited on hand and foot.

--- Oh, it was lovely there, Stan.

--- I'm glad you took my advice.

But just then we heard footsteps and a knock at the back door. It was the vicar. My father seemed to perk up at his arrival...as he usually did whenever he encountered people of, let us say, local standing.

--- Hello, Douglas, he suddenly piped up, miraculously more effusive and cheerful than he had been all morning. You're just in time for coffee.

This feature of my father's was something which always irked Peter and me: often sour and uncommunicative around his immediate family, he would instantaneously become jovial and deferential, almost fawning and obsequious, to these people who, we felt, hardly deserved this attention. Why did **they** merit this treatment and not us? Father was about to be made Diocesan Architect for the Episcopalian Church on Royal Deeside: he regarded this appointment as a huge honour, and would give him something to occupy him in his retirement. In truth, he was to be treated as a landowner would treat a menial, but this didn't really bother him, it was the kudos which appealed.

Anyway, I quickly made my excuses and scarpered home with the letters.

1941

1

Back home, I felt quite invigorated by the freshness of my mother's letter. I returned to its chattiness: *'Yesterday George took us out for the day in his car. We went to Portsmouth via Eton (saw the famous college) Windsor (saw castle) and Ascot (saw the racecourse). We went miles around but lo and behold your silly old Phyl had to keep stopping to be sick. My face was green when I got home.* [All her life my mother suffered from travel sickness].

Darling I dream about you nearly every night and when I wake to find I am alone and you are thousands of miles away from me I just put my head in to the pillow and sob my poor old heart away. Oh darling I hope you don't get these heartbreaking dreams, but we are so alike in every respect, that it is only natural that we do. [She then fantasises about being allowed to visit her husband in India]....*I can picture it now. Stan standing there in his tropical outfit, while his Phyl walks into his arms – her face a dark shade of green after being sick all the way !!!! Darling I have bought quite a few nice clothes. I bought a mac, a riding coat, also I have several pairs of superb stockings (pure silk) I got from Marble Arch, London, one Saturday. I feel quite smart and well dressed in my grey costume with burgundy shoes (the ones you helped me to choose).*

Ah, this is pure Mother. Throughout her life she had an incorrigible obsession for buying clothes, much to my father's chagrin – Oh, Phyl, what do you want another skirt/dress/blouse/pair of shoes for? Yes, I would look forward to more of her letters. But it was my father's diary which enticed me more. It was headed:

DIARY OF VOYAGE TO INDIA
DERA ISMAIL KHAN
25th July – 27th September 1941

25th July 1941 Friday

10.00pm. Left Halifax by train. Went to Glasgow, Scotland, via Wakefield, Normanton, Holbeck (Leeds) Shipley, Skipton, Carlisle, Kilmarnock. Back into Shipley Station to pick up more troops. [Oh God. Pure facts. No feelings.]

26th July

Arrived Glasgow 10.00am.

Boarded H.M.T. Cameronia (Anchor Line) at 10.45am. H.M.T.Cameronia a passenger vessel of 16,400 tons, rather small but looked sturdy. Later in the morning allotted cabins, mine being A Deck No.65. Cabin contained four bunks, mine being a top one beneath the porthole. Companions are fine fellows. Sent a letter to my wife. [This must have been the letter I read out to them earlier. But 'To my wife'! This is a diary, for God's sake...why not 'To Phyl'?] *In the afternoon luggage came aboard. Meals were excellent. After dinner went a stroll around boat but felt rather lonely and became rather depressed and worried about Phyl.* [Ah, that's better!]

11.00pm retired to bed very tired and fretful.

27th July

7.35am Arose and shaved. Spent morning strolling around ship. In the afternoon at 4.15pm had lifeboat stations drill. Retired to bed at 11.15pm. My mind was on my wife all day.

28th July

7.40am Washed and shaved. In the afternoon read until 4.30pm then went a route march with the other officers of my draught [sic]. *Walked towards Renfrew. 9.30pm saw the tail end of a concert for the troops. The padre finished the concert by asking everybody to sing 'Abide With Me'. After the hymn he prayed for the wives of all the men present. I felt very lonely and downhearted.* [That's more like it! Some emotion at last.]

29th July

Wrote a letter to Phyl and her father. I was forced ['forced'?] *to write to father because I was rather upset about Phyl staying in Liverpool and I thought he could help.* [Reading the diary so far, I felt puzzled by his authorial 'voice'. He seems to be explaining his actions to some mysterious third party. It was an odd dislocation, I thought.]

3.00pm Left Glasgow. Both sides of the Clyde workmen gathered to cheer us on our way.

7.00pm Anchored outside Port Glasgow facing Rothesay and Greenock.

30th July

10.30am Boat drill. In front of the Cameronia the Empress of Australia cast anchor. To the left the Windsor Castle, both ships appeared to be full of troops.

2.30pm Counted 40 ships of all types and sizes anchored around the Cameronia. Whether all these ships will move with the convoy remains to be seen.

31st July

During the night many of the ships in the Clyde had moved – apparently sailed on the morning tide. After luncheon had a short lecture on URDU.

1st August

7.10am Arose and did PT from 7.15 to 7.35.

At 10.30am the Action Stations sounded i.e. three rings on the ship's bell. This was only a practice. On action station the decks are cleared for action. The 3" and 6" guns are manned also the anti-aircraft weapons – such as Lewis, Bren, etc. All the remainder of the personnel go then to their respective cabins and close all portholes.

10.40am Boat stations sounded which was a continuous ringing of the ship's bell. All personnel then proceed in an orderly manner to their respective boat stations, mine being No.3 Station, Starboard side. At the station men and officers line up in six ranks with the officer in front nearest to the rail. Each section of 5 lines (i.e. 30 men including 5 officers) are commanded by a captain.

2nd August

7.30am Arose and discovered I was too late for PT. Two of the other fellows had got up and left myself and another chap asleep. They thought it rather a pity to get us up. At 4.00pm along with 12 other officers had to report to Lt/Col Barclay Smith for not attending PT. Thought of an excuse which did not involve the other fellows who let us sleep on. Orders posted up that we had to sleep in our full battledress during the next four nights – also that there would be no more post to England. It seems that we will be moving on tonight's tide. God bless Phyl until we meet again.

7.10pm First boat of the convoy commenced to move down the Clyde.

7.45pm Cameronia weighed anchor. Altogether in convoy I was able to count 18 vessels, mostly liners. On moving I felt a lump come into my throat and somehow wanted my eyes to absorb as much of the land and scenery before nightfall because I wanted to see as much as possible of my dear country. It is a horrible feeling to see the land you loved and the people who lived there slowly move away. Farewell my love. Farewell.

3rd August
_____

There were 9 destroyers, one cruiser and one auxiliary cruiser escorting the 18 vessels in the convoy.

During the early part of the morning a huge box kite was flown from the rear mast. This acts as an anti-aircraft measure against dive-bombing.

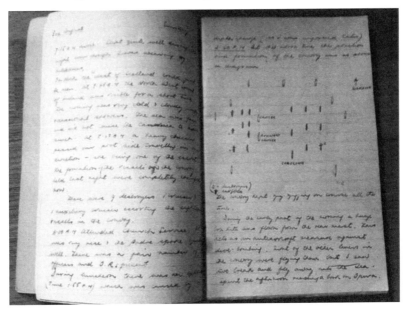

A detail from my father's sea diary showing arrangements of the convoy.

4th August

7.15am Arose and went to boat deck for PT. Not many turned up because PT is now voluntary. The sea had quite a swell. The Cameronia was pitching quite a lot.

10.30am One of the destroyers commenced firing into the sky with anti-aircraft guns – white and black clouds of smoke could be seen in the sky. A number of ships on the port side commenced machine gunning. Whether this was only practice or not I could not say.

After dinner went to my cabin and talked. Listened to the 9pm news and felt relieved when the announcer said there had been no air-raids on the North West. Oh! I hope my dear Phyl has left Liverpool for a nice quiet place in the country.

5th August

After breakfast commenced washing dirty underwear and handkerchiefs. Thanks to Rinso the job wasn't too bad – except the water was rather cold and I put too much Rinso in it and could not get the Rinso out of my clothes. [This episode was rather typical of my father, a man who could not even boil an egg successfully.] *Felt rather dismal all day.*

6th August

12.30pm While playing deck quoits with four officers I did not know the mist suddenly cleared and the sun shone brightly, but lo and behold there wasn't another ship in sight. Had we lost the convoy? At 1.40pm the other ships were sighted away on the horizon waiting for us.

7.10am Arose. Weather very misty again. Throughout the night the ships could be heard blowing their sirens. The escort was now much smaller – in fact there was only one cruiser and one destroyer left. After dinner studied concrete until 10.15pm then went a stroll on deck. I saw a magnificent sight. There was a clear star-lit sky and a full moon. The reflection of the moonlight on the water was one of the finest sights I have ever seen. The air was balmy. Somehow I felt that if Phyl was only with me how much more beautiful the sight would have been to me.

Elsie, Jimmy and my mother.

A studio picture of Nanny, my mother
and Jimmy taken around 1924.

My brother Peter.

My mother with my father's parents.   Nanny, Fan in her carriage, and James my grandfather.

2

I sensed a kind of growth as this diary went on: the short, fearful and factual entries of the first few days were becoming more expansive and he was now writing in complete sentences imbued with feelings. But at this point I will leave him, sailing towards the Azores, swatting up on his Urdu and the intricacies of reinforced concrete (his speciality), because I feel it's time the reader learned a little about my parents' backgrounds.

My father, born in 1917, was the only child of John Wilkinson (1888-1958) and Elizabeth (nee Seddon) (1888-1950). The former, a somewhat dour man, was a builder's labourer and his semi-literate wife was a devout Methodist, my brother remembering a harmonium in their home, the common accompaniment to Sunday hymn-singing in those days. Home was Premier St. in Anfield and clearly they only knew great poverty. At the age of 16 he entered Liverpool University and graduated with 1st Class Honours in Architecture. He was called up in March 1941 and married my mother at St. Saviour's Church, Everton, on April 12th 1941. In June he received a commission in the Royal Engineers and was sent to India almost immediately. Now, I do not know how much his humble background, the fact that he was an only child, or his braininess affected his outlook on life but as I matured I increasingly recognised in him a, to me, crippling sense of shame about his origins.

My mother came from a similarly deprived background but, polar opposite to my father, her attitude to her family was always one of great pride ; perhaps as a consequence, my father always nursed a barely disguised animosity towards" her people", as he called them. In later life, visits by my grandmother or my mother's brother, Jimmy, or sister, Elsie, were preceded by a week of brooding silences, gruff responses and seething anger. The visits themselves were punctuated by more silences and a stiff coldness.

My mother's father was James Moore (1886-1951) whose Irish forebears fled the potato famine in the 1850s and settled in the Liverpool slums. By all accounts a very amusing man, he was a labourer with Liverpool Tramways Corporation for 51 years. My mother's mother Agnes (nee Clark) (1886-1975) had Kirkcudbrightshire roots. They had four children: Elsie (1905-95), Frances (always called 'Fan')(1908-96), my mother (1918-2013) and Jimmy (1921-98). As a very young child Fan contracted polio and as a result lost the use of her legs. Brain-damaged, too, she would remain a four year old forever. Almost to the very end of her life, my thin, fragile-looking grandmother cared for her at home.

Home was 31, Rockley St. in Kirkdale, Liverpool 4, a two-up two-down terraced house with a backyard and outside toilet. As a child I loved that house. Similar to Seamus Heaney's own attitude to his Aunt Mary's home I recognised what *he* did:

'And here is love

Like a tinsmith's scoop

Sunk past its gleam

In the meal-bin.'

Elsie, much older than my mother and Jimmy, was a motherly sister, acting as a foil to my mother's skittish and often frivolous ways. As the only boy in the family, and the youngest, Jimmy was always the apple of his parents' eyes. He and my mother got on famously.

My parents first met when my father, collecting for the University Rag Week, entered the Co-op offices where my mother was a clerk. Apparently they fell in love immediately.

Time passing allows you to generalise about the past, to make assumptions, even to make up stories, turning fiction into fact. My father's odious attitude to his wife's family culminated in his refusal (based on an alleged illness) to travel to Jimmy's funeral in 1998. Fact. What on earth happened so long ago to warrant this complete derogation of duty (as I saw it)? Somehow, somehow, I hoped this diary and these letters would shed some light on the family's dark corners. A thought even crossed my mind that this could be the reason my father was so reluctant to let Peter and myself read the correspondence in the first place. In the past, direct questions about his attitude to the Moore family met with obfuscation --- It was a long time ago.....I can't remember now....It doesn't concern you. My mother was almost as unforthcoming, and Jimmy, himself, was reluctant to speak about it at all, perhaps not wanting to create a division between father and sons.

I was in a quandary, though. I was losing sight of the main purposes behind my investigation of the letters: to take my father's mind off his debilitating illness; to give them both pleasure in their dying days. How would he react if I discovered some horrible truth lurking, buried, in the two containers?

Yet I decided to carry on because my parents clearly revelled in my readings. In his eyes I could see my father transported to what he regarded as his halcyon days; my mother, too, could experience family life again in Liverpool. We had motivation.

So I cracked on.

3

1pm   One of the islands of the Azores was seen on the starboard side. The weather is becoming hot and sultry.

11.15pm   Retired to bed – heat terrific in the cabin – door open and fans full on but still no air.

11th August

7.10am   Arose. Tropical kit was worn for the first time: felt very cool in aertex shirt and khaki shorts.

2.30pm   Lecture by Dr Fava, captain in RAMC, on Tropical Diseases and Hygiene. He made some very interesting facts about disease generally, especially malaria.

5pm   Watched boxing by the men on the boat deck until 6pm.

7pm   Dinner. Wore khaki drill tunic and slacks for the first time. Felt very very hot probably due to the newness of the clothes.

12th August

After lunch the sun was so hot I wore my topee most of the afternoon.

4.30pm   Saw quite a large number of flying fish – these looked like herrings and seemed to skim over the top of the water for quite some distance.

10.40pm   Retired to bed. Finished off letter to Phyl and read it through. Strange how words fail to express what is in the heart.

13th August

As soon as dinner was over went a stroll around the deck in the dark. I mingled amongst the ordinary men on their own decks. I listened carefully to their talk and I purposely tacked myself on to groups for this purpose. After about one hour of this I came to the conclusion that most of the talk was about women and sex – especially the latter – this sort of thing absolutely makes me sick and I left feeling rather depressed and sad. Retired to cabin at 8.45pm and studied concrete until 9.45pm.

[When I was reading this extract to them my father became fidgety. I knew why. Sex was a subject never broached by us as a family. When I was a child, I remember, any TV programmes containing 'smut' were greeted by the words, 'Oh, turn that rubbish off, Phyl!' Benny Hill was anathema. Programmes depicting the working class were never tolerated either: *Steptoe and Son, Till Death Us Do Part* (the list seemed endless)...and when my grandmother visited she was cruelly banned from watching her favourite show, *Coronation Street.*]

14th August

During the morning 5 more destroyers and a flying boat joined the convoy. Received news today that letters would be collected for the return mail at Freetown – very good news – because it meant Phyl would receive a letter before I got to India.

16th August

8pm Met Guard Sergeant for inspection of Guards on the ship. Gosh this was a terrible job in the bowels of the ship – the heat was almost beyond my endurance. How the men sleep down in those converted holds is beyond me. At one place where there was a thermometer it read practically 100F.

17th August

6.30am Saw the coast of Africa for the first time – Sierre Leone. After breakfast the convoy steamed into Freetown Harbour. Immediately the boat stopped, dozens of canoes full of natives came from the shore. Some of these sold fruit while others dived for coins. The negroes sold bananas, mangoes and various other fruits.

8pm Quinine parade. Freetown is very bad for malaria, hence the precaution.

18th August

7.10am Arose. The weather was too bad for PT. Rain was simply coming down in torrents and torrents.

8.15pm Went to a concert given by the troops for the officers. At 8.30pm I left because of its 'blueness'. ['Oh, turn that rubbish off, Phyl!']

19th August

Both yesterday and today oil ships and water ships had been beside our ship filling her up with fuel and fresh water. After lunch studied concrete. Later in the afternoon became very depressed and longed for Phyl. This is a horribly monotonous and wearisome kind of existence, especially when there is life and love and happiness at home with my precious wife.

---*Was this a real low point for you? I asked.*

He nodded almost imperceptibly and said, 'Remember, I was only 23...a mere boy. Go on.'

21st August
_____

Read all morning until 1.00pm. Never seen such torrential rain in all my life.

11.00am Waited outside Lt/Col Berkeley-Smith's cabin for particulars about my educational and military career.

1.30pm The ship's anchor was weighed.

8.00pm Went to the first meeting of the Shakespearean Society. Read parts from Henry IV Part 2. Decided to produce Macbeth as the most suitable play. Retired to bed at midnight. Longed for Phyl. If I get into a good station I think I will send for her.

--- What do you mean by a 'station'? I asked.

--- Well, the interview was to help decide whereabouts in India I was going to be sent to.

--- Like a posting.

--- That's right.

23rd August
_____

Crossed the Equator at approximately 2100 hrs.

28th August
_____

Had a very nasty cold all day – made me feel quite rotten – slightly sore throat. Longed and longed and longed terribly for Phyl.

I stopped again. It had started raining heavily and Mother was looking at the washing dripping on the clothes line.

--- I must get the washing in, she said, and went through to the kitchen. There she put an old jacket over her head and went out into the garden.

--- Father, I notice your diary entries are becoming shorter, terser, and you've missed out complete days in places.

--- Well, I think the routine was getting to me. Besides, we were nearing our destination and I must have been thinking of the journey which lay ahead.

An awkward silence descended until Mother finally resumed her seat after rearranging her hair.

30th August

11.30am Went along to the ship's hospital for inoculation. Had two in left arm, one T.A.B. and one T.T. After lunch went to a cinema show called 'Oil for the Lamps of China'. Began to feel a little shaky. Head started to ache. Went up on boat deck and saw an albatross flying behind the Vollander. Felt worse after dinner.

31st August

Did not sleep all night – pain in my head was terrible. After breakfast returned to bed and slept until 1.00pm. Felt better.

9.00pm Went to a meeting of the Shakespearean Society. Given the part of Fleance in Macbeth.

--- Not the biggest part in the play! I said sarcastically.

--- No, he chuckled. Not many lines to learn.

1st September

Sea choppy. There was quite a swell which made the Cameronia pitch and toss a little. We were nearing the Cape of Good Hope, hence the reason for the very heavy sea.

2nd September
_____

Cape Town is supposed to be 40 miles away. The remaining ships in the convoy were dispersed.

Felt very lonely and down-hearted since dinner tonight, especially when I seem to be left on my own because I do not play cards, smoke or gamble. Nobody satisfies my power of friendship except my dear Phyl. Whenever I am without her I feel very uncomfortable and unhappy with other people. Oh may we meet soon or else I shall go completely mad.

--- So you did go mad!

--- Just get on with it.

Gargled twice during the evening with TCP because my tonsils felt very sore indeed.

3rd September
_____

Got up with a terrible throat.

11.30am   Went along to see the doctor. He said that my glands were inflamed and told me to gargle with water as hot as I could bear.

5th September
_____

On awakening was informed that DURBAN was in sight and only about 5 miles away. Went up on deck. The landscape of the city was wonderful. Told to pack by 11.45am. In Durban docks saw the new Mauretania [which was launched in Birkenhead in 1938].

2.30pm   Paraded on quay.

3.00pm   Boarded transport wagons and taken 8 miles outside Durban to a transit camp to await the new ship.

3.30pm Arrived at Caerwood Camp. Put in tents, two officers in each. Next to us was an Italian Prisoner of War camp – felt sorry for the poor devils!!

6.00pm Went to Durban on Army Transport lorry. Wandered around and went to the Maypole Café for dinner.

8.00pm Went to the pictures and saw 'Billy the Kid'.

11.35pm Caught special troop train back to camp.

--- Do you want me to stop at all?

--- What do you think, Phyl?

--- Carry on if you want. I'll start getting lunch ready. I'll be listening.

6th September

Spent the morning cleaning buttons etc. After lunch went into town. The architecture was very modern and followed the American style. Many of the stores, principal buildings and hotels were over ten storeys high. Came across a snake zoo. I touched a gigantic python six feet in length and 4 inches thick. [At this point my mother, with her lifelong fear of all insects and snakes, uttered a yelp of horror.]

7th September

Took train to Durban.

7.00pm Went to St.Paul's Church which was packed with people. Today was a national day of prayer throughout the Empire.

8th Septmber

Took train to Durban.

2.30pm   Met three fellow officers and went a tour in a private car driven by a very nice and wealthy lady. The tour consisted of visiting an old fort, a drive along the beach for a couple of miles, aerodrome, the huge park belt where there were comparatively tame monkeys. You could feed them by hand.

Arrived back in the city at 5.15pm.

8.00pm   Went to the Playhouse to see 'The Ghost of St.Michael's' with Will Hay.'

9th September

6.30am   Boarded army transport and proceeded towards the docks.

7.50am Arrived at the docks only to find that no boat had arrived. Told we could go in to town for breakfast but must return by 9 o'clock. I dashed off because I had heard there was a shop which would send silk stockings home if you bought them there.

--- I remember those arriving! Mother shouted out from the kitchen.

With good fortune I arrived at the shop quite quickly and with beating heart found it was open. Bought two pairs of really beautiful stockings which almost finished off £1.

11.15 am   H.M.T. Britannic sailed in. Gosh I felt delighted about going aboard her.

1.05pm Commenced to cast off ropes and move out of the dock.

10th September

After breakfast commenced to make my long thin drill trousers into shorts.

Today the convoy sailed 384 miles. After dinner played cards until 10.30pm.

--- I thought you just said that you didn't play cards.

--- I was only being sociable I think.

--- Mmmm.

12th September

After breakfast attended lecture by Major Burnett on 'Indian Customs' – a very interesting and amusing lecture. I learnt that the Britannic was built in 1928 and is capable of 20 knots.

13th September

11.15am – 12 Urdu lesson as usual.

17th September

Wrote to Phyl and felt really happy for the first time since leaving Durban. Heat oppressive today.

19th September

10.30am Lecture on Venereal Diseases by a doctor in R.A.M.C. Did not enjoy lecture one bit because the 'actives' treated the whole thing as a joke which to my mind was going too far.

20th September

...

--- I think that's enough for today. Don't you, Phyl?

---But why? You've almost reached Bombay.

Whether the subject of venereal disease ['Turn that rubbish off, Phyl!'] had sparked this sudden interruption I don't know. Anyway, he brought a physical end to the session by stalking off to the toilet.

4

--- Right, are you ready then?

Next day, as a lover of routines, Father again parked us around the dining-room table.

--- This shouldn't take too long, I said. I'll have to stop when you arrive in India anyway because that's where your diary ends and the letters begin – and I haven't read those yet.

--- Carry on then.

--- Are you enjoying it so far?

--- Very much so, aren't we, Phyl?

--- Oh yes.

--- Right. Here we go then.

20th September (again)

7.00am Arose, washed and shaved. There was no sign of land yet visible. After breakfast watched numerous native fishing vessels sailing by – DHOWS. The ships in the convoy were all in line in the following order: Aranda, Stirling Castle, Britannic, Strathallan, Windsor Castle.

9.00 Land was sighted.

10.00 Bombay and the surrounding country was plainly visible.

11.00 Convoy sailed into harbour and the Britannic cast anchor.

2.30pm Lt/Col of the Indian Royal Engineer services came aboard and issued forms to each officer to fill in giving qualifications and military experience etc. After dinner went to see Lt/Col again who had made the various postings. He informed me that I was going in Works Services (which is just what I wanted) at Waziristan on the N.W. Frontier, building defences and fortifications. Felt very elevated and uplifted.

22nd September

11am Docked at Ballard Pier and it was very hot indeed.

3.45pm   Went ashore to the Customs and I was given particulars of the train (for officers only) I was to travel on. From the Embarkation Officer I then got hold of a native porter who carried the baggage to the platform.

--- That porter was called a 'boxwallah'.

--- What?

--- That was his job, to carry our boxes and luggage.

--- I've heard of a punkah-wallah. Wasn't there one in *'It Ain't Half Hot, Mum'*?

--- That's right. A punkah-wallah operated the fan to cool Westerners in India. Originally it was a palm leaf he wafted using his feet – that was in the days of the Raj though. Later the leaf was replaced by a long piece of cloth like a curtain. There were other wallahs. A chai-wallah made and sold tea, a dhobi-wallah…

--- OK, I've got the picture.

--- They were menials. The lowest of the low. Dirt, in fact.

--- And the boxwallah?

--- Long ago a boxwallah sold things from the boxes he usually carried on his back. A sort of pedlar.

Then he paused as if in thought.

--- You're **our** boxwallah.

--- Thanks very much.

--- Carting my Indian boxes from house to house.

--- Am I dirt, then?

--- Don't be daft.

--- Can I get on, please? We're nearly finished.

22nd September (continued)

Weiss [a friend from on board the ship] and I decided to spend a little time in Bombay itself and get a meal there. On the road from the station we were accosted by various beggars and vendors. The educated natives seemed to be haughty and cynical. Wandered around until we came to a 1st class café in the Green Hotel. Arrived back at the station at 8.45pm where there was a tremendous messing around getting a berth. Eventually four of us were fixed up in a compartment which had a private lavatory and shower attached. The train moved off at 12.30pm.

23rd September

7.00am Chai-wallah brought tea and toast.

7.30am Arose, washed and shaved.

8.30am Went to the restaurant car for breakfast. There are no corridors on the train so consequently you have to get out at a station and walk along to the restaurant car. Had porridge, fish, bacon and eggs, marmalade and toast.

Cost 2 rupees. After lunch the train went through scrubland and bush – saw monkeys, flamingos, herons, cardinals etc. During dinner we were pestered with moths and insects of all sorts.

--- You've listed all the stations you passed. Were you sitting there, notebook in hand, jotting down every blinking stop?

--- Why not? It was a new world to me. A new experience.

24th September

The whole land was now very dry and parched. Saw many camels, monkeys, and oxen turning water-wheels. Arrived at New Delhi at 12.15pm. Removed baggage in order to find another compartment nearer the top of the train since the last couple of coaches were being left behind.

25th September

2.00am Awakened by much shouting and noise. Discovered it was Lahore, a place where a large number of officers of my draught [sic] were bound. Suddenly a railway official (a native) popped his head around the corner and informed myself and another officer that we would have to change coaches since this one was not going on to Rawalpindi. Gosh what a mix-up.

12.30pm Arrived at Rawalpindi. The next train to Mari Indus was not until 9.20pm so I wandered around in a tonga and bought a few odds and ends.

26th September

6.55am Arrived at Mari Indus station.

[My father's diary ended here, never to be resumed. He perhaps thought that letters home now served his purpose better. The final stages of his journey are described in a letter dated '2.10.41'.]

'At Mari Indus station eleven officers were put in a second class compartment designed to take four. You can imagine what it was like with the luggage piled up in the middle. The heat was terrific by ten o'clock. The distance to Bannu is only 87 miles but it takes the train (narrow gauge –2' 6") eight hours. It is nicknamed 'The Heat Stroke Express'.

When we arrived at Bannu there was nobody there to meet us, so we took a tonga to the military camp. There we were directed to the Garrison Engineer's Office. He was not expecting us but he immediately telephoned C.R.E.D.I.K. who assured him that two new officers were coming and that he (the C.R.E.) would come to Bannu the next morning to interview us. We were then shown our quarters for the night which were in a Rest Bungalow. This was a grand place, Phyl, full of fans etc. I had a bedroom to myself.

This is a very wild place out here, especially the tribal people who shoot officers quite often. Next morning I was interviewed by Lt/Col Whitehead who appointed me ASSISTANT GARRISON ENGINEER, DARA ISMAIL KHAN on the banks of the River Indus. Just after 3pm I left Bannu in the Lt/Col's car with an escort of 8 armed native troops. Three hours later we arrived in D.I.K. and I was given very pleasant quarters. My long, long journey was over.

All my washing is done by a man called a dhobi or dhobi-wallah. There is no sanitation here, consequently chambers are used which are called 'thunder boxes'. These are emptied by a very low caste of people. My immediate chief, the Garrison Engineer, is an Indian but [!] a really splendid fellow. He was educated in England and holds a B Sc from London University. He is Captain P.R. Ahuja. The job is not too bad but I have got to deal with native contractors and native labour. All my instructions are done through an Indian overseer who talks English and Urdu. We have to sleep under mosquito nets because of insects. Last night a gigantic creature got into my bedroom –it had a black body the size of the top of a teacup and a big head like a cockroach. Crikey, it made a shiver down my spine.'

And there, for a time, we must leave my father, now safely garrisoned.

5

There was little doubt that the diary readings had a generally beneficial effect on my parents, albeit briefly. There were frequent curry evenings for the whole family (my mother excelled at curries and they were often so hot that sweat used to trickle down my face) and my father even dug out his photo albums to show his doting grand-daughters, but they seemed disinterested as, indeed, were his own children at that age. My brother Peter approved of what I was doing so that was an added incentive to continue, but what I had embarked on was quite a task: I had only read one tiny diary and two letters so far. I was an English teacher whose every breathing moment was spent marking, or so it seemed: how could I find the time?

There was another factor to consider: when he was Professor of Architecture my father was steeped in work, and as a visiting examiner vetting degree courses he flew about the country with alarming regularity. Now retired, and with a rapidly dwindling private practice, there seemed little enough to occupy his days : so my parents had constructed a weekly routine which consisted of the weekly shop at Sainsbury's in Aberdeen, the Wednesday visit to the bank to collect my mother's allowance (all her life she received this weekly housekeeping money) and wherever they went they always had to rush home to see 'Countdown'. They always went abroad twice a year, always with Saga, to Spain, Portugal, Malta or Yugoslavia. The dead days in between needed to be spiced up, and this was where the letters came in. That was my incentive;

besides, I selfishly hoped for 'discoveries' buried in the past.

My best plan, I thought, was to read out extracts from each set of letters covering a relatively short period of time. This, I hoped, would keep them separately interested. About a fortnight later we reconvened.

6

--- Mother, I began, after we'd sat down in our customary positions around the table, 'I know you're expecting me to start with **your** letters, but I want to go a bit further with Father's so that he is finally established in his station. You don't mind?

--- You're in charge. I don't mind at all.

--- Thanks. You won't have long to wait.

13th October 1941

My dearest and most precious darling,

While I am writing this letter there is a terrific thunderstorm raging outside. First of all it started at 7.00pm with a colossal sandstorm. I could see the sand coming towards Mari Indus in the form of a huge black cloud. Suddenly it struck the village with a mighty roar. Sand was flying past at such a speed and such a thickness that it was absolutely impossible to see a few feet ahead. After the sandstorm the lightning and thunder started. The lightning here is fork and you can see the path of the lightning zigzagging and forking across the sky. The flashes are continuous and I could easily carry on with this letter without the electric light.

This morning I was told that an epidemic of cholera had broken out in Kalabagh, a place just across the River Indus from here. Consequently I decided to have an injection immediately since a large number of workmen come from that place. In another 3 or 4 days I expect I shall be leaving here and returning to my own station (Dera Ismail Khan). At the moment I am superintending the erection of new petrol tanks, pumps, pipes etc. Each tank weighs seven tons so you see they are fairly heavy thing to lower into pits.

Kalabagh is a native village – gosh, I have never seen such filth and smelly places in all my life. The animals (cows, goats, dogs, sheep etc) just do their excreta in the streets and it is just left.

[Reading these first Indian letters was a great relief to me: gone is the stiff, frightened religiosity of his first letter written on board ship; gone, too, is the clipped formality of his diary. These recent letters are expansive, descriptive and fascinating, I thought.]

27th October 1941

Thanks so much for your very very much awaited cable. That cable made my whole life bubble up with joy – it was like water to a man dying of thirst. I noticed the cable was stamped 'Reading': do I gather from this that you are living with Mr and Mrs Meadowcroft?

Well Phyl I have moved again, this time to Wana on the Afghanistan border. In order to reach here I have travelled through the most dangerous country for a white man in the whole world. The tribal gangs in this region shoot every white man they see. I will now tell you the whole story: as you know I was stationed at Mari Indus for 3 weeks. When I returned to D.I.K. I was informed I had been appointed Assistant Garrison Engineer in Wana 160 miles away because they needed a man with reinforced concrete knowledge. The area between here and Wana is frightfully dangerous and you can only travel there on convoy days. The convoy consists of armoured cars and army lorries laden with troops. The country between Wana and D.I.Khan consists of wild rugged mountains soaring up to 10,000ft.

The road cuts up and down the various valleys in circles and bends. In this very wild and desolate country are bands of tribesmen with rifles and machine guns.

However, I learnt that on the 27th of October there was no convoy and I had to travel entirely on my own with 3 or 4 'badruggas' (enlisted tribesmen) as my escort. Of course I was armed with a special revolver sling used out here – I look just like a cowboy.

Eventually, without mishap, we arrived at Wana at 4.30pm. The old A.G.E. met me at his bungalow – he was surprised to see me and considered I was a brave fellow to risk coming so late in the afternoon "especially after the affair last night": apparently the previous day an officer had been shot and wounded in his leg.

My father (fourth from left) with his bedraggas. Note his gunsling.

Well dearest I have been given a beautiful bungalow overlooking the most beautiful gardens. Wana is situated 4500ft high and surrounded by the Himalayas. I suppose you will be pleased to hear that I have been promoted to Lieutenant!

--- What did you feel at this point? I asked, as Mother went out to make a pot of tea.

--- Well, Wana was to be my home for the foreseeable future so I felt as if I had 'arrived'. But five days later I was summoned back to D.I.Khan.

--- Why was that?

--- I was simply told I had to keep my original position. I was glad because D.I.K. was safer. I later heard that the previous day tribesmen had held up three lorries and killed four people.

Suddenly he laughed.

--- I decided to grow a moustache, I remember, as it was the custom to grow one.

--- *Yuck!* was my mother's response from the kitchen.

20th November 1941

About a week ago I moved into a nice quarter of my own. It consists of a sitting room, a bedroom and a bathroom. Of course the bathroom is not an elaborate affair, it just contains a round tin bath and a commode. I have hired the furniture from a native bazaar shop for 8 rupees a month (approximately 10/-). I get my meals at the officers' club. In the evenings I play tennis to keep my body fit. It is rather strange playing with full colonels and majors – but here they mix in with the subalterns very well indeed.

My Garrison Engineer to whom I am assistant is a Hindu and a really fine fellow. So far we have worked really well together. I look after the construction and erection of all the new buildings, so I am still using my architectural and reinforced concrete ability. In the evenings I employ a teacher to help me learn URDU. This language is most peculiar and things are said backwards way round. For instance in order to say 'Here is water' you would say 'Water here is'. If I pass the Easter examination in Urdu I get an increase 100 rupees per month (about £7).

Is Jimmy still studying at the School of Architecture? Tell me darling – how are my people doing? Do write to them and let them know how I am getting along.

I stopped there. Something puzzled me.

--- Did you not write to them yourself?

--- Well I didn't really have time. The letters to Phyl were the priority and I didn't want to have to repeat to them everything I told her. I knew she would keep them informed.

--- But they were your parents!

---They were always moaning that they hardly ever got any letters, Mother added. I thought it was awful.

3rd December 1941

Sweetheart, your letter was grand, probably because it was the first I received since leaving England.

--- Hooray!

Well darling you kept your promise loyally. Liverpool was not safe for you and Reading seems really fine. Fancy my Phyl being sick during a car drive, well well well! Ever since I received your cable about the silk stockings I have been trying to purchase some pairs for you but unfortunately my quest has been hopeless. My servant went into D.I.K. and brought back the dearest and best samples but sweetheart they were antique and old fashioned in style and completely out of date for the beautiful legs of my darling Phyl.

My work is interesting darling: I am designing buildings for the government in my division. I do quite a lot of touring since many of the new buildings are many miles from my headquarters. Tomorrow for instance I am going to inspect some work 89 miles away. Whenever I tour I have a personal escort of badraggas.

P.S. I have just had good news. I am now a Lance-Corporal!!

17th December 1941

Dearest you very nearly lost your husband yesterday. He was involved in a nasty motor car accident. I arose early because I wanted to motor up to Manzai and back, a distance of 62 miles each way. At 9.00am I started off in my Ford V8 Vanette with my escort of six men, a clerk and a spare driver. I was driving about 40 miles per hour and the road was clear when I spotted two loose bullocks being driven by a small boy. When I was about 20 yards from them one bullock suddenly decided to cross the road. Before I could breathe I was on top of the beast. The car hit the bullock

The vanette in which my father hit a bullock.

49

around its head and shoulders. The impact caused the car to swing around and away we went over a steep embankment, across a ditch and through a lot of bushes.

Never in my life have I ever had such a shock. When I got out of the car I was absolutely dithering. I expected to see the poor bullock all cut up and bleeding and lying in the road. Lo and behold the animal was quietly walking away. The damage to the car was very bad but nobody was hurt. The engine was not touched, however, so rather dolefully we returned to D.I.Khan.

On Xmas Day I have received an invitation to dine with the Colonel and his wife. Mrs Whitehead is a lovely lady, not in looks but in nature I mean. Dearest, how are my parents doing? I sent them a couple of telegrams but so far I haven't received a word from them. Sweetheart they do not know my address, but I anticipated you would send it to them. I would like you to write to them whenever you receive a letter from me giving them up-to-date news.

--- Did you not write to them throughout the whole war? You just left Mother to be an intermediary between you and them?

--- They were upset about that, Stan.

--- Oh, just get on with it, will you?

--- Well, the last letter of 1941 describes how you spent Christmas.

28th December 1941

Phyl it is no use beating about the bush, without you my life is complete hell. I go about my tasks but without any zeal. It was for your benefit that I really studied hard at university and so graduated with 1st Class Honours – like an olden day knight who showed off in tournaments and duels so I tried to prove my cleverness for your benefit.

On Xmas Eve a medical colonel gave a party in the mess. The dinner was really grand: turkey and Xmas pudding. There were about 45 people present including a number of officers' wives. After dinner there was dancing and drinking but that sort of entertainment did not interest me.

--- Surprise, surprise! I interrupted rather meanly.

So I went home and went to bed.

On Xmas morning I played a round of golf with a Staff Captain from District Headquarters. I like golf very much indeed and I think I will take it up. [He remained an assiduously awful golfer all his life, insisting on clutching his clubs with a cricket bat grip, hands apart.] I expect you will be tickled pink to see me playing in a white shirt and white short trousers, and long scraggy hairy legs. For my Xmas dinner I went along to my colonel's bungalow. There were nine people present. The dinner was very homely and Mrs Whitehead tried her very best to make the young subalterns a little happier...but I readily admit that tears came into my eyes when I came back to my lonely bungalow.

A long, weepy silence followed which I was keen to interrupt.

--- Your turn now at last, Mother.

7

11th October 1941

My own darling Stan,

It only seems like yesterday that we were together in our little 'love-nest' in 1A Walpole St., York. Some nights I lie awake for about half an hour or so just thinking about our courtship and how it started, our introduction on May 16th 1938 and how we met every evening in the Co-op doorway. Then I recall your 'degree day'. I felt so happy and proud to be at St. George's Hall and watch you looking so marvellous in your cape and hood. Then our holiday in Keswick. Then the ghastly war came. One night we had a 'lovers' tiff' and fell out. Next morning you phoned me to say 'Well, Phyllis, I suppose you are glad, but I'm leaving you next week. I've got my papers'!! We 'made it up' by corresponding from office to office. Then, do you remember, we were engaged on May 1st 1939 the day before you entered the army. Then I recall a day, a Thursday, April 10th 1941, when I met you at Kirkdale Station, the day of our marriage. Oh darling I thought our little home in York was our abode for the duration where I recalled poor old Stan teaching his 'empty-headed' wife to cook!!!

18th October 1941

Since I last wrote, Stan, I have got another situation. My job at the Milk Marketing Board was a bit monotonous so I wrote to the GPO....and am now engaged as a clerk in a sub-post office. I am in charge of the National Savings certificates, telegrams, insurance stamps etc. My pay is £2.10.0 a week.

Darling I have not seen you for three months and to me it seems like three centuries. The last I saw of you, you were walking up

Woodlands Terrace with your mac on, your dress hat, your haversack and your respirator. You kept turning round and waving to me and I thought I would die when you went out of sight.

I received a letter from the Institute of Structural Engineers requesting your original degree diploma. I replied and said that it must have been destroyed when your home was bombed but actually I know where it is. I packed it away (and your R.I.B.A. one) with my wedding presents in trunks at Rockley Street.

9th November 1941

I have bought several things towards our home, necessities really. For heaven's sake, darling, DON'T bring home all sorts of rarities, I don't want my home to look like a museum. Don't bring any stuffed birds, animals or insects because I will only burn them!!!!

I have just got over a most painful process which affected my heels. I went a hike blackberrying with Mrs Meadowcroft, Lil [a new-found friend] and a neighbour. We walked about 3 miles (it was a boiling hot day and I wasn't wearing stockings) when my heels and feet became inflamed. I still walked on another mile or two but had to stop I was in so much pain so we went in to a chemist's. When he took off my shoes there was no skin whatsoever on my heels – it was raw flesh, my shoes were full of matter and blood. 'I'm afraid you have blood-poisoning', he said. My feet were simply RAW MEAT!! I even had to be carried to the bus. Anyway I haven't been out for 10 days and am forced to wear George's very large slippers.

15th November 1941

I have still not received a single letter from you.

One night last week I went to see Charlie Kunz [Kunz (1896-1958) was a popular pianist and bandleader during the Dance Band era]. Gosh, darling, he is a brilliant pianist! I did not *enjoy the other part of the show. In fact I hated it – it was vile. The jokes were absolutely repulsive then there was a most disgusting scene of two girls dancing some native dance. They were almost naked. I said loudly to Lil so others could hear, 'Personally I detest this type of entertainment, it is acted only for vulgar mentalities'.*

--- Oh, Mother, what do you sound like?!

We would have left but Charlie Kunz was playing again at the end. Next week I am going to see Laurence Olivier in a film called '49th Parallel'.

24th November 1941

'Mother, in this next letter you spend a lot of time planning your future after the war. This bit's quite funny:

When you come home I think we will spend a fortnight's 'honeymoon' in Keswick [they did!] *amongst our wonderful lakes and fells. We will settle down together and bring up our own 'Angela Barbara' or 'Peter', preferably the latter. I have the names of our children all readily* [sic] *planned darling. If it's a dear little boy 'Peter Clark-Wilkinson will suit him.* [My brother was actually christened Peter Derek Clark]

--- It's a good job you didn't christen me Angela Barbara then! The two of you sent poetry to each other pretty often. This letter ends with something by Patience Strong:

<u>I wait</u>

I try to fill the empty days and live them patiently –

But time goes at a jog-trot pace – they're all alike to me,

For now that you're away Life goes unheeded past my door,

Autumn, Springtime!....Does it really matter anymore?

--- Isn't that lovely?

I made no comment.

--- You've got beautiful handwriting, Mother, but the next letter is typed, and the majority of all the others are too. Why was that?

--- Well, writing words smaller meant I could write even more rubbish. So the typewriter was the answer, an 'Imperial' portable it was. [I threw that into the local dump a week ago.]

12th December 1941

I've had the typewriter 6 days now and I can't leave the thing alone. But so far nothing from India. Anyway, since I last wrote darling I have had some of my teeth out. [I only ever remember my mother with false teeth. She was often prone to making up stories: she peddled a myth that she lost most of her teeth when she tripped going upstairs in a Liverpool tram and her mouth collided with the edge of the metal step. Maybe that's where **my** myth-peddling came from.] *Last week I received a severe ear-ache and the doctor reckoned it was due to a tooth. I went in my lunchtime to the dentist who extracted 5 teeth. Meanwhile he is fixing me up a plate.*

To cheer myself up, yesterday, darling, I bought myself a very expensive pair of pyjamas. They cost 45/- [about £75 today]. I've never worn anything so delicious in my life. I am saving them for our '2nd honeymoon'.

22nd December 1941

My own darling hubby,

Many, many thanks for your wonderful three letters which I have received during the past week.

--- Hurrah!

--- Gosh, the shivers that went through me when I saw them.

--- I bet. And just before Christmas too!

--- Yes, even though they were posted two months earlier I couldn't have received a better present.

[This particularly long letter ends with a wonderful character assassination of an RAF couple who were billeted at the Meadowcrofts.]

Remember me telling you of the RAF officer who is billeted here with his wife? Well last week she got a job in Reading. She is passionately fond of children but can't have any of her own. She put an advert in a Reading newspaper for afternoon work taking care of somebody's children. She got a reply and is now a nursemaid to a famous doctor's baby boy. His name is Anthony, aged nearly 3, and is a sweet child. Her husband did not know anything at all about her job – she did it <u>underhandedly.</u> He was out last Tuesday with a squadron leader when lo and behold he walks into her pushing a pram with 'dear little Anthony' in it!!!

Crikey I can imagine him. He did not lower himself before his squadron leader but walked past her and ignored her.

However when he got home that night, darling, you should have heard him!!!!! He absolutely wiped the floor with her. Mrs Meadowcroft and I listened through the wall (cats!!). We heard him say 'You lowdown little hussy doing that sort of work behind my back. Do you realise how you are degrading yourself, an officer's wife minding other people's kids. Let me just catch you at that game again I will give you something to cry about. You can just go to Dr Murphy tomorrow and tell him you have resigned, if you don't you cannot stay here with me one minute longer'. We heard 'Yes, yes' between all the sobs.

However, darling, yesterday I saw her out pushing Anthony's pram again, she is <u>secretly</u> going on nurse-maiding this child. Her husband is a terror of a man when he is furious. I wouldn't be in her shoes if he finds out again!!

She is terribly jealous of me because I have been exempted from National Service as I am the wife of an officer. She was jealous of my stockings you bought so she tried to show off by bringing down all her underwear to show me. It was vile. How awful to be jealous. They have been married 3 years and are not a bit in love. He told Mrs M that he married out of pity. She is a good wife about the house but her taste in clothes is awful. Her husband I know is ashamed to take her out.

I left work at the GPO on Saturday morning. I became so fed up of the usual office stuff that I decided to resign my position. So at the moment I am a 'lady of leisure'. Jimmy has sent me 'Gone With the Wind' so I am enjoying reading that but, for me, you can't beat Sir Philip Gibbs [now virtually forgotten as an author].

Goodbye, my own sweety pie.

--- And, finally, your last letter of 1941.

29th December 1941

As you will have heard from my cable, I have spent Christmas in a beautiful little place called Henley-on-Thames. Gosh, darling, it is a heavenly spot. Of course I didn't go there alone. My friend Lil asked me if I had ever spent Christmas at an hotel. I had not, but could imagine what fun it would appear. She booked a room for us at an exclusive hotel where the food was marvellous – you wouldn't have thought there was a war on.

I've just received a letter from my mother. And before I forget darling I want to tell you off for being very laxative [sic] before Xmas.

[We all had a giggle at this point: Father, who seemed to be permanently constipated throughout his life, devoured food that was supposed to have laxative properties: figs, prunes, my mother's Senokot pills, and especially cartons of Liquorice Allsorts.]

While you were at the job of despatching Xmas cables to your people, don't you think it would have been an easy job to have written one out to my mother too? She has just mentioned that she is very disappointed that you should forget her at Xmas. I think it was very mean of you darling and I am taking this opportunity of telling you off about it. I think it is simply dreadful of you.

Now that I am free from work again I have decided to pay a visit home next week.

Coincidentally, we were approaching Christmas as well. A few nights later my brother, his then wife and I were invited for an evening of Canasta. An appallingly wet holiday to south-west Ireland in the 1950s was the reason why Peter and I were taught the card game which became very fashionable at that time. As a family we played it very regularly and Peter still does. So, on that particular Christmas evening, the four of us sat down for the usual cutthroat game. The fifteen cards were dealt, Mother picked up her hand, shuffled them about and suddenly started crying.

--- What's the matter, Phyl?

--- I don't know what to do.

--- Oh, don't be silly. Have you got any red 3s?

--- Why?

--- They're worth 100 points.

There was a long pause.

--- I've completely forgotten how to play.

She had. No amount of gentling her along worked. It had all completely gone. In the days after that evening broke up we didn't discuss this occurrence, nor did we consider its ramifications at all. It was tacitly brushed under the family carpet. We never played Canasta again.

1942

1

It took me about three months to sift my way through the letters of 1942. My mother's circumstances were to change quite drastically later that year, hinted at, perhaps, in her opening letter. So, there we were, seated around the dining-room table as usual, on a snowy March day, my father having greeted me at the door with that irksome appellation of 'Boxwallah'.

16th January 1942

My dearest darling Stan,

I am afraid I was unable to write last week for the simple reason that I spent a couple of days at home in dear old Liverpool. I was certainly glad to return here to Reading as during the previous night in Liverpool we received a nasty air-raid. We were all ready to go to bed when it commenced (11pm) and it continued until 3.30am. I was absolutely scared stiff. However, it did very little damage except I heard later that the Rialto and Stanhope Street received a bombardment.

I spent 2 or 3 nights with your mother and dad in Roby Mill. I did not tell them I was coming, but dropped in and gave them a surprise. By the way, I have resigned my position as clerk at the post office. I was absolutely fed up at having to get up early and catch the workmen's bus with a mob of cockney shop assistants and clerks. I left on Christmas Eve. I am now 'Lady Wilkinson' with very little to do, except that on various occasions I travel into town and bring home some errands for Mrs Meadowcroft. A fortnight ago she and I went down to London to do a bit of shopping. We toured all the biggest shops in Piccadilly Circus, Marble Arch etc. Darling, believe it or not I have bought a beautiful fur coat. It is superb. You will like me in it. It cost 26 guineas [about £600 in today's money!]. *I know you will not mind me spending so much money but it is what I wanted for a long time now. It is a three-quarter coat and is very, very modern. I wore it to go home to Liverpool. My mother made an awful fuss over me. I bought it at Marshall & Snelgrove.*

While at home I paid a visit to the Co-op office. All the girls begged me to come back, but gosh I could never go back to a place like Liverpool after having lived in Reading which is so clean and peaceful.

Jimmy is still at school. He has done some lovely drawings darling. I'm sure you would approve. All the same he was up till 3 and 4am while I was home. He is 21 on the 1ˢᵗ of April, so I guess I must think of something to buy him.

We still have the airman and his wife staying with us. Last night she begged him to take her to the pictures. He said 'Go to blazes, I want to read' but he eventually relented. We found out later from her that wherever he takes her he always makes her pay for herself. We would never do that would we? But, gosh, I often think of the row we had once in York. I bought a lovely magazine and for some unknown reason you snatched it from out of my hand, ripped it into two pieces and flung it into the hearth. Afterwards I badly needed something to tear or break to relieve my stored up tension. So I decided to take my revenge out on your face...I smacked your face full belt, broke your glasses, then had to pay about 6/- for repairs.

When we are older darling and you die first before me, I swear that I will take a coward's way out and take my life. You must do the same.

--- I felt like that when I heard about the fur coat you'd bought, quipped my father.

--- Hang on, he interrupted. What's happened to the letters between this one and – what was it? – the 13th of January one?

--- The 14th. Well, I hope you realise I am editing these letters. The missing letters are just full of less interesting stuff, like the problems of sending cables or various shopping trips. I'm not reading every word or we'd be here till the cows come home.

--- I see. Well, OK. Go on.

We have had (and are still having) 5 feet of snow. [My mother was always prone to exaggeration but I suppose we must trust her on this].

--- Your fur coat would have come in handy!

--- Will you stop interrupting! Do you still resent, after fifty-odd years, Mother buying that coat?

--- Oh, of course not, he lied.

Every time I see a fall of snow, darling, I think of you at Xmas two years ago. It was so severe that particular winter that you had to come down to our house with brown paper tied round your legs and trousers. You looked most comical but it proved then that you loved me for wanting to come out in all that snow. Then the very next night you had a frightful row with me because I confessed I had walked home from work with a young man who was good enough to keep me company during a miserably lonely walk. It was a silly thing to argue about but 'jealous Stan' decided to leave there and then. You marched from our house in a temper, got to the top of the street, then you came back having second thoughts.

--- I don't remember that, Mother said.

--- Of course you must remember, Phyl. What's the matter with you? My mother had great faith in brown paper.

--- Let's get back to you now, Father.

3rd February 1942

Do you remember how we used to talk of our future married life and home? At this moment my mind wanders back to our weekend hikes in Thurstaston [an area of parkland on The Wirral] *and our 'loves' in the ferns. Gosh we were terribly in love.*

--- Why've you included that? Father spluttered.

--- Well, it's interesting. I'm not going to censor these letters for rudeness [I must admit that I debated about including this rather embarrassing titbit, so to speak].

--- A good job you're not publishing this.

--- 'That's an idea!

--- Don't you dare. Right. Finish this letter and then we'll have lunch.

I also remember the very hectic return we had one Saturday evening which ended in a Birkenhead shelter and a crossing through a blazing Liverpool. Yes, dearest, I agree with you when you say that the time we spent in 1A Walpole Street, York, was the finest in our lives.

--- It was, wasn't it, chick?

--- Yes.

--- Look, if you're going to interrupt again I'm going to stop altogether.

But I stopped anyway because the soup was ready.

9th February 1942

I saw Jimmy off this morning. He spent a long weekend here, from Friday until today (Monday). He thoroughly enjoyed himself, having spent the entire Saturday in London with George. They inspected the Royal Academy, St.Paul's, Buckingham Palace and dozens of other notorious [!] buildings. Yesterday I took him a walk to show him how beautiful our countryside and surroundings are. He was impressed with Berkshire!

--- The address on Mother's next letter was altered or redirected from Dera Ismail Khan to Jandola so at this point I'm going back to Father's letters to find out why. I use the word 'letters' advisedly because from this point on you used airgraphs.

--- Yes, they'd just been introduced and they were guaranteed a much quicker delivery, three weeks from time of posting in fact.

--- Unfortunately, Mother butted in, you were tempted to write very small to try and cram as many words in as possible, so I had to buy a magnifying glass to read them.

--- Me too! I said.

--- But I *did* continue to write nice long airmails too.

25th February 1942

Once or twice I have thought of my courtship with D.R. with a...

--- Dorothy?

--- Yes.

....shudder. In view of my love for you I cannot understand why I was such a complete idiot to think I was in love (with

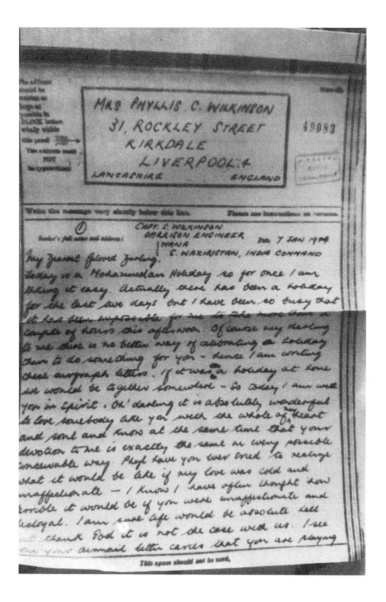

Example of an airgraph

her). In one sense I am glad I went through that ordeal before I met you, because it certainly made me appreciate you more.

Well dearest I expect you would like to know a little about my affairs. A couple of weeks ago I received the full powers of a Garrison Engineer plus the officiating rank of Captain. Unfortunately this is not a real promotion because I would lose it immediately the Garrison Engineer returned from his course. A G.E. constructs new roads, erects new buildings, reservoirs, water supplies, electrical works, bridges etc which are required in this area. For all these new works my office prepares the drawings, makes the contracts and in many cases does the work. When a new job is being constructed I have to measure and inspect the work and do all the calculations necessary for foundations, beams etc. So you see darling I am an architect cum engineer cum mechanical expert. All my work is scattered over an area about half the size of Wales. Due to this I have to do a lot of touring to the most outlandish outposts of the British Empire. On an average I travel 200 miles per week. The surrounding mountains rise up to 12,000ft with the tops covered in snow.

5th March 1942

Phyl, my precious sweetheart, I am sorry if I forgot to send your mother and father a cable at Xmas, but to tell you the truth I completely ran out of money. You did right in telling me off over this. I deserved it.

8th March 1942

My poor darling really told me off in her last letter and I will try not to be so neglectful in future. I have read 'Grand Hotel' (by Vicki Baum) which you sent me. It was a very interesting and enjoyable story but I am afraid to say it was very 'blue' in places!!! In D.I.K. we have a little cinema in the officers club – of course the films shown are years old but still it is a welcome break. Unfortunately there is only one projector which is continually breaking down. It broke down the other night so I only saw half of 'Pride and Prejudice'.

17th March 1942

Well, sweetheart, at the moment I feel rather 'down in the dumps' of despair. As you know I have been acting G.E. since 2nd January while our G.E. went on two courses. At the end of last month he was posted to another command and did not come back. For almost three months I have been doing two men's work without even getting the payed [sic] rank of captain so I was hoping to take his place. The Captain of District Headquarters told me that I was a brilliant engineer in every capacity and the best in the Division but too young for a position like a Garrison Engineer. Gosh I was wild – that is the thanks I have received for my labours.

Well I then received a letter this afternoon posting me away to another Division, but not out of Waziristan. I am to take up an appointment of Assistant G.E. over a little area of my own at a place called Jandola which is situated away in the mountains. The Colonel told me that I had been selected for a very special job. My precious darling I am going into a very dangerous area....pray to God for my safety.

18th March 1942

I am sending this particular airgraph in commemoration of the anniversary of our wedding day. I can remember every little detail of that never-to-be-forgotten day but then a bit later how the whole outlook of our lives changed with the arrival of my commission. Do you remember, dearest, how I broke the news to you? I came in the back way of our little home – you were cooking something on the stove. As soon as I entered the kitchen I told you the bad news. We just put our arms around each other and cried, do you remember?

21st March 1942

Oh darling I wish the war would end quickly so that we could be together again. I envy other couples' happiness rather bitterly and wonder why we have been separated like this. India, I am afraid, darling, is in many ways rather corrupt and a little immoral – I mean the English people. During the hot summer months the wives and sweethearts have to leave their husbands behind in the plains while they go up to the cooler hill stations. This separation every year upsets all family life. Not only that but many women are left behind because their husbands are overseas. Another very important factor is sex. Very hot climates always tend to make women more sexual, and their menses start much earlier in life than in England. Darling you are better in England where such goings-on do not exist on such a scale. Also children's education is badly neglected. The wealthy people send their children to England from the age of 7 years and never see them again for years and years. Gosh I certainly could not do that – I want to be with my Peter and Barbara and see them grow up under our care and guidance.

--- That last remark is absolute tosh, I said. How come, then, that you banished Peter to boarding school for most of his teenage life, something he always resented? [Peter was a boarder at Hutton Grammar School, just outside Preston]

--- Well, that's different. Anyway, it was only 30 miles away; it wasn't as if we had sent him to the other end of the Earth. It didn't do him any harm.

--- You'd better ask him that. And that other remark about English women becoming more sensual, that's pure E. M. Forster. He believed that Indians are more true to their feelings *because* of their warm climate as opposed to the repressed, bottled-up Brits who are afraid of showing their cold climate emotions.

I stopped suddenly. Why am I always picking holes in him? I thought. My continued smugness was beginning to irritate even me.

--- Can you two stop arguing? my mother chipped in.

--- OK. I'm sorry. There's just a small bit of this letter left.

I am studying very hard for my language examinations which take place on 5th April. I do hope and trust that I pass this time and get the menace off my shoulders forever.

--- Was this an exam in Urdu?

--- It was. And it was a struggle.

24th March 1942

Last Sunday morning there was an earthquake in N. W. India. Just as I was getting out of bed at 7.45am I suddenly heard my bathroom door shake, then my bed and bungalow followed suit. The roof then commenced cracking, so I dashed right out on to my veranda in case the building collapsed on me.

29th March 1942

As you can see darling I am now living in a place called Jandola, a fort. This is like a small village surrounded by large castle walls. Jandola is situated in the wildest part of India with ferocious hostile tribes all around. This part of the world is not inside British Territory and is like a kind of no-man's-land between India and Afghanistan.

A few days ago I went up into Tribal territory for my last visit to various stations as G.E. D.I.K. before handing over to the new G.E. Just as I was leaving Darazinda one of my workmen came up to me and said, 'Sahib, a man comes to show you a tiger skin which was killed last night – he wants to sell it to you.' Well I consented to have a look. Gosh, I liked it straight away. The tribesman said he would sell it for 15 rupees but even though it was worth more I answered no. He then offered 10 rupees but I still refused. I pretended to leave but shouted '8 rupees for tiger skin.' Immediately he ran after me and accepted.

When they saw it my fellow officers said that it was worth about £7 yet I had got it for 12/6 only [about £20 today]. Since then I have had it cured and treated which cost me another 5 rupees. In England, Phyl, this skin would cost about ten guineas [£350 today]. Now it makes a beautiful carpet and I have placed it in the middle of my room in front of the fireplace.

The other night I got a terrific fright. I returned to my bungalow after dinner and went to my desk in order to get a book out of the drawer. On opening it I heard a scuffle inside. It was a long drawer so I looked towards the back: suddenly a large rat jumped out and ran away. Oh Phyl I have never seen such a place as India for insects – gosh there must be millions and they are all five or six times too large.

--- 'God, that must have been awful, I said, showing some sympathy for him for once.

--- 'I'd have died, was Mother's response.

--- 'What happened to that tiger skin? You didn't bring it home.

--- 'I was tempted to. But it had deteriorated too much by the time I left so I had to leave it behind, sadly.

We left it at that for the day. I was invited to join them for a walk around the cricket ground, a much loved walking area when we had dogs. Mother had told me that the doctor had recommended that Father went a walk every day 'to improve his circulation'. It would have been churlish to refuse.

2

Conversation during that walk revolved around how much they missed Utsi, the family corgi which had to be put down the previous year. They were now too old to cope with another dog and clearly felt this new vacancy in their lives. As a matter of fact they left me in sole charge of organising this: they decided to visit friends in Edinburgh and when they returned home they arranged for his remains to be cremated and we scattered his ashes on the cricket ground a few days later. Ever after the park was a place of pilgrimage and sadness. I never resented what I had agreed to do. Not then.

6th April 1942

Well dearest I am living in a real fort, something similar to the one in the film 'Beau Geste' only instead of being surrounded by sand this one is surrounded by high wild rugged mountains of the lower Himalayas. My life here is similar to a monk's life in a monastery, only on a military scale. The fort is occupied by a civilian army called 'South Waziristan Scouts' who are like the Foreign Legion of the North West Frontier of India. The officers are English. They are fine fellows, very brave and courageous. I have a beautiful little quarter which contains a wonderful bathroom with hot and cold water laid on. My meals are taken with the Scouts officers in their superb mess. Unfortunately I am not allowed outside the fort unless I am accompanied by at least a dozen of my own little army of 'bedragga' protection.

The Scouts can protect me but they are greatly disliked by the hostiles and are a sort of legitimate target for them. On the other hand they would think twice about firing at their own tribesmen who surround me. The hostile tribesmen are continually blowing up bridges, causeways, culverts etc and it is my job to design and build new ones.

Last Friday I was going to go out on a tour of inspection but I was suddenly advised not to under any circumstances because a large hostile gang was only 3 miles away. A few moments later the Scouts went out to attack the gang. The battle went on all morning and there were many casualties on both sides. However the leader was killed, which was something.

Meanwhile I was beginning to sense that as the afternoon wore on Mother was becoming more and more fidgety and unfocused. Was she bored?

--- Two more letters, Mother, and we'll get back to you.

--- Oh good.

14th April 1942

Well dearest I am actually writing this airgraph from a fort called Sararogha, even further afield than Janola. Quite near this place are cave-dwellers and I took some photos yesterday from the fort but I did not go too near in case the inhabitants went for me.

15th April 1942

A few hours ago I received a letter from my mother and father which brought tears to my eyes: oh gosh dearest it was awfully sweet. The most touching part was 'Well your mother still has her cough [she suffered from heart disease], I don't think Roby is doing her any good it is too foggy and damp for her. She longs to see you.' She is a good mother, the best the world could give a lad so don't forget her.

At the moment I am living in a fort called Sararogha, about 20 miles from Janola. It is 4,000ft high. Always before I go out to work I kneel down in my room and ask God to protect me and often in bed at night I break out in a cold sweat when I think of the tremendous risk I am running. I received today a beautiful letter from your dear mother. I like her letters because they always contain a lot of warmth and genuine affection. Your parents have been good to us and I shall never forget them.

--- Now it's your turn, Mother.

--- Hooray!

19th March 1942

Darling, whatever possessed you to send me such an incredible telegram: 'Cease correspondence with Kenneth Amey'? Ever since I received it I have felt most horribly unhappy and humiliated, especially the latter!

Why do you ask me to do this, Stan? Have you reason to doubt my faith in you? When I opened the cable I must have proved a surprising sight standing reading it with my mouth gaping open. It is merely a platonic relationship – good heavens, I've not even <u>met</u> the fellow. I've no wish to, but as it was he who wrote asking for your address, what more could I do? I did it for YOUR sake as I realised that you and he were excellent friends in Bradford. <u>I do believe you are jealous!</u>

--- Gosh, I remember that row we had, said Mother, a long distance row. I had only received five letters from this man I had never met and you just flew off the handle.

--- Well I.....

--- And this was nothing compared to the rows we had later, one to do with Reece's Restaurant in Liverpool, I remember, and an even worse one that I call The Typing Incident. It's all coming back.

--- I haven't come across those yet.

--- You will.

--- What do you say, Father?

--- Yes I was jealous. Who wouldn't be, parked thousands of miles away and not knowing what your wife was getting up to.

--- What do you think she was 'getting up to'?

Things were getting unusually heated around the table so I decided to move on quickly.

--- Let's get on. Peter will be here soon anyway.

One of the oddest things about reading these letters, and one I hadn't predicted at all, concerned these long-distance rows that they had. Of course, at the time, the immediacy of these arguments was partly nullified by the time-gap between writing a letter and its arrival (about three weeks) so my father, say, writing an angry epistle would know that its effect was ruined because by the time the letter arrived my mother had moved on regardless. But, now, around this dining-room table, these rows were rekindled with much more immediacy because there was no passage of time to dampen their effect. I admit that this was a bit worrying experiencing their arguments spring back into stronger life than they ever had before.

Conversely, and this was what kept me motivated, idiosyncratic comments, moments of humour, expressions of forthright love seemed to re-energize the two of them, perhaps kick-starting something which had lain dormant for years : a clear love based on shared experiences. To put it somewhat crassly...had I, perhaps, reignited their love?

24th March 1942

Last Friday I had 6 teeth out. I had some out before Christmas but I decided to have more extracted.

--- Why was that? Seems a bit extreme.

--- I was having aches and pains all the time. The gas had a bad effect on me, though, and I was still being sick two days later.

--- I'm not surprised!

Tomorrow I go for an interview at an aircraft works. It is where George works. I definitely <u>don't</u> want to go to work. In fact I'm dreading it. I enjoy being free. But George said I will soon be forced into work by the government. Had a nice letter from Ken Amey yesterday, but I will obey, darling, and <u>ignore</u> it!

12th April 1942

I went home for a couple of days at Easter. I spent a day with your mother and father. We had a house full of people one evening. Some of the guests included Elsie and Dick [her husband] and Jimmy's friends. Jimmy was 21 on April 1st and we sort of celebrated. By the way, darling, I asked you to send him a greetings telegram but you did not – I am annoyed (again!!) with you. I bought him a silver cigarette case because he smokes very heavily.

In my last letter I told you I was going for an interview to Elliott's where George works. The man asked me if I could do shorthand typing. I said 'No' and told him of my clerical experiences. He asked if I could <u>trace</u> or draw. Again I said 'No'. I could see he was getting irritable and then he said he had nothing to offer me. He even had the audacity to ask me to <u>learn</u> shorthand. He finished by saying,

'Well, Mrs Wilkinson, I will drop you a line and let you know if anything turns up.'

Next morning a letter came from the Labour Exchange requesting I should attend another meeting <u>immediately</u>!! I did so, and believe it or not I was actually BULLIED into factory work. The first gentleman had obviously rung up the L.E. and told them I was IDLE!! I was given an 'appointment card' which read : Mrs Phyllis Wilkinson has been appointed a fabric worker in the wing covering dept of _____ Aircraft Works. I was dreading coming back to Reading from my trip to Liverpool because I knew I was starting work. When I got there a welfare officer examined me, fitted me into overalls and cap then showed me the aeroplane wings. As soon as I saw what I had to do, <u>sewing</u> [Mother was never ever very good at this] *and the riff-raff with which* [sic] *I had to work I immediately asked to see the Works Manager. When I saw him he could see I was 'full up', so he said 'Yes, I can see you are not cut out for factory work, but seeing you are a Liverpool girl and I am a Wallasey man I will see what I can do'. He then said, 'Take those horrible factory things off, they don't suit you, and come with me. I have a job ready'!!!*

So there and then darling I started in the office of one of the largest aircraft works in England. I am a costing clerk for the Admiralty and I do nothing all day long but decimals!! My job is working out the costs of steel and aluminium, as they are all invoiced in decimals.

--- What a fuss, Mother, I said. And all that stuff about working with 'riff-raff' when you were from the working class yourself! What a snob you sound!

--- You wouldn't understand, Tim, said my father.

--- That's a bit harsh.

--- Well, it's true, he continued, and I understand Mother's feelings. We felt we were rising in the world, and taking this job, well....she must have felt she was being dragged back down again.

--- That's exactly right, Mother added.

19th April 1942

Today I wore my new costume, it is perfectly tailored and very smart. It cost me 9 guineas [£300 today]. My shoes cost 2 guineas and a pair of gloves 20/- too. However I felt very "well turned out" today. My mother wrote me a nasty letter last week saying that I spend all my money on clothes – your mother did the same. When I was home at Easter your mother was disgusted with me when I showed her my pyjamas for which I payed [sic] 45/-. People who criticise are only jealous, I think. My mother also said that Jimmy has recently passed his University military exam (Cert A and B) and within the next 4 weeks he is to be posted to an O.C.T.U.

Last week I had to go to the doctor about my left ear which had been painful for days. He syringed it about 8 times. Gosh it was an odd feeling, it sounded like the Niagara Falls in my brain. He then asked what I'd been doing to my ear: 'You've been using an instrument of some sort to clear the wax.' I couldn't lie to him, for he already knew. Actually I had put a hair clip down and it had injured the drum.

The work [at her office] is interesting at times and I did not realise how many various nuts, bolts and screws went into an aeroplane. It drives me mad when I get an invoice which says,'320 aluminium rivets @ 3.58d per oz' and I have to work out the cost.

--- Sounds riveting, I joked. Nobody laughed.

Just then Peter arrived: a bit like Jimmy, Peter's jokey, extrovert character tended to lighten a room, a complete foil to my taciturn grumpiness.

3

Peter wanted to know how what he called 'the memoirs' were getting along and I was grateful to hear that everyone seemed to approve. So, to give him a taster, I embarked on a few more entries.

24th April 1942

Well dearest my job is the most horrible thing I have ever done!!! I never knew I could possibly loathe a thing so much. It is detestable. It is an aircraft factory under the supervision of the Admiralty. My hours are really shocking: 8am until 8pm week nights. Saturdays until 12.30pm.

I hate it more and more each day. The 5 girls I work with are nice and friendly with me but I have no interest in the place or the employees, because I loathe the very sight of it.

--- Gosh, Mother, that's all a bit strong, isn't it? Peter interrupted.

--- No. They assumed I was educated because of your father being an architect. They didn't know I was thick as a wall.

--- To continue, I said.

I nearly died of fright at first because it was work far beyond me, but now I can do it as simply as anything. I still wear my little locket dear. To me it brings all the sweet memories of our last 2 hours together in Halifax. Remember that terrible, TERRIBLE farewell.

2nd May 1942

Today during my Saturday half-day I have been to town where I made a rather expensive purchase! I bought a bicycle!!!! I bet you are doing one of these two things: laughing, or pulling a long face.

--- Almost certainly the latter, laughed Peter.

It is a sports model with a 3 speed. I will save about 7/6 a week on bus fares, also the fresh air and exercise will do me good. It cost £10. 10s. cash.

All the girls in the office went hysterical when I showed them your snaps. I heard cries of 'Isn't Mrs Wilkinson's husband lovely' and so on. They think you are frightfully good-looking, which is of course true.

--- What a hunk! These letters are quite feisty, Mother, Peter went on. Can I hear a sample of Father's scribblings?

--- Sure.

23rd April 1942

Now sweetheart there is one particular worry which I would like to get off my chest.

--- Here we go! Peter butted in.

You have mentioned in your letters that you have gone walks into the country on your own at night – darling, please don't do this unless you are accompanied by someone else, especially if the walks are near soldiers' billets and camps. Phyl, my precious, I have served in the ranks and I know that there are some men who are sexual maniacs who will attack any girl and rape her if the opportunity presents itself. Please follow my advice.

Well dearest enough of that, let us change the subject after my little lecturette.

--- I was going to say, said Peter, that it sounds like you're being written AT rather than TO.

Since I have been in this country I have had a little trouble with constipation.

--- So what's new!?

One or two times blood has come with my motion but the doctor told me not to worry, it was nature's safety valve. I have just had a lovely cooling bath after a very strenuous game of football. This afternoon I promised to play for one of the native teams – they all belong to the South Waziristan Scouts. Gosh I feel sore from top to bottom.... 'Especially your bottom!' Peter cut in... not having played for 4 years.

In order to disguise myself I now dress up like a real native whenever I visit outposts. Gosh you would simply die with laughter if you saw me: when I return home I will dress myself in the garb just to attack you one dark night. [Here Peter chortled to himself]. On my head I wear a pugri and a cula. Instead of shorts I don a pair of very big native trousers. They are very wide around the waist, 10 feet in fact. The reason for this great width is that the natives in their religion believe that when they are in danger Mohammed comes to help them so they wear very wide trousers in order to make room for Him when He comes to their aid. On my feet I wear native sandals which are beautifully cool. Don't think I am rude, darling, when I tell you that there is no slit in front in order to make water. When the girdle is pulled tight and the 10ft of cloth is tucked in all around it is a frightful bother undoing the cord and rolling the blessed things down. The native wallah (fellow) just squats down and rolls his trousers down but I am blowed if I can. What I do is roll up one leg of my trousers right up to the top and produce Little Stan from amongst the heap and do my No.1 down the side of my leg.

--- Little Stan?! Peter burst out.

I could see my father cringing with embarrassment. Mother was now giggling uncontrollably.

--- Oh, carry on, will you?

--- That's it, I said. Little Tim has finished.

After lunch, while my parents were filling the dishwasher and pottering about in the kitchen, I was able to have a few words with Peter in the garden about what I was doing. Solely on the evidence of what he'd heard today, he thought it was a splendid idea mainly because they hadn't stopped talking about it since I started.

--- But it's not all like this, you know. I'm afraid Father's going to come across as some kind of ogre, and Mother isn't the little angel we imagined her to be.

--- Well, if that's how they were, it's how they were. You can't lie or try to make them out to be better than they actually were.

--- Yes, but I know what's coming and I'm afraid they may feel hurt. Maybe I shouldn't have started this....I'm just worried what cumulative effect it may have on them.

--- You make it sound as if you're going to reveal that one of them is a murderer or something.

--- It's more subtle than that. Much more subtle.

--- How do you mean?

--- It's hard to explain. Are we meant to learn their secrets? I feel slightly dirty doing this.

--- Well, they can always tell you to stop.

--- True.

--- But if you ask me, I think the boxwallah is doing very well.

And so I decided to blunder on.

4

Work is still awful for me. I go all the way there and back on my bicycle now, Stan. There I go full speed along the Basingstoke Road. It is a lovely long road and winds through some beautiful countryside. I still find the work difficult but it is not so bad now because I have been there 5 weeks. I generally have my lunch at midday in a country café overlooking the Thames. It is called the 'Lakeside Café'.

Yesterday, Saturday, my friend Freda and I went for a bicycle ride to a heavenly place 8 or 9 miles away called Mapledurham. Gosh it's a magnificent spot, very 'Olde English'. Stan, sometimes I long to go home to my mother. Many and many a time I'm tempted to ask for my release and ask them to transfer me to an Admiralty office in Liverpool. Would you mind very much darling if I went back to Liverpool? My people are fine. Dad has had his teeth out, all of them. Fan has a colossal new carriage.

23rd May 1942

--- This letter is written from Rockley Street, I said.

--- Oh, yes. I decided to go home for Whit, I think.

In Reading there is nothing to remind me of you, Stan; consequently, when I arrive here memories hit me wherever I go. In my room I have your books, journals, drawings etc also my wedding dress. I simply <u>had</u> to try on my veil once again. Gosh, the train journey here was terrible. The compartment became packed like sardines, people were sitting in corridors. Everybody in my compartment went off asleep. Women talked in their sleep. A couple of soldiers took off their boots, undid their battledress, thoroughly made *'a job' of it, got down full length on the confounded floor. I had nowhere to put my legs, then they commenced snoring and whistling. 'Crikey, 'I thought. 'This is a bally madhouse.' So I got my coat from off the rack, picked up my things and climbed out of the compartment. I stepped over prostate [sic!] bodies the whole length of the corridor until I came to a 1st class compartment where I remained undisturbed for the rest of the journey.*

Darling, I have a <u>gorgeous</u> new coat. It was frightfully expensive and cost me £9. 9s. [£300 today]. *It is a camel hair, fawn, fluffy material with colossal pleats at the back. Lil also bought a similar one but hers is a new 'utility' one which cost the Government controlled price (a third of mine).*

Jimmy is awaiting his call-up at any moment. He has passed his military exam, consequently when he is called up it will be an immediate posting to an OCTU. Fan is still as fit as ever, and still as cheeky!!

Now, some news. Yesterday I was requested to call at the Managing Director's office immediately. Gosh I went hot and cold and I was so nervous I could hardly walk straight. I imagined I had been doing my decimals and algebra wrongly and I would have to work on the factory floor. However, darling, it turned out totally different from what I expected. In fact Mr Preedy summoned me in order to <u>give me promotion.</u> What do you think of that, darling?

Tomorrow morning I commence in a new office which is entirely to myself except for one man who is the Works Manager. I was introduced to this man, a Mr Compton. I am more or less his secretary and the hours are better, 8.30-5.30.

--- You're on the up, Mother!

--- Yes, but it wasn't to last: a couple of months I think.

--- You never seemed to stick at things, my father cut in. Always restless.

--- I think I was beginning to miss home, even though I didn't say too much about it in my letters to you. Deep down I was.

--- OK, let's get back to Father.

6th May 1942

Next week I am going to ask for a month's leave in either June or July. While serving in India I am entitled to 60 days in two periods. If it is granted I am going to a place called Gulmarg [?] which is a tiny place situated in the middle of India's Switzerland, Kashmir. The mountains in this part of the world are the highest in the world.

I have just returned from one of my tours along a very dangerous tribal road. On this road I am building a number of reinforced concrete bridges and causeways but I am

My father dressed in native 'trousers' outside his bungalow.

having a frightful job getting them started. The hostile tribesmen force the coolies to go on strike so I have to be a sort of diplomat and adjust things finely between the different tribesmen.

I think of your mother a lot. I always remember how pleased she used to be standing on your doorstep watching us depart up Rockley Street arm in arm. When we reached the top she always gave us a last wave.

11th May 1942

My most precious darling, I am spending four or five days at Sararogha Fort. I have quite a lot of work near this place in a dangerous area. Two days ago one of the biggest maliks (a sort of hostile head man) promised to protect my life from danger. I was very pleased to hear this because his influence is tremendous. When I went out on the road he accompanied me, the first time he had travelled with a British officer.

16th May 1942

Yesterday I returned from Sararogha after one week's tour in that part of my sub-division. I was accompanied by my bedraggas and head men of the various villages who promised to safeguard my passage through their particular pieces of territory. Darling, these villages are peculiar places. All the houses are made of mud bricks in the middle of which is a tall tower for protection. In the little sketch below you will see what I mean. [Insert sketch?] Every night all the animals sleep and eat in here also, so you can imagine what the smell is like. A house with a tower and compound is called a 'cote'. These tribesmen fight amongst themselves hence a strong tower is essential.

26th May 1942

Please forgive my delay in writing to you, but due to a quick move to another post I have been in a frightful mix-up during the last couple of days. Last Tuesday I received a letter from my colonel telling me the wonderful news that he had appointed me 'Assistant Commander Royal Engineers' (A.C.R.E.). As you know, darling, I was longing to become a Garrison Engineer but I never anticipated rising higher in such a short time. My promotion carries with it a Captaincy and captain's full pay and allowances.

27th May 1942

Well dearest I never anticipated such a colossal promotion. Instead of becoming a G.E. of a small division I have to check and direct all the work of a number of Garrison Engineers in my new capacity. The actual rise in pay from Lieutenant to Captain is quite considerable. Anyway darling I left Sararogha at 3.15pm last Monday and arrived safely back at Razmak two hours later without an incident or a shot despite it being one of the most dangerous roads in India.

Razmak is a hill station and it is situated at 7000ft amongst very high mountains where it is lovely and cool. Gosh I feel the difference terribly after leaving Jandola where the temperature was 109F in the shade when I left. The heat was so great at night there that I found sleep almost an impossibility. Now here in Razmak things are quite the reverse – it is just like an English spring.

7th June 1942

I am sorry I had to make such a peculiar decision about stopping you writing to Ken Amey. I am quite sure, Phyl, that you would not like me to correspond with another girl even though there was nothing in it and you know the person concerned. Perhaps I was a trifle jealous. Probably you think this is rather foolish of me, but I am sure that you know by now that I have some funny ideas about different things.

--- Really? [That was me]

At the moment I am in the very best of health. The little bleeding I had every time I went to the lavatory has completely gone. The doctor told me to take Liquid Paraffin every day and as a result the bleeding has stopped. Between 8 and 9 every night I have a native teacher in order to learn the language, since I am compelled to sit for the elementary examination before the end of September. Having to sit this blessed exam is a bit of a blow, but still if I try hard I might be able to pass by then.

11th June 1942 (Airgraph)

Yesterday my colonel promoted me to Field Engineer for the whole of Waziristan.

14th June 1942

[Six letters had arrived from Mother in one bundle, describing her unhappiness at work]

That evening I had arranged to go to the cinema to see 'Bitter Sweet' [a film of the Noel Coward operetta] but after your letters I felt that I could not go. After some persuasion by my friends, coupled with the remarks you made about this film in one of your letters, I decided to go. Unfortunately the sad story and beautiful singing made my condition worse. Oh, Phyl, I have a confession to make: I cried in the pictures for the first time in my life. I was so awfully upset over your work that the very opening song (one of my favourites) brought tears to my eyes with tremendous rapidity:

'I'll see you again

Whenever spring breaks through again

Time may lie heavy between

But what has been

So past forgetting.'

Darling, when I got to my bungalow I broke down completely. Oh, Phyl, I cannot bear to think you are unhappy. I asked God to make your work easier and happier. Sweetheart I want you to buy expensive clothes – don't take any notice what mine or your parents say. Buy anything you want and please do not consider the cost.

Last night the other officers who work in my office gave a party in celebration of my promotion. My colonel turned up also and he made a little speech in which he said he was very pleased to see me with three pips and that he had me in view for this position for quite a long time. After he left the party became a trifle rough. We started playing tricks with a bath tub. Actually this was very good fun darling – when I come home we shall have it at some of our parties. A long pole is inserted between the handles of a tin bath and the pole is made to rest on the back of two chairs so that the tub swings freely on the pole. Now the trick is to sit on the pole (one leg on each side) and stand up in the bath. Gosh, if you do not balance properly you go crashing sideways at a terrific speed.

21st June 1942 (Airgraph)

I am really happy now that you have been promoted to secretary and have better working hours. When I heard the news I actually broke down.

21st June 1942 (Letter)

This evening a tribal overseer came around to see me at my bungalow here. His name is Amir Sahib Khan and belongs to a tribe called Shabi Khel Masud in whose territory I did quite a lot of work. He gave me a beautiful hand-embroidered pillow case made by the women of his tribe as a token of gratitude for the work I had done on their land. I treasure this little gift because of the poorness of the people who gave it to me. I expect when I bring it home you will stow it away somewhere out of sight.

--- That was a funny thing to say, I said.

--- Well, your mother had a thing about me bringing home lots of native junk, didn't you, Phyl?

--- Yes, stuffed animals in particular.

This afternoon I went to the military hospital to see a friend of mine. He is a fine fellow and I used to play golf with him quite a lot when I was stationed in D.I.Khan. Poor fellow, he has had a pretty bad time during the last few months. First of all he cut his hand and his arm turned septic. No sooner had he recovered from this he then went down with dysentery. After Capt. Shinnie had had 3 weeks of this he suddenly cracked up completely. At first the hospital people could not find out what was wrong with him. In the meantime HQ moved up to Razmak and consequently he had to be moved the 150 miles by ambulance. For five weeks he has lain on his back hardly able to move. A week ago it was discovered finally that he was suffering from Rheumatoid Arthritis. He was a fine big fellow, now he is thin and haggard. He is married and hails from Aberdeen. Probably he will be discharged from the army and sent home.

28th June 1942

A few days ago I received a beautiful native dagger with my name carved very nicely on the blade. Gosh it is a beautiful thing and the handle is made of ivory with a lot of local carving in many places. The whole thing fits into a wooden sheath overlaid with black leather. It was presented to me by the Jandola badraggas who protected me so well during my A.G.E. days there.

5th July 1942

Two days ago I received a letter from Jimmy. It was a very very pleasant surprise which I greatly appreciated. He thanked me for the birthday greetings which I sent him. He told me quite a lot about himself and his university work. Poor kid, I never realised what a terrific struggle he had had in getting through his first year. In your mother's last letter she said that Jimmy collapsed due to overwork a couple of months ago. Only for this confounded war I am sure my help would have aided him quite a lot. Yes, darling, I would have helped him with everything in my power, even though I once told you before we were married I would not.

--- What was that all about? I asked.

My father hesitated for a long time, glancing occasionally at my mother rather sheepishly.

--- Well, let's just say Jimmy and I never really got on.

--- Why was that?

--- I never really knew. Whether he thought I was an unsuitable match for his doting sister....or it might have been simple antipathy.

---He was very young then, you know, my mother said defensively. He was only eighteen when we married. Hurry up and finish, I've got a headache.

--- OK, chick. Finish the letter and we'll stop.

--- I'm stopping. There's not much else in it except you talk about a reshuffle in your work.

--- Oh, yes, that was a worry.

5

Mother's headache persisted for a few days more. When I restarted I went back to her letters.

8th June 1942

Stan, I am surprised at you. You were very nasty to me in one recent airgraph. First of all you 'moaned' because I'd made a request for some cosmetics. You were awfully rude in one sentence over the lipstick. I know you dislike me using it but I am afraid it will have to be so darling because no matter how much I am coaxed I could never stop using it now, so there....I don't feel 'dressed' without it. It's like asking you to go without shaving.

My new job is very interesting now. It is mostly typing. I have a really lovely office to myself. A colossal mahogany desk with endless drawers. Mr Compton is the Chief Inspector. He is very rarely in the office but spends most of his time in the works making tours of the various stages of the planes.

I have been upset recently over Jimmy. He suddenly took ill one night and the doctor had to be called. He was delirious all night and my mother and dad had to sit up and sort of hold him down. He has been shouting out and screaming all night long. Gosh I hate to see him suffering. The doctor reckoned it is diphtheria.

11th June 1942

Jimmy is very ill darling. I feel frightfully upset over him. I wish I could do something. He has had diphtheria and a nervous breakdown. He is terribly cut up because, due to his illness, he has been unable to take his final exams, consequently all his labour has been in vain.

12th June (Airgraph)

I am secretary to a fine old fellow. This morning he presented me with a bunch of red and peach roses from his garden. Tonight I discovered an extra 10/- in my wage packet. I consulted him and he said, 'I made the arrangements with the Pay Office because your work has helped me tremendously, and also your work is more important than anyone else's'. So, darling, what do you think of that?

--- What *did* you think of that, Father?

--- I wasn't happy.

--- Surprise, surprise, mumbled Mother.

19th June 1942 (Airgraph)

Tonight I am fed up. I'm in a filthy temper.....I come home from the office and find Mrs Meadowcroft in another of her moods when she decides not to open her mouth. Darling, this sort of thing makes me homesick.

Jimmy is much better now but far from well. He has been back to school to see if Professor Budden will let him sit for his final exams because he is expected to be called up at any moment.

29th June 1942(Airgraph)

Jimmy has arranged to take his exams privately. All of his colleagues were called up last week.

1st July 1942(Airgraph)

Well, darling, I am feeling upset today. Jimmy has had his calling up papers and reports to an OCTU in the Highlands of Scotland [Dunbar] today. My mother is awfully worried because he is not properly recovered yet.

5th July 1942

I am going away in a week or two to Bude, Cornwall. I wouldn't be going but for the fact that a holiday is a necessity for a 'war-worker'.

Darling, do you think the war will last much longer? The Russians are, at present, rigidly retreating everywhere. The Germans have occupied Tobruk and we are retreating in the Middle East. I wonder what will become of us! As long as the Japs keep clear of India darling I am content to wait!

Jimmy has been called up and is in North Lothian, Scotland. My poor mother and dad are heart-broken. Here is an extract from a recent letter from dad: 'When I got home your mother was crying, then Fan started, then I had to go out I felt so lonely'.

Well darling I have waited till the end to tell you this because I don't want it to spoil your temper which would naturally change the mood of my letter: I am going home darling. I have been frightfully homesick for the past couple of months that I feel I cannot stand it much longer. Darling, do you mind? My mother is lonely without Jimmy and me.

--- Well, that was quite a bombshell, I said.

--- I should say so.

29th July 1942

At last I have arrived home from my holidays and can settle down to tell you about it and myself. First of all, I must say it was the most awful holiday I have ever spent. Needless to say Lil had a 'hectic' time – plenty of soldiers to amuse. She used to leave me every evening and go off with a few boyfriends. One day one of the soldiers with whom she was friendly actually had 24 hours leave off duty, consequently they spent the whole day together bathing and dancing, while your poor Phyl was sitting at the other end of the beach absolutely down-in-the-mouth and lonely.

One day, darling, we took a bus to Clovelly. Gosh, you've never in all your life seen anywhere so quaint, so pretty. What a better companion you would have been than Lil who immediately discarded me the moment she made an acquaintance with some soldiers. It was then that I realised what a 'friend' she was! A young couple in the digs took so much pity on me that they started taking me here and there for little outings, surf-riding etc. I felt a proper 'gooseberry'! I loved the surf-riding though. You carry a little 'board' out with you. It is wooden. Then ride back on the crest of the waves. Gosh it's grand. I also went diving, my highest one was 40ft. How is that, eh?!

Jimmy is having a tough time at the OCTU. Terrific training, motor cycling and mountain climbing in full kit. I ring him up once a week.

2nd August 1942

Darling we had bad news from my dad yesterday. Poor Frank Unwin is reported missing in the Middle East since June [Frank Unwin was a lifelong friend of Jimmy; Frank's parents ran a grocer's shop in Kirkdale]. *Dear old Frank – I do hope and pray that he has been taken prisoner. He was in all this recent Tobruk business, tank battles etc. I still like my clerical position, but I've been homesick lately, and when my mother and Fan come home from their holidays in Goole I will get a release and go home.*

16th August 1942

Recently I've worried and wondered what to do about going home. I've become so absolutely fed up and homesick lately that on Thursday I filled in a form of application for my release from work. In order to obtain this one has to produce a very excellent excuse. I said that my mother has been in ill health for some time now and as there is nobody to take care of her or my invalid sister I found it necessary to return home and look after them. It is definitely not a lie, darling.

--- Really? He said.

Darling don't be annoyed at me : this is a home from home for me, and George has been wonderful but increasingly Mrs M has been talking behind my back.

Jimmy is still at the OCTU but is now in the Isle of Man.

4ᵗʰ September 1942

[This, and all subsequent letters from my mother, is written from 31, Rockley Street, Kirkdale, Liverpool 4]

As you see I have now arrived home and am with my mother once again. Gosh! It's grand to be back after 12 months away. I came home 3 days ago, had just set foot in Liverpool for five minutes when the Labour authorities were after my blood. Yesterday morning I received a letter asking me to attend for an interview. As soon as I told [them] of my qualifications as Chief Inspector's Secretary down south they immediately pounced on me and said, 'By Jove, you are just what we want for Napier's!' As a result I am compelled to start here as clerk/typist on the Aeronautical Inspection Dept of Napier's (Engineers), East Lancashire Road, on Monday!!

Mother and Dad are delighted that I am home again. They are awfully thrilled. Dear old Fan is too.

--- Well, Mother, out of the frying pan into the fire, eh? But I bet you were glad to be home.

--- Gosh, yes.

--- I was not happy, grumbled Father. Not happy at all.

6

Next day my parents had to be taken out to buy a microwave oven because their old one had 'exploded' not long after I had left. The new model seemed a vast improvement, but the main problem was that my mother just could not use it, could not *learn* how to operate it and, as my father said, kept pressing the wrong pads. He thus became the official microwave master while my mother scowled at the contraption with malevolence.

We resumed the readings with my mother safely ensconced back in Liverpool and my father about to blow his top, presumably.

12th July 1942

At the present moment it is 5.30pm on a very pleasant Sunday afternoon. From my bungalow I can see all the troops and the mules returning after a very long day piquetting the hills on either side of the Razmak road in order to ensure the safe passage of a Government motor convoy. The poor sepoys look very tired after their very long walk and climb. It is quite likely that many of them have hiked for over 20 miles. Darling the area around Razmak is very very dangerous from tribesmen because the hills and mountains are very close to this camp which allows easy sniping. The whole camp is surrounded by a perimeter wall and each foot of it is guarded night and day. My bungalow is one of a block of eight and faces the perimeter wall, so all the occupiers have to be very careful not to show too much light in case some wild fellow on a hill takes a pot.

An example of my father's engineering work.

The garrison of Dara Ismail Khan.

Officers' living quarters at D.I.K.

My father's 'bungalow'.

A local map of the time. D.I.K. can be found in the centre, a third of the way up.

I am going on a month's camouflage course commencing 3rd August at Kirkee near Poona. I am rather pleased I have been selected because it is near a large city, Bombay. I have been wanting to go somewhere like that so that I can buy you some clothing – undies and stockings etc also cosmetics.

18th July 1942 (Airgraph)

Dearest, I am sorry to hear that Mrs M's moods upset you and make you long for home at times. Sweetheart, I would be a little unhappy if you returned to Liverpool especially now that you have such an excellent position.

19th July 1942

Last week, Phyl, I sent your brother a long airgraph. I told him that even though we never really seemed to hit a real friendship he had nevertheless a real companion in me who would never let him down and would stand by him through thick and thin. He has had a very nasty time of it, especially during his recent illness which resulted in not sitting his examinations.

Darling, I am so glad you have a pleasant job – and an important one too. I sincerely hope your chief does not mean anything by bringing you flowers and slipping an extra ten shillings in your wages. Sweetheart do be careful : some of these old chaps are a menace to a nice girl.

26th July 1942

Well, sweetheart, when I heard about your little holiday an awful sad feeling crept into my heart. Tell me – why are you going with Lil? If I remember rightly you had told me you had broken off her companionship because she was flirty, cheap and definitely not your type – yet now you are going on holiday with her. I definitely do not wish you to make a friend of a person who is fond of men and uncertain company.

I have just come back from a tour of inspection of some of my engineering work around D.I.Khan. D.I.K. in summer Phyl is one of the hottest places in India. One afternoon the temperature was just over 120F in the shade : gosh, the air was like hot water and everything one touched was like the top of a red hot oven. That night I saw fireflies for the first time and my bungalow was absolutely alive with insects. Sadly I learned that my camouflage course has been cancelled – sad, because it meant a little holiday for me and a chance to buy you various things.

29th July 1942 (Airgraph)

Today I sent you a parcel containing: a jar of Pond's cream, a large box of Coty face powder, a tube of the best American lipstick, a tablet of Lux toilet soap, a pound of sugar and a pound of the best Indian tea. I have also written to a shop in Bombay for 3 pairs of silk stockings for you, payable on delivery.

9th August 1942 (Airgraph)

This letter is written from a little tiny Frontier Constabulary fort called Moghol Kot. It is right at the end of the civilised world and many many miles from a large camp or town. Last Friday I left Razmak by car and reached D.I.Khan after a long journey of 151 miles. At 7.15 the next morning I left with the G.E. for Moghol Kot. A very large portion of the route was under water consequently I had to travel part of the way on the back of a camel. Once or twice I really thought my last had come because in many places there were only a few inches to spare or else the car was over the side of a horrible precipice. This morning I started off for Dhanasar in Baluchistan. For protection I took 25 men from the fort. On the way we had to walk through Dhanasar Gorge. What a phenomenon of nature! The sides, darling, rose to about 1,000ft on each side, the width could not have been more than 50ft. Only a few white men have ever walked through it....

11th August 1942

....The little narrow ledge which I walked along was only a few feet wide with a drop of 200ft or more to a roaring torrent below. At 12.45 'Y' (I cannot name the place) was reached where I was able to inspect recent engineering works. Gosh it was grand to get back to the cool climate of Razmak again.

Your latest letter, darling, was not as nice as usual for some uncertain reasons. There were a number of little points which rather hurt my feelings and made me wonder why you had written them. And then an airgraph from your mother arrived saying that you were thinking of returning to Liverpool. Honestly, I cannot understand your attitude at all – you have an excellent job, you are free from air-raids. Phyl darling if we are to come through this war together we must endure home-sickness and other longings and not make foolish moves which may jeopardise the wonderful future happiness which is waiting for us. I was so worried about this that I was compelled to send you a cable over it. It reads: "Annoyed at your Liverpool move proposal darling affectionate love".

18th August 1942 (Airgraph)

Fancy Jimmy wanting you to ring him up once a week – that is certainly a very unusual request from a brother.

--- Don't start arguing again, I interrupted, but why was that such an unusual request?

--- There's so much of this you don't understand. Nowadays you can just phone anyone quite cheaply but then it was much more expensive. I imagined your mother wasting so much money, not wanting to get off the phone to him. Jimmy wasn't a baby.

--- He was to me, Mother said. Besides, Jimmy didn't want me to do the ringing. You got that completely wrong.

21st August 1942

I cannot understand why you suddenly want to go back to Liverpool. If you do decide to return I will never think of you the same.

23rd August 1942

My own precious darling, I am sorry I let off a tremendous amount of steam in a recent airgraph about your probable move to Liverpool. Darling, if you are able please hold on in Reading for a little longer. This evening I received your airgraph in which I read that my parents had returned to Liverpool and were now living in Friar Street [this was the next parallel street to Premier Street, where they were bombed out.] *I could hardly believe my eyes. I cannot understand them making such a move.*

26th August 1942 (Airgraph)

I haven't received any airmail letters from you for quite a long time now.

27th August 1942 (Airgraph)

I received your latest airgraph this morning. It has upset me very much and I feel pretty foul about it. So you go on holiday and get into conversation with soldiers on the beach and then you stated that it was the worst holiday you had ever had. I find it 'fishy' and paradoxical that you suddenly go on holiday with someone you had previously told me you had given up being friends with. So! MY WIFE IS ACTING LIKE THIS WHILE HER HUSBAND IS SWEATING AWAY IN THE TERRIFIC INDIAN HEAT MILES AWAY HELPING HIS COUNTRY AND YOUR COUNTRY TO VICTORY.

I am afraid under the circumstances I am unable to correspond with you any further until I receive a satisfactory reply to the above comments.

Yours sincerely,

Stanley.

--- Honestly, Father, I said. What do you sound like? A grumpy dad more like, trying to turn his daughter into a nun.

--- Just get on, will you.

2nd September 1942 (Airgraph)

I suppose my last airgraph gave you rather a bad shock – which it was intended to do. Dearest it was sent in the form of a joke and nothing else.

--- Backtracking now. Wriggling out of it?

--- I didn't find the 'joke' very funny, said Mother.

--- I'm not surprised.

Sweetheart, please forgive me for not writing for about one week but I have been on a tour again for about five days.

4th September 1942

I expect the joke airgraph I sent you rather upset you in connection with your Bude holiday but I know definitely Phyl that if I knew you were acting double I would finish with you like a shot out of a gun and my love would melt into galling bitterness. Anyway forget that now.

--- Not much trust there then. You don't come out of this too well I think, Father.

Well dearest going down to Bannu last Friday from Razmak my vanette was fired upon by hostiles hiding in the hills. I was driving the car. Just as I was rounding a bend in a very rugged and barren part of the mountainous valley I heard the whistle of a bullet as it flew just over the top of the car. By Jove, did I step on the accelerator! After that there was no other incident and I arrived in Bannu safely. Over lunch that afternoon a medical officer suggested having a party.

--- Any girls involved? Mother asked.

--- Don't be silly, chick.

He suggested bringing along five nurses from the hospital in order to liven things up a little.

--- You were lying!

--- Just wait a moment, Phyl.

Well darling I immediately told him to count me out – naturally I was ridiculed for being so Victorian and narrow-minded. Anyway their rather sarcastic sayings and jokes did not worry me. These nurses by the way are Chichi which means half and half i.e. Anglo-Indians.

The organisers of the party asked me if I would kindly take out my bed and sleep outside that night because my room was most suitable for dancing. The party wasn't due to start until 10 o'clock that night and I wondered what to do while my bungalow was being used so I borrowed an old bicycle and aimlessly rode up and down various roads. Eventually I came across a native cinema so I decided to go and see a native film. I paid my 2 annas (approximately 1/6) and went in. My seat was on the back row of the balcony which wasn't too bad except for the terrific heat. The film was just about understandable but I was a great object of curiosity to those around me.

At 12.15 I left and cycled back to the bungalow. There I found the game 'Murder' in progress but no murder had been committed for over an hour; instead I found couples in the various rooms. My arrival unfortunately upset things because I switched on the lights and asked them if I could have my room back again. The party members went outside and sat on the lawn drinking while my servant brought my bed back in again and I left them to it.

--- So what is the moral of this story? I asked.

--- I think I was just showing Phyl I had integrity.

--- A quality you thought she lacked?

--- Exactly.

--- What did *you* think, Mother, about Goody-Two-Shoes in India?

--- I just laughed.

---And of course, by the date of this letter, September 14th, you were now back in Liverpool!

--- Yes, and that would mean more letters full of spitting feathers.

--- One more letter and then we'll have a break, I added.

18th September 1942 (Airgraph)

Dear Phyl, I received your cable last night telling me you had returned to Liverpool. Well! I am absolutely discusted [sic] with you – so you went after all the cables, airgraphs and letters I sent advising you not to. Naturally I count for nothing!!!! The other airgraph which I sent you telling you off in a funny way was a joke but this one is certainly not and here I mean every word I say. Phyl I am going to cease writing to you as often: instead I will send you a formal airgraph once a fortnight letting you know about my health but everything else will be cut out – my love and worry has gone.

Yours ever,

Stan

With that we broke up for lunch, but some echo of this fifty year old antagonism simmered under the surface because the atmosphere was palpably frosty to say the least. Mother banged down the cutlery in a manner which always indicated something boiling inside, so I was understandably anxious to sail on with the letters and reach calmer waters.

7

Mother's return to Liverpool was now a 'fait accompli', back with the people she loved and with a full-time job. I was hoping that the happiness resulting from her 'escape' from Reading would improve the increasingly sour feelings around the table.

10th September 1942

(Airgraph written from 31, Rockley Street)

Much to my disappointment, the moment I returned from Reading I was immediately put into compulsory work again. I had only been back in Liverpool <u>one day</u> when the confounded Labour authorities were on my heels. They considered that my secretarial experience was much too useful and vital to the country. Consequently I have been put into another Aircraft place but after 3 days' work I felt that I just could not go on a minute longer. My head had the most queer pains across the crown, and I felt I wanted to be sick. When I stood up my legs trembled, then I FAINTED. When I came around, Mr Hunt (the boss) was speaking to me, asking how I felt. He then gave me the rest of the week off.

15th September 1942

Early this morning at 3am I was wakened by a most horrible explosion. Crikey, I honestly thought the world had come to an end. The sky was lit up by fire too. Fire engines were flying everywhere. However after half an hour's wait we decided to get back in bed. Tonight's Echo was full of the verdict! It was a barrage balloon which exploded and demolished 20 houses in Matlock Street!!! I've been down to see the damage. The row of houses is completely wiped out. Narrow shave, eh?

---And that was exactly why I didn't want you to return to Liverpool.

20th September 1942

[This letter is written from 'Appleby Bridge, Wigan']

As you can see from the address I am spending the weekend with your mother, dad and Mrs Halliwell [their friend].

This is a Sunday morning; we have just finished our breakfast. Your mother is still 'gassing' to Mrs H while your dad is sitting next to me, <u>watching me</u>, and firing endless questions about my new job, etc, etc – you know the way he does. Last night I slept with Mrs Halliwell. When I awoke I found her standing over me with a cup of tea. Wasn't that nice of her?

I dread tomorrow morning when I have to go back to work. I wish I could leave. It's really awful having to do a thing against one's will. It is grand money, over £3 a week [today, the equivalent of £100 a week], *fine hours, lovely people I work with too, but it is the work itself I cannot tolerate. The office is called 'Internal Auditing and Stock Scrutineering'. My own job is to deduct the income tax from the wages of 10,000 people. Crikey, Stan – it doesn't half make my poor old head buzz.*

Jimmy is still having tough training. They have to do the most peculiar exercises: in fact recently they have been undergoing a course of Commando Training. They have to get up at 2ish, blacken their faces, don little woolly caps and do motorcycling in the dark and climb cliffs in the dark. He has another 2 months before he gets his commission.

Hope I am forgiven, darling, for coming back to Liverpool. If you had a little more sense you would see that I did a wise thing.

24th October 1942

Personally I do the most idiotic things. Every night before I get into bed I pick up one of your numerous photographs and nearly squeeze the life out of you, then a goodnight kiss. The first thing I do in the morning before coming downstairs is [say] 'Good morning, darling, one day nearer!'

Last night we were all invited out for supper to my Auntie Gert's in Mauretania Road. We stayed there from 7 until 12.30 but had to walk home as there were no trams running. They have a stunner of a home. My cousin – Freddie [Jones] – is a subaltern with the King's Liverpool Regiment in Secunderabad. Last Sunday I took Jimmy to see your people. Your dad made an awful fuss over him, then your grandfather came in and wanted to know who the fine big soldier was. [Father's grandfather was David Wilkinson (1864-1944)]

Just had a break for tea. My mother came in with Fan, then my dad from an outing somewhere. I felt very domesticated all of a sudden and showed my skill at cooking hake and chips. You know how funny my dad is, he said that he has never tasted anything so lovely in his life, which is not saying much for my mother, is it??

2nd November 1942

[A birthday card and letter from Father's mother]

Dear Stan I am sending you card for your Birthday what would you like I will send it to you Well your mum and dad doe miss you terrible the war will soon be over if we will trust in God and pray and pray every minute of the day that God will guide you and under-take everything you do I trust you do the same this war as hit your mother Father terrible put us out of home and your dad feels it such a long way for him 55 next birthday we are both getting on so speed return son from your loving Mother and dad God bless you and spair you   xxxxxxx

21st November 1942

Darling I am painfully upset over the cable I received from you this evening. It was to tell me that you were now <u>out</u> of hospital and working again.

--- You had dysentery, didn't you? I asked.

--- Yes, it was pretty nasty too.

--- Gory details later, no doubt!

This afternoon, having a half-day, I went to Bold Street where I sacrificed 5 coupons and 18/11 in order to purchase the most heavenly woolly bed-jacket. Yes! I am so cold because it's got so frosty and dark here. My dad is just off to bed and he said: 'Give my very best love and wishes to Stan and tell him we will have a happy reunion in August 1943, for it is then that Stan will be home.' Fan still sits and weighs everybody up and gives her usual straightforward, no nonsense, comments!!

5th December 1942

We are all going away for Christmas – to West Derby!!! [Another area of Liverpool]. *Elsie has invited the whole family. Elsie has a nice new bed-settee downstairs. Fan will sleep on it. Jimmy will be home too. He will have to sleep with my dad. Mother and I together. Dick and Elsie in the other room.*

Darling I have £220 in the bank [£7,500 today].

26th December 1942

(Written from Elsie's: 14, The Fairway, Blackmoor Drive, Liverpool 12)

Christmas Day was very quiet for us. Jimmy, Dad and Dick went for a walk and called at '31' to feed the cat. I helped Mother and

Elsie with the cooking of the pork, chicken and turkey. While they were cooking I made some very pretty-looking jellies in glasses with cream and fancy decorations on the top. When my duties were done I set the long dinner table and then listened to the Forces Wavelength broadcasting soldiers in Cairo Cathedral singing 'Silent Night'. My tears were uncontrollable. Just then my mother came in to the dining-room and had a weep with me in harmony.

After our Christmas dinner, which consisted of turkey, pork, sprouts, plum pudding, mince pies, whisky, port, orange wine and fruit (apples), we sat round the fire listening to carols sung by members of the Wrens. The men all smoked cigars, then one by one they fell asleep. Jimmy and I then went a long country walk. Then when we came back he [Jimmy] had to pack his valise to leave on the midnight train for the East Coast. His friend Rodney [Peden] came for tea after which we helped him to clean his uniform and belt. After he had gone (N.B. He kissed us all on this occasion, the only time I can ever remember him doing this) we all went to bed. Darling Stan I have not had an airmail letter from you for about <u>2 months</u>.

--- Was this deliberate? I asked.

--- Yes, it was Mother's punishment.

---Ah. I wondered when this would appear. It was a bit of a damp squib, though, wasn't it? Where is Mother's reaction to your punishing silence and formality?

--- Well, Phyl wrote a number of nasty airgraphs, didn't you, chick? In my anger I destroyed them, that's why there are some gaps in your dates.

--- That's a pity.

--- Not really, Mother interrupted. I said some silly things. Besides, I thought it was all hot air. I was back in Liverpool and my life had moved on. I was much happier too.

--- Right, well let's get back to Father's last letters of 1942..... and his dysentery!

22nd September 1942

I haven't written to you for over a week now for punishment over your move to Liverpool, but I am inclined to think that I am suffering the most. Anyway, I have broken the custom by this little note.

12th October 1942

Phyl darling I suppose you are still rather upset over my recent action of only writing to you twice in one month. I wanted to impress upon you that I was very hurt over your return. For the last fortnight I have been in Razmak conducting a Court of Inquiry. Thank you for giving me permission to join the Brotherhood [of Masons]. I am sure it will benefit our family in the future.

26th October 1942

Do you remember me telling you that I had designed some special timber bridges on a new road which I had been working on? They are now finished and quite heavy loads taken over them. On Saturday I heard that Sir Somebody or other had been down the road with the Deputy Commissioner and wished to congratulate me on them.

1st November 1942 (Airgraph)

Please do not be alarmed if I tell you that I am at the moment in Hospital in Bannu. Remember me telling you I was serving at a Court of Inquiry at a place I can't name.

Towards the end of the 2 week meeting I was walking around and suddenly wanted to go to the lavatory and felt rather feverish. In the afternoon we went on some reconnaissances and I was compelled to go behind a couple of bushes in order to do a call of nature. It was there that I noticed that the stuff I passed contained blood and mucus. Feeling worse, on return I went to the hospital. The doctor took a sample of my stool and sent me home to my bungalow. Well dearest I spent a terrible night and I went to the lavatory about 20 times. Back at the hospital the doctor told me I had a bad form of Dysentery and I had to go to a bigger hospital, the one in Bannu.

4th November 1942

(Written from C.I.M. Hospital, Bannu)

Well dearest the doctor this morning stated that I will be in a fit condition to leave the hospital tomorrow. I have received wonderful attention here. Darling, we both have something most wonderful to look forward to – just imagine how happy we shall be with our little Peter and tiny Barbara. Your Stan will be lying full stretch on the floor playing trains with Peter.

At this point Mother snorted. I knew why: Peter did, indeed, have a Trix train set but was rarely allowed to play with it on his own in case he broke it.

14th November 1942 (Airgraph)

Well, sweetie, your Stanley is getting stronger and stronger. Yesterday I played tennis for the first time for weeks.

23rd November 1942

I have been playing a little golf lately but dearest I have been really awful. Honestly, you can't help but lose your temper at times – it is so exasperating especially when the caddie grins. One evening I was so disgusted that I threw my club about ten yards away into the jungle.

I laughed. Father had done this twice in my presence on Aboyne Golf Course, once nearly hitting a woman on a nearby tee. He was, at the time, President of the Club.

7th December 1942

I have been studying hard for my language exam in Urdu which I had today. Unfortunately the examiner told me he thought it advisable for me to try again next month, in other words I had failed. What I am most worried about is the fact that if I do not pass I shall lose my Captaincy and revert to Lieutenant.

Tonight I received a letter from Jimmy. He started off by discussing our none-too-friendly relationship during the good old courting days. He said that he did not know who was to blame but he would take his share. I am glad that he now knows what I originally told him in your father's presence one night was the absolute truth. I am sure that at the time your father and Jimmy thought I was trying to put him off going to the School of Architecture and at the same time boosting up the Honours side of my degree. I am sure he must have thought me the most conceited individual imaginable. I am fully convinced your dad was hurt with me because he said, 'I am sure if you got through Jimmy can also, no matter how difficult you make the study appear to be.' I was a funny chap then and also said some nasty things to you : the cause was really always your Stan's rather jealous mind.

--- 'I'm just interrupting at this point, I interrupted, because I discovered what may well be [it was] the only letter/

airgraph sent by your parents. Why did you only keep this and the earlier one from your mother?

--- Well, I did for a while. But after the war I decided to get rid of them.

--- Why?

--- They were sort of formulaic, not saying very much really. It was a sort of reminder of how uneducated they were.

--- That's a bit harsh.

--- I know. I regretted it afterwards.

--- Can I read it out?

--- If you must.

21st December 1942 (Airgraph)

Dear Stan

Just another airgraph to let you know that we are receiving your airgraphs saying that you are on the mend + now back at your work again so look well after yourself + if you can get a leave I would have one it may embrace you up you can see by the date that we will be looking forward to Xmas we don't know where we shall be going Becky [this is Marion Rebekah Wilkinson (b. 1903), my father's aunt] has asked us to go there but John [Joan?] Rice may want us to go to her house so we don't know what to do I hope you will have a nice Xmas + that this New year will see you home again the war seems to have take a turn for the best + Germany may crumble up any moment I wish they would Pleased to know that you go to church there is nothing like it, it will keep you from Temptations, We can thank God for His goodness towards you they prayed especial for you at the Police mission when they got told you was in hospital it was very kind of them + I sent word to Mr Procter thanking them We are sending your Hairbrushes after the Xmas holidays we thought they may get lost in the Xmas rush We had Phil here on Sunday for dinner + tea she looks well + don't worry over her she is all right pleased you liked the photo of your Mother + I + Phil so don't you get down hearted it won't do you any good make the best of a bad job look on the bright side It will be grand to see you again + to tell us your experience which I know will be a thrill to hear.

Love from Mum + Dad.

--- They were good people, Mother said.

--- Now back to Father.

21st December 1942

I am afraid your poor old hubby has been in the wars again. I haven't been able to write for the last four days because I have been ill in bed with malaria. Last Tuesday I felt rather shaky about the legs and had a slight pain across my forehead and behind my eyes. On Wednesday I was infinitely worse, the pain in my head getting unbearable and I was losing my appetite. Somehow or other I got to my office, but work was absolutely beyond me. So I went around to see the head military doctor who is a friend of mine and a mason. He took some blood and sent me home. Next day the doctor, Captain Gilmour, came round to say he had discovered malaria germs in my blood. That night I suffered the worst pains in the head I have ever had. I suffered absolute hell. Next day I was treated with Quinine and powders and this morning I felt quite fit.

Darling I have a little dog, a poor little fellow on whom I took pity last Tuesday in the rain. On my way to the office

I found a tiny little pup dying in the mud just outside my bungalow. It couldn't have been more than a fortnight old. I took it to the office, warmed it by the fire and gave it a little milk. The poor little thing couldn't stand on its feet but after two hours he began to pull round. I decided to keep him! I thought of a good name 'MILA' (a Hindustani word pronounced MEELA which means FOUND). He made himself quite comfortable in my bungalow.

27th December 1942

Darling I have got over my malaria and I got up on Xmas Eve for the first time. Xmas Day I went outside and the doctor allowed me to attend dinner at my Colonel's bungalow. He very kindly arranged a car to take me and bring me home.

It is beautiful in D.I.Khan at the moment. I am sitting on the grass in front of my bungalow writing this letter in the beautiful warm sun. In the trees around here I can hear the very very noisy twitter of parrots, linnets and mynahs. High above in the distant blue sky I can see vultures and Kite Hawks circling round and round.

1943

The kites were certainly circling. I made a concerted effort to speed up my summarising of the letters over the next few months because of an event which was to have a profound effect on my parents' lives.

The following February I received, at school, an urgent message to call at their house on the way home. To this day I am still uncertain about the exact details of the accident, but it seems that my father had parked their car (a chunky, automatic silver Honda, far too large for his needs anyway, Peter and I always thought) outside the local chip shop while he went to Rotary and my mother had lunch with the Rotary wives. Somehow, and this is the source of the mystery, somehow on returning to the car he got in a fankle with the pedals, smashed into other parked cars and ended up half-way up a wall. The police were called and my parents, unharmed but in shock, were taken home. The car was a write-off.

The first thing he said to me when I entered the house was

--- Oh, Tim, we're finished.

His licence was to be taken away and the car had been towed to his garage. It was difficult to placate them, (he in particular) because I sensed he knew that his freedom was to be severely curtailed, and that they were effectively imprisoned in their own home. Rather lamely, I tried to explain how Peter and I would take them everywhere, and that the neighbours would help.

--- And what about my trips as Diocesan Architect? he whined.

--- Well, I can take you on those, I replied.

The following Saturday I drove him, quiet, beaten and humbled, to the local police station where he meekly surrendered his licence, and then on to his garage to rescue the odds and ends from the car : an umbrella, dusters and a cushion. I was appalled by the damage to the Honda – it was, indeed, beyond repair, and looked as if it had hit the wall at about 60 mph. Clutching his driving cushion, he wept as he made his way back to my car.

Not long after, when they slowly fitted in to their new routine of lifts to church, to Rotary, to the shops, Peter and I urged them to go on holiday and they readily accepted the kind offer of staying in a solicitor-friend's Portuguese villa for three weeks.

It was when they returned, and surprisingly upbeat, that we resumed their other routine, the letter-reading.

--- We discussed it on holiday and we want our boxwallah to continue his good work!

1

1st January 1943 (Airgraph)

My dear dear sweetheart I am frightfully upset over your work and the faints you are having lately – I really cannot understand the reasons for them. As regards it being due to 'your age' I think that is rather silly.

4th January (Airgraph)

Precious sweetheart you <u>MUST</u> go to a specialist if your health does not improve shortly. <u>Darling this is a definite order from your hubby</u>. When I come home I do not want to find you a wreck due to overwork.

5th January 1943 (Airgraph)

I am delighted you have been transferred to another office and away from that most detestable fellow named HUNT. Darling I hope I have the opportunity of meeting the fellow after I get home. He will certainly wish he had never treated you in such a horrible way.

6th January 1943

Well my love I am very glad I have joined the Masonry – it will help me and you in the days to come. Now that I am a mason I realise its very great significance and extremely high ideals which must be lived up to. If a man takes it very seriously, and I propose to do so, he will become almost morally perfect. Last Saturday evening we had our Installation Meeting. It was a marvellous ceremony. I invited my own colonel but he was rather scared of coming. He thought he would have to go through all sorts of weird and wonderful rites. After I had assured him that our secrets are kept solely to ourselves he decided to come.

8th January 1943 (Airgraph)

For the next three weeks I am going to be in Wana. The present Garrison Engineer has to go on an Urdu course at Bannu and he asked me if I didn't mind officiating. I didn't mind in the least because I felt like a change after my malaria and the doctor said the extremely cold climate of Wana would do me the world of good.

16th January 1943

At the moment in Wana I am the only British Officer in the G.E.'s office and I have to deal with the work of about 1000 people which amounts to thousands of pounds.

18th January 1943 (Telegram)

Consult specialist over faints/ hubby will bear costs/ darling please obey.

18th January 1943 (Airgraph)

Dearest I would like to be home again in order to give your boss a really good smack on the jaw, gosh I would smash him up into tiny pieces for the way he has treated you. Darling he should be out here on the frontier where men are men.

23rd January 1943 (Airgraph)

In the batch of letters I have just received was an airgraph from your parents. Sweetheart your mother told me that the doctor said you were anaemic. Dearest this is not a bad condition but you must drink iron tonics like Parishes Food etc. Darling I feel for you and your little troubles and mine also. Yesterday afternoon I left Janola at 2.30pm to visit a new job I am doing. We were there for half an hour or so then I pushed on to Wana while the C.R.E. returned to Janola. I was in my tribal lorry with a protection of 22 badraggas. At 4.10pm I reached Sarwakai Fort and finally reached Wana at 6.15pm. Anxious faces greeted me and much relief because they had learned that a large hostile tribal lashkar (gang) was hiding on the main Wana road ten miles away. I must have gone right past them!

29th January 1943

I am sitting for my language examination again on Monday – I do hope and trust that I do pass this time. Honestly, Phyl, I am really a duffer at this Hindustani. If I do not pass I then have to go on a three weeks concentrated course at Bannu.

1st February 1943

Phyl, my most precious darling, you very nearly lost your Stan today. I decided to inspect a road with the Assistant Political Agent and a Lt. Colonel of the South Waziristan Scouts. This road is never used and neither of us had ever been along it before. For tribal protection we took a large number of bedraggas. I have been on most roads in Waziristan but this was by far the worst. Suddenly at a bend on one rock-face the lorry would not round [it] because it was so acute. The driver did not realise this until it was too late. The front wheel on my side swung off the road. Due to the load of the men at the back and the weight of some cement I had on board the other three wheels held the road until the fourth came on again. Instantly I opened the door and was ready to jump in case the lorry plunged over the cliff.

6th February 1943

I am writing this letter from Bannu. My colonel told me that I had failed the oral examination again so I was immediately *sent here to attend the new course. I will be here until 2nd March.*

--- That must have been a bit of a bummer, failing that exam.

--- A what? What a horrible expression!

--- A...disappointment.

--- Well, yes, it was holding me back. Hindustani left me cold, I remember. Such a backhanded and peculiarly phrased language.

--- Let's get back to dear old Mother's world.

--- Less of the 'old', please.

2

4th January 1943 (Airgraph)

Don't gape in amazement darling. I played 'gooseberry' to my friend and her husband who was home for weekend leave. They insisted that we three should go together. We saw a show, then tea and home. I thought it a very kind action, don't you darling?

7th January 1943 (Airgraph)

Many, many thanks and kisses for your very generous Birthday Present received this evening. Darling, I have just tried on the undersets and they fit perfectly. You would think they had been tailored for me. Darling, Stan, that party I attended was not 'sloppy'. There was not a <u>game</u> played all evening!!!! Merely talking and eating.

9th January 1943

Stan, you seemed awfully uncertain about that party I attended in November. This is entirely silly and wrong of you. It was a very classy affair indeed. It took place in the Carlton House dance-hall in Eberle Street off Dale Street. 'Games' never entered anybody's head. I don't mix with 'dubious' people, as you remarked- you should know this by now.

Jimmy is getting on very well. He has a batman for 2/6d per week. He brings him tea in bed, cleans his belt, shoes and does everything possible for him. The camp is so large that he has been issued with a bicycle!

17th January 1943

This is written from your parents' at 312 Ormskirk Road. I came here last night at 7 o'clock for the weekend. I came straight from my

131

shopping expedition via Exchange Station and bus from Ormskirk. We had rather an amusing evening, your father was very funny. I slept in the big bed with your mother while your dad slept in the 'Guest Room'. Fancy him sacrificing his own bed for me! This was my first Sunday off for four weeks and I slept so well that I was awoken with the words: 'This is the BBC Home Service and here is the 1 o'clock news.' Your dad then got some rainwater and I washed. Darling, you would love this little cottage. It is ever so tiny and quaint. It is 300 years old.

19th January 1943

Darling, don't be too upset over my return to Liverpool. I hope you have got used to the idea now. I suppose I will remain at Napier's now for the duration. I have an excellent position. My salary is £3 12/6 per week. Pretty good, eh?

Miss Sutton with whom I work has suddenly taken ill so tonight I went to see her. She lives in Aintree. Gosh you should see the Americans out there. They are all on the racecourse. I was surprised to see Eunice looking so ill. She has suddenly taken a nervous breakdown, plus a heart attack. The doctor warned her that this is due to the overtime we have put in.

['Auntie Eunice', as we called her, remained a lifelong friend, never moved from her house in Melling Road in Aintree where she lived with her ailing mother, never married, came to visit us in Scotland in the early 70s, and died in the 1990s.]

20th January 1943

Tonight I am going to the Royal Court to see Terence de Marney and Zena Dare in 'Watch Over the Rhine.' I am going with two friends, Stella Middleton and Irene Mitchell. This morning we had an air-raid practice. Gosh it was rediculous [sic]. *We sat for twenty minutes in the shelter, listening to all sorts of danger signals bellowing through the loudspeakers. Just think of the production lost in 9,000 industrial workers and 1,000 office staff for merely sitting doing nothing for 20 minutes, while some poor devils in the Middle East and India are crying out for more aeroplanes.*

29th January 1943

Stan, I hope you have completely recovered from your most terrible attack of malaria. The night I heard this news I cried my eyes out in bed. I was telling a chap in the office about it and he said that it will recur the same time every year. Is this true darling?

I am enclosing a small photograph of my friend Stella. I knew her at St. Lawrence's Sunday School when we were 15, then when I started at Napier's she was there. She went to Evered Avenue School and is next to you darling on a photograph taken of House Officers 1931-2!!!

[Napier's] makes me sick actually. It is an awful place for scandal. All the bosses go out with their secretaries, married or otherwise. The goings-on are dreadful. Here is an instance, darling. One day I went to the A.R.P. Office. I merely opened the door, peeped in and looked around but for the moment did not see anybody there, and was just about to leave when I heard a tittering in the corner. There was a typist at her desk, and over her was the chief A.R.P. Controller. They had obviously been making love because the girl's eyes were absolutely 'blotto', and his face was flushed and his hair unruly. I couldn't think of anything to say!

--- 'Oooh, Mother! [She then started giggling in her inimitable way].

--- 'That's not all, she replied. I once caught red-handed the head of the Costing Department making an adjustment to a girl's suspender.

--- 'Oh, Phyl, you didn't!

--- God strike me dead if I am telling a lie. [One of her favourite expressions]

--- To get back to the letter.....

Jimmy is progressing nicely. He is being congratulated all around from various high ranks. He said that this Major-General watched him personally one day drilling his men and he told him that his was the Best and Toughest in the British Army!!! Please, Stan, send me some <u>lipstick</u>. It is not just scarce, but absolutely UNOBTAINABLE.

31st January 1943
_____

Darling Stan, I hope you are not annoyed with me but I have sold my fur coat. The truth is that I have never felt really comfortable in it. Strange, but I sold it for the price I paid for it (£25)!!

1st February 1943
_____

Darling, 5 years yesterday (31st January 1938) I lost my nanny. I suffer her loss even yet and I am so grieved that you and she did not meet. You'd have loved her too, darling. [This was Agnes Smart (1865-1938)]

4th February 1943 (Airgraph)
_____

Tonight I am meeting my mother and Elsie outside the Paramount at 7pm. We are going there to see 'The Road to Morocco'. I am hoping it is a travel film, I don't know exactly who is in it.

--- 'That was a Bob Hope and Bing Crosby comedy, wasn't it?

--- 'Yes, with Dorothy Lamour, I think. It was very funny though. Even Nanny laughed.

7th February 1943
_____

I have just returned from your people's home. As usual I went to town on Saturday afternoon with Stella, where we did our weekly shopping. We had tea in Reece's then walked to the Pier Head because we were too early for our respective trains. I had a lovely time but had a nasty experience getting off the train at Kirkdale. A young lady about my age got on the train at Maghull. She had with her a brand-new baby draped in shawl and christening robes. Also she had a little baby boy, aged about 18 months. He was ever such a dot.

As I stepped out of the train (it was one of those trains which has doors that automatically open themselves) I heard somebody fall. I turned round and saw the little boy flat on his face, while the lady was kneeling on the platform with her right leg caught between the train and the platform. The train was about to move off so I put down my handbag and the baby I was carrying and heaved the lady as hard as I possibly could so that her leg came up on to the platform just in time! Once she recovered from the shock I walked her home.

Unfortunately your people have not heard from you for 3 weeks. While they told me of how few and far between your letters and airgraphs were, darling, I there and then decided that I must write and tell you that if you do not write more often to your mother and dad I will have to stop writing to you, Stan. I mean it!!!

--- That's me in trouble again.

--- This seems to be a constant bone of contention throughout these letters, I said.

It obviously still rankled with Mother after all these years because she suddenly interrupted, with some degree of emotion.

--- I felt very sorry for them, especially your mother who wasn't in the greatest of health at the best of times. You were their only child, for heaven's sake.

--- All right, all right. Stop ganging up on me.

At this somewhat frosty juncture we left it at that for the day.

3

Peter came for dinner that night. Between marriages, he was able to give our parents a bit more attention than usual. Ever the joker, he arrived wearing a monocle and proceeded to send Mother into a paroxysm of giggles with his own version of the Bertie Wooster way of speaking. Despite her complete inability to understand how to operate either the new microwave or the main oven (a newly domesticated husband was now in charge of the timing of the cooking apparently), she produced a wonderful goulash.

While they were clearing up in the kitchen Peter began asking me about my summary of the letters.

--- How's the Boxwallah thing coming along?

I put down my glass of wine and broached a subject which had begun to bother me.

--- Well, I'm not sure what purpose it's serving really. First of all, they seem completely different people from what they are now....it's almost as if they've totally changed. I'm not expressing it well, but Father was intensely jealous of Mother, and that's a characteristic we have never experienced. And I don't like him for it. But – and this is what's odd – as the letters progress I'm beginning to feel sorry for him, almost being able to understand his jealousy and even admire him.

--- How?

--- Imagine it. Out in India he must have suffered the most thorough and complete loneliness, exacerbated by the fact that he virtually had no friends to discuss things with. He never mentions anybody he could call a 'pal' in any letter so far. He even reminds me of Crooks in 'Of Mice and Men' – you know it, don't you? – a man who craves companionship and, because he hasn't a single friend because of his colour, *he got nothing to tell him what's so and what's aint so. He got nothing to measure by.* I think I've got the quote right. And what's worse, I don't think Mother could even begin to perceive what it was like out there.

--- Why? The isolation, you mean?

--- Exactly. She was with people she could talk to, she had things to distract her. Yes, they were undoubtedly desperately in love, but could it last over such a long distance? To Father she was in constant danger from leering, libidinous bosses and lonely soldiers.

--- You're certainly getting a lot off your manly chest.

--- That's because you're somebody I can share this with.

--- Anything else before they come back in?

--- Two things, quickly. Mother keeps extolling the virtues of Jimmy and his meteoric and successful rise in the army. Now, I can understand Mother filling her letters with loving accounts of her baby brother's military activities, but how do you think Father must have felt, hearing about all this marooned in a forgotten cul-de-sac of the British Empire, building a few oil dumps here and there? I exaggerate, you realise.

--- Obviously. So, you're saying Father was jealous of Jimmy then?

--- It's beginning to look like it. At least that's my theory. And one final thing : I'm not sure my two dimensional accounts do justice to their three dimensional experiences.

--- How could they? You're doing the best you can. What are you expecting? Movie cameras in Liverpool and India?!

--- No, but....Shush, they're coming back in.

--- Have you switched the dishwasher on?

My parents had finished in the kitchen and when they sat down and got their drinks, Peter embarked on a completely different subject altogether.

--- Father, where were we going when we had that awful crash on the East Lancs Road?

--- Do you remember that?

--- Of course I do.

--- What do you remember then?

--- We were in the blue Standard 8....

--- PKD 477! Mother shouted out.

--- That's right, Peter went on. We were coming back from somewhere and some drunk American G.I.s crossed the central reservation and smashed into the car in front.

--- Go on.

--- Tim was asleep on Mother's lap in the front. After the impact, I stepped out and said to you, 'Daddy, there's a man lying in the road with a hole in his head.'

--- Go on.

--- That's it. Oh, it was dark.

--- Chick, what do you remember?

--- I can't really think. I was asleep in the front....I do recall going into a council house and they were watching a TV programme called 'Seton of the Yard' which involved car chases. I was getting upset so I asked them if they would turn it off.

--- Oh, I forgot, Peter butted in. I remember cans and bottles in the road.

--- Boxwallah, what about you?

--- All I remember was being carried up a slope and us going into a council house where we were given cups of tea. And there was a budgie.

--- But you were a baby! Peter cried out. How on earth do you remember that?

--- Well I do.

My father seemed to be enjoying all this, almost as if he was pulling some invisible strings.

--- OK. Final question. When do you think the crash took place?

--- 1953. Tim was a baby.

--- Tim?

--- Gosh....when do babies begin to remember? 1953, when I was two?

--- Phyl?

--- Oh, Stan, don't ask me.

--- This is like '*Rashomon*', I said.

--- What?

--- Oh, never mind.

Father then left the room and we could hear him fiddling about in the bureau, a ghastly oak monstrosity which had a permanently squeaky pull-down lid, the hinges of which were never oiled. This section was flanked by two glass-fronted compartments built to house a complete set of Encyclopaedia Britannica for 1946, a gift for my newly born brother who mostly ignored the leatherette tomes. The bureau seemed to contain, as far as I ever ascertained, pigeon-holes stuffed with cheque book stubs and old passports.

He returned with a piece of paper. He sat down.

--- I have a letter here from Forshaw, Richmond & Co, solicitors from Warrington, asking me to make a statement about my experience of the accident which took place on the 19th March at about 7.30pm...in <u>1955</u>.

--- What?

--- Yes, Tim would have been three and a half, hardly a baby! And Peter eight and three quarters.

--- So?

--- Tim would have been too big to be sleeping in the front. He was with you in the back. And at 7.30pm in mid-March it would only have been starting to get dark. And, Phyl, the programme that upset you was called *Fabian of the Yard* and starred Bruce Seton.

--- Well, I was nearly right. What does all this prove?

--- Four different people, having four different experiences of the same event.

--- Yes, but you haven't told us what *you* experienced.

--- I've got a headache. Anyone want a cup of tea?

We never did learn where we were returning from on that fateful night. And I never **fully** understood why Father went through this rather tortuous analysis of the accident.

And then I started thinking.....do we ever really get to know our parents and they us? They become the beings **we** got to know, for a brief time, because of what impinged on their lives earlier, before we existed, and then, as we age and grow apart, we become different again.

As he was leaving that night, Peter did say one thing which hit a nerve: 'What you are doing means more to you than it does for me....but keep going, old chap!'

When I got home to my flat that night, I lay in bed mulling over some of our conversation. Out of nowhere I remembered, as if it was yesterday, something I said as a child to my best friend Charles. We were on a bike ride to Formby I think:

--- I wish your father was my father.'

I have regretted these words ever since. What a lousy thing for a seven year old to say! Harold Price, his father, was a wholesale grocer who seemed such a jolly man compared to my father. He had a Vauxhall Velox PA, an Americanised monstrosity of a car, and in it he took the pair of us on trips, a thing I never remember my father doing (I vaguely recall some kind of regatta in Derbyshire and a stronger memory of a day out to Portmeirion before it became famous because of *'The Prisoner'* TV series).

There, in bed, I suddenly feared I was editing these letters to reflect the subconscious dislike of my own parent. Surely, surely, not.

4

8th February 1943 (Airgraph)

Darling I will take your advice about a rest – in fact I have asked for a month's leave in May. I have decided to go a trek from Kashmir to Tibet. I am quite looking forward to this since it will be quite an adventure. I shall take my servant with me and hire a donkey to carry my luggage, and I shall hike about 15 miles a day.

21st February 1943

Honestly darling I simply cannot be bothered writing to other people except you, your parents and my own. Actually my epistles to you are the only real enjoyments I have out here.

While I was in Wana I was given a beautiful Persian bedroom carpet. It was given to me by an old Subdivisional Officer of mine who used to work under me when I was G.E. D.I.Khan. I asked him why he presented it to me and darling this is what he said, 'Well, sir, you are the finest British officer I have ever met – you are fair, honest and just. I give this present to you on behalf of myself and my Indian brothers.' Wasn't that marvellous?

24th February 1943 (Airgraph)

Darling, I read in one of the Echoes you sent me that Liverpool was target No.2 in the whole of the country after London. Oh Phyl do you remember the long sessions we used to have in your sitting-room – we were so happy together we did not worry about the enemy planes overhead dropping bombs all around us. Bombs did not disturb our 'loves'!

144

27th February 1943 (Airgraph)

Well darling my language course in Bannu came to an end today. I enjoyed [it] very much indeed and it has certainly helped me a lot. I am now able to talk in it with natives which is perhaps something.

2nd March 1943 (Airgraph)

I returned from Bannu yesterday. At the end of the language course I finished top of the class in the written work and second in the conversation. I am now all keyed up for the final exam at the beginning of April.

6th March 1943

Next Wednesday I am going through my last degree at the Lodge – after this I will be a Master Mason which means that I am then a really fully-fledged member. I will be most delighted when I return home to take you to the ladies' night at the Masonic Lodge.

--- That didn't happen, did it?

--- Not on your nelly, Mother replied. I'd rather have died than go to one of those dos.

--- So, did your Masonic membership lapse?

--- Oh, unfortunately. Mother just refused to go, couldn't abide me going either.

Somehow I was secretly pleased.

20th March 1943

My trek to the border of Tibet will give me a marvellous opportunity to study and take photographs of the ancient Tibetan architecture which is absolutely unknown in Architectural Academical studies. I intend to make a proper study of this subject when I am there in order to write a thesis so as to obtain my M.A. degree when I return home.

--- That didn't happen either, did it?

--- No, unfortunately. Raising a family, lecturing, etcetera, ate up all my time. I wished I had though.

20th March 1943

I received a letter addressed by you but written by dad. In it he said that you are looking absolutely beautiful. Wasn't that nice?

23rd March 1943

Yesterday I received a number of letters from you. Two letter cards written from Upholland [where his parents lived] only took 16 days to reach me – that certainly beats the record. I was awfully sorry to hear about the accident Jimmy had during part of his training at the Infantry School. Of course I didn't mind in the least you sending him some pyjamas of mine. He must have been in a terrible position not having any dry clothes to wear after nearly drowning in the river. In another letter you certainly gave me a good telling off for proposing to go hiking in the Himalayas. Phyl, do you remember the time you broke my glasses and made my teeth bleed during a row? Gosh they used to be grand times. I cannot obey your order to go to a city instead – it is not dangerous and the walking will do me good.

28th March 1943

Well darling last night I was a bit fed up and disconcerted. All day long I had been doing three people's work and somehow felt it was going a little too far: the D.C.R.E., a major who is over me, went on tour so I was left with his work, the Surveyor of Works was on leave so his stuff came along and then there was my own work. What made me furious was that my Colonel who had not very much to do did not volunteer to help me. So at five o'clock I packed up and went home even though I could have stayed there until 10pm. My work is not easy Phyl – all day long I am constructing things, answering difficult questions on building construction, transfer of personnel, signing at least 200 letters. I really believe I earn every penny of the £64. 12. 4 I receive each month [about £2500 today] *but I feel I am being taken advantage of by higher ranked people.*

31st March 1943 (Airgraph)

Well dearest your wish about my leave has come true. Due to an outbreak of Typhus Fever in Kashmir I am not allowed to go there for my leave. Instead I have decided to go to a quiet little place called Dalhousie and spend a simple holiday in the Himalayan hills.

5

I had been noticing that Mother seemed to be nodding off during the reading of the previous letters.

---She seems to be doing this a lot recently, Father commented.

But then we heard....

--- I can hear you. I'm not asleep. Just resting my eyes.

--- Right, Mother, we're returning to your letters now.

9th February 1943 (Airgraph)

Darling Stan, I am terribly sick and tired of my work. My boss is the most impudent 'pig' one could wish to meet. He was very sweet to me all morning, telling me that I had such a clean personality then in the afternoon he asked me to take a letter. After I typed it up he took it and crossed out one word with a mighty daub of ink. He then said, 'Don't look like that, Mrs Wilkinson, don't pull a face, did you learn to spell at your school?' I said that I'd always been regarded as a fine speller and that the word which he has crossed through – 'accommodation' – was definitely correct. He said it only had one M. He was adamant so I had to retype the letter complete with the spelling mistake!!!

12th February 1943 (Airgraph)

My mother has just gone to the Whist Drive and I am entirely alone except for dear old Fan. My dad, after much persuasion, has finally decided to go to the pictures; he has not been for about 18 months. I've recommended 'Mrs Miniver'. I have just finished my tea, the time is 7.35pm and am listening to a lovely programme of music by Jack Payne and his orchestra. Do you remember how we loved those plays at the Liverpool Playhouse? Do you remember 'The Corn is Green' at the Winter Gardens, New Brighton? Weren't Sybil Thorndike and Emlyn Williams [who wrote the play] *marvellous?*

19th February 1943 (Airgraph)

Jimmy has been having a terrible time at his School of Infantry which he is attending for one month up in Northern England [Durham]. It is for all newly commissioned officers. At the time of writing his letter to me he was in the M.O.'s office after being treated for shock and water on the knee caused when he had to cross a river, in full kit, chin-deep. The other officers were all six footers but Jimmy is only 5' 10" and when his turn came he was absolutely lifted off his feet by the current and carried downstream underneath the water. Two Czech officers rushed to his aid and after bringing him out applied respiration and took him to the hospital. He had hurt his leg and had to be treated for shock. My mother is terribly upset, she said he would be better off in the Middle East or India.

22nd February 1943 (A letter from Elsie)

You ask me to look after Phyl for you, Stan. Well, my dear, I am her slave just as you are, I positively worship the child, and I would do anything for her, as you know. When Granny Clark told me to watch over Phyl, I promised her faithfully I would.

2nd March 1943

Today I received 5 airgraphs from you. I confess I was rather startled and frightened in one when you said you nearly lost your life over a hairpin bend. Darling, please try not to travel on these roads again. Must you accompany the men? Can't you ride a horse or a camel rather than drive? You want my care there. If I could be there with you I would make myself your personal bodyguard, then you and I would die together.

Father burst out laughing.

--- I'm trying to imagine you, Phyl, as my bodyguard, fighting off the natives, a rifle held before you.

--- Well I would have done. God strike me dead.....and stormed off into the kitchen.

--- Oh, Phyl, I'm not laughing at you. Come back. It was a wonderful, touching thing to imagine, chick. Quickly- go on with the letter.

As Mother slunk back, her pride hurt, I continued.

I am busy saving up for my holidays, darling. Elsie wants me to go to our relations in Scotland, just over the border. Remember me telling you about my mother's, especially my 'nanny's' brothers and cousins, who live in Kirkcudbrightshire? Elsie would like to go with me, not to live at their homes, but to book at the one hotel, called the 'Lochinvar'. I went when I was 7 and they thought the blind world of me then.

--- The rest of the letter, too long to read, I added, is taken up with Mother's interest in renting a house at 19, Cecil Drive, Eccleston Park, Prescot [8 miles east of Liverpool city centre], and living there with her parents and Fan until the war is over but *'Needless to say my mother refused.... Gosh I could have hit her.'*

5th March 1943

I'm glad that everything between you and Jimmy is now on the level. The army has certainly made a difference in him and he respects you even more than you think, darling. I admit that he was very young when we were courting; this accounted for his impulsive reactions to me.

6

The next day I was anxious to get back to Father's letters as he was about to embark on his trip to Dalhousie. I had arranged to pick up Mother at the hairdresser's and when she emerged she looked ten years younger. Back at Wilson Road, and over coffee, the ritual continued.

1st April 1943

Phyl I am sorry to hear about the terrible 'carryings-on' which take place in your work – it is because of the filthy loose morals of the nations today which has caused God to bring war upon us for retribution of these ghastly sins.

--- You make it sound like Sodom and Gomorrah, I said.

--- Well, it seemed like that at the time.

France was politically corrupt and without any fighting stamina when this war started because for years she has been the sexual playground of Europe. Nothing nauseates me more than the loose morals of men and women – it makes me feel like vomiting with rile and disgust.

--- Blimey!

5th April 1943

Tonight I searched the D.I.Khan bazaar and bought you the following articles: 2 jars Pond's cream, 1 box of Evening in Paris Face Powder (shade Neutrelle), 1 box Coty Face Powder (Neutrelle) and 2 tubes of Tangee Lipstick of the shade you required. They cost me rather a lot but that of course means nothing to me. I expect you will be pleased to hear that today I learnt that I passed my language examination Part II Oral.

--- Hooray!

9th April 1943

Well darling today I am going on leave to a little quiet spot called Dalhousie. Before going [there] I am staying in Lahore for two days in order to do some shopping and visit a proper cinema. Major Hill is going there for the weekend and is going to act as my guide. On Saturday evening we are going to see 'In Which We Serve', Noel Coward's first film.

12th April 1943

[Written from STIFFLES HOTEL, DALHOUSIE, Nr LAHORE]

My Dearest Most Precious Darling, as you will have noticed from the above address I have landed at the destination which will serve as the centre for my three weeks leave. I left D.I.K. at 1pm last Friday afternoon with Major Hill. The train eventually reached Lahore five and a half hours later i.e. 11.30am Saturday morning. Hill was staying on in Lahore until Sunday evening so I decided to spend the weekend with him. He arranged everything, rang up the best hotel (Faletti's) and booked a combined room. Dearest it was awfully strange being in a big city once again – the traffic sort of took my breath away at first. As soon as we had lunch we both retired to bed for a nap: during the night on the train Jackie had been very ill with his stomach. Due to him getting up all the time and putting the light on and running to the lavatory every other minute I could not get a proper sleep. I felt awfully sorry for him, especially when he took cramps in his legs also.

After the little snooze we decided to go to the cinema and see 'In Which We Serve' which I did enjoy. We then went back to the hotel for a really grand dinner and watched the dancing until 11.30pm.

Next day we went to the zoo and in the afternoon I packed up in order to catch the 5.20pm train for Pathankot. I spent the night in Pathankot Station and at 8am I left in the mail lorry and arrived in Dalhousie at 12.30pm.

14th April 1943 (Airgraph)

I am writing these few lines from my little hotel sitting-room. Through my window I can see the Punjab plain stretching miles away to the distant horizon. Dalhousie is 6,500ft high. Every building is built on a terrace. The scenery is magnificent: lovely valleys and mountains covered with tall deodars and pines. If I walk around to the other side of the hill I can see the rising snow-capped Himalayas.

During the last few days I have been strolling about the countryside in order to get myself acclimatised for the little trek I hope to do next Saturday into Chamba State. Tomorrow I am going to climb a nearby mountain called Dain Kund, about 9,000ft high, with my servant.

16th April 1943

At the last minute my servant decided he couldn't come because he couldn't make a proper arrangement for his food. So I placed my small automatic pistol in my pocket fully loaded in case I encountered any wild animals on the way and started out at 9.30am. The only animals I saw were about 30 or 40 wild monkeys – gosh they were delightful fellows, beautifully clean and of a silvery-grey colour. They were very amusing jumping from tree to tree. The last 1,000ft of the climb was most difficult due to the thin air and I was breathing twice as fast as usual. But at 1.00pm I reached the top. Oh, Phyl, the view was marvellous, both the Himalayas and the Simla Mountains were visible. The descent was quite difficult and when I got back to my room I was absolutely tired out.

Today I received a written permit to enter Chamba State and I also saw the Chamba State vakel (a kind of ambassador) to arrange some mules for me. The trek to Chamba is 20 miles.

18th April 1943

(Address : Dak Bungalow, Chamba State, Chamba)

As you see I have arrived in Chamba. It is a delightful spot and is situated in the finest valley I have ever seen in my life. If ever there was a land which approximates to a country flowing with milk and honey – well this is it. The little town of Chamba stands in the valley of the River Ravi and looking south-east there is a gigantic snow-capped mountain called Kankot, about 18,564ft high. Chamba is not very large and has a population of 6000 people. Behind it rises Shah Madar hill, crowned by the ziggurat (tomb) of Shah Madar, a Mohammedan saint.

After breakfast this morning I went a stroll through the town and took various photographs of temples, etc. When I got back to the bungalow I found a note waiting for me from the Resident asking me to come round for a chat. From him I learned all I wanted to know about the country and regulations. When I got back to my room I found it in a frightful state: clothes and bottles were scattered all over the floor, a new film I had bought was ripped to pieces. At first I thought a thief had been searching for money but the owner of the bungalow said it was definitely the work of a wild monkey!

Looking towards the main Himalayas and Chamba State from Dalhousie

Looking towards the plains.

Six temples near the raja's palace, Chamba dating from 920-40 A.D.

Map of Chamba State.

raja's palace, Chamba, overlooking the
ve bazaar.

The entrance gate to the city of Chamba
with the temple of Hari Rai.

h the place of a night's rest.

"Three of my boxwallahs."

20th April 1943

[Written from Dhargate Rest House, Somewhere up the Ravi Valley, Chamba]

On Monday I left Chamba at 8.30am with three coolies carrying my bedding and food supplies for 7 days. Also amongst the baggage were cooking utensils of various sorts. I bought the following things: 1 tin of cheese, a packet of salt, a tin of butter, a bottle of coffee, two large packets of biscuits, 1 packet of Corn Flakes, a small sack of flour, a tin of native cooking fat called Ghi, a small sack of potatoes, two dozen eggs, a jelly. I hired the following cooking utensils: a frying pan, a kettle, a large iron plate on which my bearer could cook chapaties.

It was thrilling starting out on this 40 mile hike. Eventually we arrived at Rakh where there was a rest house where I could sit in comfort and put my feet up for a while. My servant prepared some chips and boiled eggs for my dinner.

At 7.30 this morning I started out from Rakh. Instead of three coolies this time I had one horse. By 1.15pm I arrived at Dhargati 15 and a half miles away and I am writing this letter to you in candle-light while sitting on my bed. Tomorrow morning I am setting off for Bharmaur, 10 miles away.

22nd April 1943

[Written from Dhargati Rest House]

The valley was now like a narrow gorge with the Ravi rushing madly beneath the path. Ahead I could see the path rising up the side of a mountain at a terrific angle. Actually, sweetheart, the rise is 2,000ft in 2.5 miles at an angle of about 1 in 3. Gosh this was the most gruelling climb of the whole journey. The climb, in heavy rain, took 2 hours. At the top was a little picturesque village called Khani (?) but about a quarter of a mile from there the horse carrying the baggage and supplies dropped due to fatigue. However as soon as he had a rest and a nibble of the grass he was able to proceed.

Slowly the path climbed to a height of 8,000ft and there ahead of us was the little town of Bharmaur [the letter contains a sketch of the view ahead]. *At 1.30pm I walked into the village and asked for the rest house only to be told it involved another steep climb. There and then I paid off the horseman and hired 3 coolies and eventually reached the bungalow.*

After dinner which consisted of two fried eggs and a jelly I got into bed and tried to keep warm. Next morning the rain had stopped, a lovely warm sun was out and I could admire the views which I missed yesterday. It was a revelation to my soul. To my left was a mountain called Khapransi, 17,000ft high like a dome of snow and to my right mighty Nani Mahes 18,564ft rising like a huge apex of an isosceles triangle. That morning I took many photographs (principally for your benefit later) of the scenes and old idols and temples.

At 11.30 we left and at 3.15pm Dhargarti was reached.

24th April 1943

[Written from Dak Bungalow, Chamba]

Going to Bharmaur took three days but I returned in two. Yesterday I hiked from Dhargarti to Chamba 28.5 miles in one day, thus breaking our recent tramp of 23 miles which we did in the Lake District a few years ago. "Do you remember, Phyl?"

--- Yes, it nearly killed me.

I always walked on my own about half a mile ahead of my servant, the horse driver and local guide – consequently I was left entirely with my own thoughts. I hummed all sorts of songs and hymns particularly old sentimental ones like 'Sweetheart, Sweetheart', 'I'll See You Again', 'Love Will Find a Way' and 'La Madonna [sic] e Mobile'. Throughout the whole of my trek I have been reading 'The Bright Pavilions' by Hugh Walpole, a wonderful story about the fundamental things in life.

25th April 1943 (Airgraph)

[Written from Stiffles Hotel, Dalhousie]

I have bought a little present for you from Chamba, a pair of real leather eastern slippers with turned up toes.

--- Well, I said, leaning back in the chair, that was some trip. Was that the highlight of your entire stay in India?

--- Oh, yes, without a doubt. And you, chick, were never out of my thoughts.

---And all those unlabelled photos you've got in endless albums. Your album dedicated to this Chamba visit is the only one in which you've actually taken the trouble to label each picture.

--- That's right.

The last word was mine (never without a dig).

--- Ironic, though, isn't it, that your most memorable moments in India were absolutely nothing to do with the war at all?

--- No, I suppose not. More wine?

7

Two days later we resumed the readings, this time concentrating on Mother's letters.

6th March 1943

I hope you don't mind, love, but you know your blue striped pyjamas? Well I've sent them to Jimmy. As you know he had his valise stolen and the consequence was that he had no change of underwear or pyjamas. Clothing coupons have to be given for this kind of thing, and my poor mother had to replace all his loss by sacrificing some of her civilian coupons for shirts and socks for him. I knew you wouldn't mind, so my mother laundered them, and needless to say he welcomed them with open arms!!!

7th March 1943

You certainly deserve a month's leave in May, darling, but I wish to heaven you would take my advice and not go to Tibet on a trek. I think you awfully foolish. You are not considering the possibility of being attacked by tribesmen or animals. If you go I will stop writing to you! I'm telling you, darling, that if you do go you won't hear from me again, ever, and I will join the A.T.S., the W.A.A.F.s and the WRENS and will do voluntary firewatching and everything else of which you do not approve!!!

16th March 1943

My mother has just taken Fan out for a walk. My only companion at the moment is a wee tiny kitten, aged 5 weeks, who insists on trying to walk across the typewriter. Gosh I have certainly got the miseries today. I feel wretched. I bet that when this confounded war does eventually end, you will not know me. I feel worn out through this waiting and craving for you.

160

Jimmy is counting the days towards next week when he has 7 days leave. Next Wednesday, being St. Patrick's Day, his regiment (8th Irish Btn) have to march around the town of Felixstowe, with a brass band, and wearing SHAMROCK. Gosh, he is cursing because you know how much he loathes the Irish.

--- That's odd, isn't it, considering he had an Irish father?

--- I know, Mother said, but that's the way he was. I remember him saying to my father, 'Why did you give me a name like Moore?'

17th March 1943 (Airgraph)

I have just returned from town where I bought a hat, and a black coat which cost me 2 guineas. Gosh it is lovely. I bought it at Bon Marche and the coat at George Henry Lee's. I absolutely adore going around the shops in town spending money. I came back broke having gone out with about £4.

22nd March 1943

Jimmy is now second in command of his company, but still only subaltern. His captain does all the clerical work dealing with the company of 800 men while Jimmy is left to see to the entire training of them. He says he prefers this.

25th March 1943 (Airgraph)

I have not been so discouraged for a long, long time because your mail has been most regular, but today I have certainly got a fit of the blues. Monday nothing, Tuesday nothing, Wednesday nothing and today, once again, nothing, not a damned thing.

26th March 1943 (Airgraph)

Confound it all there was nothing from you again today. Not a thing for 10 days.

--- This must have been the time you were ill with malaria.

--- That's right.

28th March 1943

Jimmy played football recently at Felixstowe, Officers v Sergeants. The sergeants obviously decided that 'NOW is the time to get our revenge on these officers' because Jimmy had to be carried off on a stretcher suffering with 2 sprained ankles caused when a certain Sgt. mistook Jimmy's feet for the ball!!! He soon recovered, though, and it will not stop him coming home in 2 days' time for 7 days' leave (which was postponed from earlier).

27th March 1943

Gosh, sweetheart, I was, and still am, terribly upset after reading the fuller account of your malaria and what pain you went through. I could never bear to see people suffer in pain, particularly the one person whom I love more than anything or anyone in the world.

Today I went to town. It is Saturday, so naturally I paid my weekly call to the Tatler News Theatre. I thoroughly enjoyed the newsreels.

31st March 1943 (Airgraph)

Early this morning Jimmy arrived home for 10 days leave, not 7 as was anticipated. He arrived at 2.40am knocking the whole house up. Naturally we all got up because we were so glad to see him after 3 months. Fan got her calling-up papers yesterday – this has caused a considerable amount of fun in our house, we have since called her the WAAF and the ACK-ACK girl etc, etc. Naturally they did not know that she was an invalid.

While I was reading all this out I noticed that Mother was leaning forward in her chair and was crouched over, obsessively (it seemed to me) nibbling away at the skin around her fingernails. I had never witnessed this action before. It struck me at once that the lights were beginning to go out, that the mental pathways were crumbling, that the waters of Lethe were creeping ever nearer, that the wolf was near the door.

--- Mother! Mother!

--- Uh?

--- I'm sure you can remember where the next letter was written from. Somewhere very unusual. Remember, Jimmy was on leave.

There was a long pause.

--- The Wirral! she suddenly announced. Somewhere on the Wirral.

--- That's it exactly! You remember. In fact you've addressed it with those very words... 'Somewhere on the Wirral'.

The waters retreated temporarily. The wolf stepped back from the door.

--- But before we get to that you got into trouble at work, didn't you?

--- Oh yes. I was very rude I think.

1st April 1943 (Airgraph)

There has been more trouble for me this morning at the office. Just before my dinner hour started Mr Hunt called me into his office and asked if I had been rude to Mr Qualtrough yesterday. I knew what was coming, and said that he had been rude to me first. When I was passing through his office one of the typists stopped me and asked if I was feeling any better. Suddenly Mr Q came along and said, 'Don't you keep my staff from their work, get back to your own office, otherwise I will report you to Mr Hunt.' I replied that, 'I don't care, you can do what you like, I'm not afraid of you or Mr Hunt.' I couldn't listen to Mr H and quickly left his office, slamming the door. Miss Sutton and I hid in the W.C. She said I was foolish and Mr Q had not meant it.

'Did it blow over?

'Yes, but I wouldn't look Mr Qualtrough in the face ever again.

2nd April 1943

With Jimmy on leave, Elsie and I booked us all seats at a variety of shows. First we went to the Empire and saw Vic Oliver [Oliver (1898-1964) was a comedian, pianist, violinist and conductor]. Gosh it was the funniest thing I've ever seen. We all laughed till our sides ached. Tomorrow evening Jimmy and I are going to the Royal Court to see a play, Wilfred Lawson in 'The Devil's Own', a new thriller.

--- Now we come to the Wirral, Mother.

4th April 1943

[Written from 'Somewhere in Wirral, Sunday afternoon]

My own darling, I have written your letters in some peculiar places, but this time I think this is the most unusual. At the moment Jimmy and I are sitting down in a country footpath enjoying a well-earned rest after a rather good hike. We took a train to Bidston and walked to Thurstaston via Arrowe Park. This by the way is full of Yankees. At one time it was occupied by the French.

Darling today was the first time I have dared to walk through Thurstaston, especially the Common, since you and I used to go there on your weekend leaves!!! After we have had our rest we *intend walking through to Hoylake or West Kirby and getting a train home.*

[Thankfully, Mother seemed to have perked up again].

11th April 1943

[Written from Upholland]

I am having a lovely time here at your parents' – I generally do. For your mother's 32nd wedding anniversary, which is on Wednesday, I presented her with a bunch of beautiful pink tulips.

15th April 1943 (Airgraph)

The other night I took my mother to see 'Bambi', a coloured cartoon by Walt Disney. I adored it – beautiful little animals in it.

16th April 1943

I have been very busy in the office all week. In two weeks' time we are having a big 'Wings for Victory' Week, and Napier's target figure is £10,000 (£1 per head). My boss is the one person who has organised the whole thing, so you can imagine the amount of work I have had to do, being his secretary. All day long I have been typing minutes of meetings and agendas for the Great Week. On Monday we had a visit from a Group Captain of an RAF station, from which we are having their dance band and military band to play daily in the canteen. Also he brought with him a Flying-Officer who is speaking (a lot of propaganda) to the workers in the lunch hours, then after he steps off his soap box there is a rush to buy Savings certificates....WE HOPE!!! This is the motive of course.

16th April 1943 (Airgraph)

Darling I am annoyed at you for not taking my advice about postponing that terrible trek through the Himalayas!! Never

mind, Stan, you can do as you please, go wherever you wish!!!!!!!!
I am thoroughly annoyed at you for doing the very thing I advised
you not to do. After this airgraph, Stanley, you need not expect
another thing, because I warned you that if you went I would stop
writing. I will teach you!!

Yours truly,

Phyllis.

--- Well, I said, that embargo didn't last very long, did it? All of three days!

--- Mother was always very impulsive, weren't you, chick?

--- I'm getting a cup of tea. Can you put the kettle on?

We decided to end the session there, but later, as I was getting in the car, Father came out and stopped me.

--- You realise she has forgotten how to put the kettle on?

--- 'What do you mean?

--- 'She can't do it. Forgotten how. And yesterday she couldn't work out how to put the receiver back on the phone, just left it dangling.

8

We resumed next day, my father and I, thinking that the more we kept Mother's mind occupied the better.

19th April 1943 (Airgraph)

My own Dearest Darling, I have a little confession to make – I am in disgrace!!! All right, darling, don't jump, it's not what you think it is. Truth is that at the time of writing your airgraph No. 260 I was unfortunately in a FRIGHTFUL TEMPER, and I there and then swore that 'you need not expect another thing'. Well I'm afraid that I have made rather a fool of myself, and I'm feeling humiliated with myself. This was all due to you going on that hideous trek. Don't think I have forgiven you – oh no I have not. You are still in the wrong for disobeying my orders. The only reason that I started this airgraph was that I was so thrilled and appreciative for you sending some more stockings!!

24th April 1943

[Addressed from Admiral Benbow Inn, Ruyton XI Towns, Baschurch nr Shrewsbury]

Edna and I [Edna Bell was her cousin] *are spending Easter here. The address is rather queer isn't it? Actually it is a little wayside hamlet tucked away 'somewhere in Shropshire'. It is such a beautiful inn. We slept very well last night in a colossal 4-poster bed. Our food is excellent too, plenty of best butter and home-made jams etc. This morning we took the bus to Shrewsbury: lovely place but very overcrowded so we only stayed 2 hours. There is a young curate and his wife staying here. They are very nice but Mr Wills will insist on playing old English folk songs, all day, on the piano,* such as 'Sweet and Low' and 'Roast Beef of Old England.' Drives me mad!!

The countryside is absolutely wonderful. Every tree is laden with either pink or white blossom. As soon as I saw it I thought 'O to be in England now that April's here.'

29th April 1943 (Airgraph)

Well I am home again after our nice Easter break. Tonight I received a rather alarming letter from Jimmy. It was a secretive one really. He asked me to tell my mother that he thinks that his recent leave _was the last_ and that very soon he will be playing a most vital part in 'something.' I wish I could tell you darling but I know you'll guess. He added that 'I don't think I will be seeing you any more, Phyl, until the war is over because when I arrive "there" it is there I stay for the duration.'

29th April 1943 [Written by Nanny]

Phyl's one delight is getting out her typewriter and banging away for hours writing to you. We often wonder what she can find to say, but of course she knows best herself. Jimmy has been on leave and went down to some old school-friends both at the Collegiate and the University but only saw some of the masters. Sorry I haven't written for a couple of weeks but I haven't been very well.

29th April 1943 (Airgraph)

I am off work at the moment as my mother is seriously ill – the doctor fears pneumonia. It came on last night and this morning she couldn't get up at all. Fan is upstairs with her. I have been making her eat some toast and Bovril, also some Horlick's Malted Milk. I also went to the butcher's where I stood in a queue for 90 minutes. When I eventually reached the counter to my amazement there were still some pork chops left. I didn't expect anything except *sausages. For dinner tonight I am cooking a little cauliflower, pork chops, onions and chipped potatoes.*

Your 'trek' sounded really interesting but why didn't you use your holiday as a <u>rest</u> like I did? But I know you, always 'on the go'!!

--- Mother, I notice you don't mention Nanny's illness again at all in your letters.

--- It was just exhaustion, I think. [Voluble, Mother seemed like her old self again]. It was also to do with the news about Jimmy. She, and all of us were scared for him since he was obviously getting ready for D-Day.

--- And what about Fan? How on earth did she get upstairs?

--- Oh yes, I remember. She wanted desperately to be with Mother so the doctor (a big beefy man) carried her upstairs and put her in their bed. She was crying.

--- Who?

--- Fan.

--- I'm going to get back to Father's letters now, because it's been a while we heard from him.

--- That's all right.

Her amenability was, for once, reassuring.

9

Last month, darling, a friend of mine did something which I think is the most dastardly trick a man could possibly do during the present emergency. Robert __ used to be G.E. Razmak and he became one of my best friends. He and I designed a new large hospital. He used to complain a lot about headaches and giddiness. [Later] he was admitted to Razmak Hospital and a medical board considered that he should return to England because he would die if he remained any longer in India. When I was in Bannu last February for my Urdu course Robert came to the hospital there on his way to Rawalpindi. So I dropped everything and visited him. When I got there I found him not in bed as expected but sitting by a fire fully clothed reading a novel. He said that his only cure was to go home. That was the last I saw of him. Last month a medical report was furnished to our office from Rawalpindi to say that he was found medically fit and capable of working in India.

Well dear it has since transpired that he was acting. As a result he has been reduced in rank. What do you think of that? The man had no backbone.

This evening Joe Newman, my friend next door, and I have been acting the fool. At about 7.30pm I called on him and found him just preparing to have a bath. He was entirely stripped except for a thin towel. I stood by his door and called him. As soon as he came to the door I dodged behind him and locked him out on the verandah. He instantly charged into my quarter in order to get into his bathroom via my back door. I anticipated this and dashed to his bathroom and locked the door just in time. Well he stayed in my bathroom a terrific time. Nothing happened for about 15 minutes so I unlocked the door and told him he could go in peace. He came out all smiles. After he had gone I went in to see what he had done to cause such amusement. Lo and behold he had used my commode and almost filled it – the smell was awful. Because the commodes are only emptied twice a day I was stuck with the smell all night.

19th May 1943 (Airgraph)

Just after I finished tennis this evening a cable was brought to me. Oh sweetheart, it was lovely but I did not know that I had some children!!!! Gosh Phyl I did laugh because this is how the cable read: 'Fondest love darling, my thoughts and prayers are ever with you. All well. CHILDREN EVACUATED.' Under the printing were the numbers representing each phrase. Apparently the Post Office had misinterpreted your last number which was 69. Perhaps the message is right and you are keeping the twins a secret until I return.

26th May 1943 (Airgraph)

I was awfully sorry to hear of your little Easter holiday falling through. That was certainly very unfortunate darling. Never mind sweetie pie you have a really grand holiday in Scotland to look forward to.

--- I'm going to get lunch ready, Mother suddenly announced.

--- That's OK, I replied. I discovered a gap in your correspondence, Mother, with only one letter between the 9th and the 30th May.

--- Oh?

--- But last night I found a whole clutch of your airgraphs mixed up with Father's....ones I hadn't read before.

10

I am feeling terribly fed up today darling. We have another new man in our office, he is Mr Hunt's 'deputy' and is to 'keep watch over us.' You can rest assured that I am not going to take any orders from him, or anybody else. He is a clever fellow from all accounts, having been to all the best schools. However this does not alter the fact that none of us like him. I can see he and I coming to blows before very long. He has a habit of coming over to us and inspecting the work we have been doing, then, with a grunt, he will return to his desk without any comment.

Darling, I hope you are enjoying yourself in Dalhousie.

5th May 1943 (Airgraph)

We had a letter from Jimmy. He is on a 10 day course 'somewhere in England' and he said that after being at the University for 2 years learning how to design buildings, he now studies the art of EXPLOSIVES to destroy them! Edna Bell [her cousin] *has had to start at Roote's of Speke where they are making aircraft.*

9th May 1943

Darling, what do you think of the wonderful news of Tunisia and Bizhta? Isn't it grand? It won't be long now when we will drive the Germans out of Africa then I'm sure the war will be over. Darling do you remember the time we went to Goole for a weekend to see my mother? There was a Home Guard practice on. You had just received your commission, and because you had no papers to prove your identity, you were marched off as a 'prisoner of war.' I have to smile when I picture you being marched away by an escort.

--- Gosh, I'd forgotten all about that.

--- Sounds like a Captain Mainwaring moment.

--- It was. It was.

And darling do you remember those little tiny puddings I used to buy in York? I used to steam them for tea and serve with custard. I think I used to buy them in fours (4 for 6d) at Marks and Spencers!!

--- So that's where your craving for steamed suet puddings came from!

Do you remember our first night in York? How the Coopers greeted us at '1A' (Wimpole Street). Then when we went to bed we found hot water bottles there. Then the sirens sounded! We didn't mind that because we were so thrilled and in love with one another. It was the first night in our first home. Darling Stan – those 3 months [April-July 1941] were the happiest of my life. And I've been crying whilst writing this!!!

[At this point, right on cue, Mother rushed out for a quiet weep in the kitchen.]

--- Oh, come back, Phyl!

--- I'm all right. You carry on. I can hear you.

Yesterday I went into the GPO and sent you a cable. There is a new thing out now, for India. It is a choice of 3 phrases for 2/6. Well, sweetheart, I had a choice of about 140 different messages. I wrote down one, then another, but I could not find another suitable one to make up the 3. All the others were such things as 'X is dead', 'Please send £x immediately', 'Son born'. I was just about to give up when, in order to amuse myself as well as you, just for a joke I put down No. 69 which meant 'Well and safe at home, children evacuated.' I roared all the way home.

This week is 'Wings for Victory' Week in Liverpool. Tomorrow we are having the Band of the Royal Marines to play during 3 lunch hours 11-2pm. Then we are having the RAF Dance Band, Will Fyffe [comedian], Nova Pilbeam [actress/film star] and numerous others.

Jimmy has passed the stage in his Military Course of 'Explosives and Dynamite' and the next one is 'Mine-laying and Booby Traps.' In July, darling, (July 10th - 17th actually) Elsie and I are going to Scotland.

13th May 1943 (Airgraph)

After a week without any letters finally one arrived written from 'Chamba State'. Darling I found it awfully enthralling, and your description of the 'record-breaking' 38+ mile walk fairly made me furious not to have been there with you!!!!!

Today I spoke to a <u>West-Indian</u> [she actually means someone from the west of India]. He works in the Engine Drawing Office. He knows that you are on the Frontier and today he asked me all about you. He knows Lahore and particularly Dalhousie (which he pronounced differently from me). He comes from Poona. He came over here to be educated at Liverpool University in Mechanical Engineering but cannot leave because of the war. He is terribly homesick but we agreed it would be lovely if you and he exchanged places.

Darling, whenever I receive news from you it sort of helps me an awful lot. I seem to suddenly possess warmth and an abundance of love and life.

19th May 1943

We had a letter from Jimmy today. He said that he had to lead his whole battalion round the town to open 'Wings for Victory' Week there. He said that, as a rule, either a Lt-Col or a Captain does this *sort of thing, never has he known a subaltern to lead the whole company unaided!! He said that he had to shout like a madman to make the hundreds of them hear his commands. According to his letters he has been undergoing all sorts of Commando training, then having to teach it, and lecture [on] it, to the men. It is so hot on the East Coast now, that he is wearing a tropical shirt.*

--- Right, I think that's enough for now, Father butted in. We've got shopping to do, haven't we, Phyl?

--- Have we? But I was enjoying that. I love hearing the bits about Jimmy.

--- Yes, but we've got things to do. Go and get ready, chick.

11

A week later we resumed our routine. Before we began, Father made an announcement.

--- Just to tell you that I am now, officially, Episcopal Architect for the diocese.

--- What does that mean?

--- Well, it means I inspect the fabric of the local churches to give advice about anything that's required architecturally.

--- Such as what?

--- Such as leaking gutters, water penetration, damp, pointing needing doing.

--- It's ridiculous, I think, Mother cut in. Why can't a younger man do it? You're not as strong as you were, climbing ladders in all weathers at your age is just daft. And it's voluntary – you're not paid at all, are you?

--- That doesn't matter. The Church urgently needs advice and I said I would.

--- Well I think you're mad.

--- Tomorrow, Tim….tomorrow I would like you to take me to St. Thomas's for our first inspection.

--- Our?

--- Yes, if you don't mind.

20th May 1943 (Airgraph)

I am going to Upholland for the weekend darling. I get awfully Stan-sick when I am there. I think it is due to your mother and dad speaking about you all the time, then on the other hand, certain ways your dad looks, and things he does, certainly remind me of you, because you are definitely the image of your father. I have always thought so. Often when your father is sitting in his chair speaking to me he has a way of blinking his eyes and raising his eyebrows which is absolutely YOU DARLING!! I've never seen such a likeness. I feel that I am watching an older version of my Stan!!

21st May 1943 (Airgraph)

In your most recent letter you had just arrived back in the office after your leave and to your joy and happiness found 27 airgraphs waiting. What a thrill for you! The papers here are full of the latest news of the bombing of those dams in the Ruhr, but personally I am rather disgusted over this – I did not think that the <u>British</u>, of all people, would do a thing like this!

'I'm jumping back to your letters now, Father.'

28th May 1943

Just before I started to write this paragraph I was rather badly interrupted by my next door neighbour, Newman. I was nicely sitting in my pyjamas by my little writing desk when he walked in 'full of beans' and devilment. He commenced playing tricks with my bed – naturally I wouldn't stand for this and consequently it ended up in a general melee on the floor with all my bedclothes all over us. Gosh it was a terrific fight. My poor old sleeping suit ended up with one sleeve missing. This sort of thing goes on quite often, Phyl – we play the most childish tricks on one another. Earlier on in the evening I crept up to his bathroom while he was having his bath and poured a bowl of cold water over him. Gosh he let out a terrific yell. Probably these actions seem very childish but honestly darling when you are 'cooped' up inside a camp perimeter and not allowed to go outside without being shot at, these sort of antics make life a little more pleasant and amusing.

178

30th May 1943

Very shortly I will be going down into the plains over a job – gosh I am not looking forward to it at all because I know I will have to suffer terrific perspiration and uncomfortableness. Actually Phyl I have found I can stand the heat extremely well during the day but it is the night-time which gets me down. You just lay on a sheet with absolutely nothing on except a towel wrapped round your middle while above a large fan swirls round and round. I have to go to this place in order to attend a conference. For the last two days I have been a member on a Court of Inquiry. The Court is trying the Head Clerk in my office for accepting bribes from people under him in order to get them out of being posted overseas.

Darling it is nice to see your photographs around my room but very often their stillness and lack of movement almost drives me insane. Yesterday, sweetest, a tribesman friend of mine gave me an embroidered Mausudi tablecloth for you which his sister has made especially for you. Her name is ALWAN BIBI.

The actual tablecloth embroidered by Alwan Bibi.

--- Is that the cloth square that's in your study?

--- That's right.

--- I've often wondered what it was.

6th June 1943

I suppose darling you must think it is rather strange that I get my dinner between 8.30 and 9.30pm because by that time the air has cooled and the warm dining-room is not so unbearable. Sunday is the 'curry' day, a real Indian curry. Today we had Kofta curry which is a sort of curried meatball. When I come home darling one day I will make a curry especially for you just to see if you like it. [Even though I never remember my father ever preparing a single meal in his life, he obviously taught my mother well since we had a fiery curry at least once a week as a family].

12th June 1943

I suppose when this letter drops through your letter-box you will be all keyed up for your little holiday in Scotland. Perhaps someday in the near future you will also take me to your Scottish relations [this never happened]. *Isn't it strange, Phyl, but each of us hardly knows our respective relations.*

13th June 1943

Lately I have had quite a lot of trouble over my servant. The other day while I was having my lunch in the Officers' Club the Abdar (Head Waiter) came over to me and said that my servant had been caught stealing eggs. I went to the back of the Mess and saw [him] quarrelling with a cook. In order to convince myself that my fellow had actually stolen the eggs I decided to search him. When I told him what I was going to do he ran for his life out of the building. This action definitely convinced me he was guilty. The cook went on to tell me that sugar, meat, cheese etc were being stolen every day and he thought my bearer was the thief but today was the first time he actually caught him red-handed. Anyway, to cut a long story short, we agreed that my bearer's 18 year old son should be my new servant.

14th June 1943 (Airgraph)

Last night I received an airgraph from your dad dated 17th May. Gosh it came as a terrific surprise to me but nevertheless a most welcome one. I sincerely hope that now he has broken the ice he will continue to write. Phyl he can rest assured that I will not pull his spelling and grammar to pieces – his thoughts and expressions are much more valuable.

29th June 1943

My Most Precious Darling,

Last night I arrived safely back in my office after a weary five days' tour in the blazing heat of the plains. I hope you will forgive me for not writing to you for the last four days but honestly, Phyl, I haven't had one moment to myself at all. Gosh the heat down in the plains was absolutely terrific and I nearly melted away. In D.I.Khan two nights ago the temperature was 100F in my bedroom at midnight. I have never been so uncomfortable in the whole of my life.

Some changes are taking place in my office shortly....and it means that I am surplus and I expect in the near future I will be posted away. It may not happen and I suppose the only thing to do is wait and see what happens.

4th July 1943 (Airgraph)

Well, sweetheart, I am going to another job but one I like very much: Garrison Engineer. I can't name the place [Wana] but it was where I was before. It is a good station with an extremely nice climate, especially in the summer.

9th July 1943 (Airgraph)

My poor sweetheart, it seems awful that you have to suffer so much unhappiness from the hands of your boss. Oh God I wish I could lay my hands on that devil [Mr Hunt] I would make him squirm. Please will you send me his address so that I can let him have a piece of my mind.

10th July 1943 (Airgraph)

I was thrilled to the bottom of my being when I heard the news at 1.30pm which announced our invasion of Sicily – at last something is appearing on the horizon and directing us nearer to the end of the war. Darling, I know how awful it must be for you to work under [such] a swine but just hold on a little longer, the end is now in sight.

11th July 1943

Oh darling, I was so pleased you had decided not to do anything definite regarding your job but were thinking of joining the Mechanical Transport Corps. To this my answer is 'I do not agree.' Phyl, my darling, I would prefer you to stay out of any sort of service which compels you to wear a uniform. I was so pleased when you sensibly said you would think it over while on holiday in Scotland.

14th July 1943 (Airgraph)

Darling, I am now back in Wana.

15th July 1943 (Telegram)

SORRY DARLING WOMENS TRANSPORT CORP NOT AGREED TO

--- That's a good place to stop for today.

--- Yes, Father replied. Because this afternoon you've to take me to St. Thomas's.

--- Thanks for telling me.

--- I thought I asked you yesterday.

--- No, you didn't.

--- Well I thought I had. Douglas [the vicar] has spotted a leak and he asked if I would investigate. Come on, get ready.

--- But it's pouring. Will he be there?

--- Unfortunately he rang to say he couldn't make it. But he's left a ladder.

--- Well, that was good of him.

After a quick omelette and coffee we headed off. Picture this then: an old, old man with a drip at the end of his nose, perched precariously at the top of a rickety ladder, poking dead leaves out of a gutter with a stick, his drenched son holding on to the said ladder with rain pouring down his upturned face.

--- Should you be doing this? I asked on the return journey. Aren't you too old? [This was cruel].

--- Of course not. I know what I'm doing. Besides, Douglas couldn't find anyone else to do it.

But I knew he **was** too old.

--- Oh, Stan, why are you doing this? You're soaked! Mother said, as we bundled him into the house.

--- Why couldn't Douglas do it himself or get an ordinary workman to help?

--- I'm the Diocesan Architect, he announced rather limply, wrapping his 'honour' round him like a dry cloak. Any old workman wouldn't do. If that leak had affected the fabric of the building I would need to know.

--- I've a good mind to ring Douglas right now, Mother added.

--- Don't you dare!

Driving back to my flat, I tried to think things through from Father's point of view. Was he clinging to the kudos of being Diocesan Architect because there was nothing else left in his life to shore him against his ruin? Except, maybe these letters.

12

Anyway, by the next day matters seemed to have settled down and we continued the readings as if yesterday's events were completely forgotten.

31st May 1943

We had a letter from Jimmy today [here Father uttered what seemed like a groan, but I wasn't sure]. *He is doing excellently. He has passed numerous examinations on 'Mines', 'Demolitions' and so on. He obtained 91% for one and 87% for the other. A Major-General had examined the papers and had written straight across Jimmy's: 'This man will go far; he knows his work.'*

On July 10th I hope to go to Scotland with Elsie. We've booked in at an Hotel Lochinvar where the fee is 6 guineas each person per week. The cost of living here is colossal. Darling, do try and send me some tea and sugar, some days we can't drink tea because we haven't any!!!

6th June 1943

My own Darling, I wish you could see me now. I am sitting in my slacks, an old woolly jumper and bedroom slippers, typing this in the sitting-room where I am entirely alone, except for the kitten which is sitting watching me. Sweetheart, I felt very sad yesterday afternoon. I think I feel it more on Saturday afternoon more than any other day, because it is then that I go to town and see other girls with their soldier sweethearts and husbands. I cut through Lime Street Station and there I watched with envy the couples meeting at the barriers and walking away arm-in-arm as though they had all they wished for at their sides.

2th June 1943

It is the Whit weekend and whilst in town darling I went into Bon Marche in order to buy a blouse for a new suit I have recently bought. Lo and behold everything I saw was 'Utility', so I made my way to George Henry Lee's where I visited the 'Expensive Dept' and bought an Indian silk blouse which cost me my last 4 coupons and also the astounding sum of 59/6d!!!! Darling, fancy £2 19s 6d for a silk blouse [about £100 today]. Still, it is a 'SMASHER'. I have bought it for my Scottish holiday.

Remember other Whit weekends we have experienced, darling? The first we knew together we went on a 5/- trip to Llandudno. The second we went to Keswick, while the third was spent 'entertaining' your mother and dad at our dear little York residence. Gosh, those were the days!

Everything about this war is horrible!! This afternoon my father started me [crying] by telling me about a little baby which had been found strangled in Stanley Park!! There is very little other news but it is 11.50pm (Mother, dad and Fan are all in bed) and I am waiting to hear the midnight news. On the sideboard I have your photograph before me. I've just looked up and seen you. I adore it. You are getting more and more good-looking. You sort of have a smile in your eyes and I can't help but smile back. I adore the smooth line of your cheek – the part where you shave – and the light is shining down one side of your face.

Darling Stan, I must be off to bed. The time is 12.30am and I have missed the news through dreaming of you. I have been writing for 3 and a half hours and my father will be knocking on the floor in his old usual way. Soon we will be one again, I know it.

--- That was a really charming letter, Mother. So in the moment.

--- Thank you.

14th June 1943 (Airgraph)

Today, after dinner, my mother took me over to Wallasey Village in order to see some old friend of hers. They are big market gardeners by the name of Sparks. We had not seen them for many years – I was only 11 the last time they saw me. They have a son aged 8, and believe me darling, if ever I wanted to shake a child, I did this one! All the time it was 'Don't do that, Norman' or 'Norman, darling, be a good little boy for Mummy.' Little Norman, in my opinion, wanted his 'behind' spanking not simply a 'talking to.' Cheeky little devil!

15th June 1943 (Airgraph)

I hate my boss. I absolutely DETEST, LOATHE and HATE the confounded little rotter. Darling, tonight about 10 minutes before it was time to leave, he gave me a division to do. I did it and gave him the answer. He got a different one to me. He came over to me (before everybody) and said, 'Tell me how you got that will you.' Just as I was finishing it he turned on me and said, 'Is that the first division you have done since you left school, don't say it isn't because I can see that it is, you are still working them out the way they teach children at school.' Oh Stan, I didn't know how to control myself and I knew everyone was watching. I was speechless with temper and anger. I said, 'Whether it's true or not I have got the same answer as you, haven't I?' I threw the pencil out of my hand on to my desk and got my coat on. He walked up behind me and told me to take off my coat, that he hadn't finished with me yet. Oh Stan I don't know what happened after that. I didn't wait, though, and I walked out with my coat over my arm and banged the door. I know I will hear about it tomorrow.

Oh I wish, how I wish, I hadn't to go back. I HATE IT AND HIM.

16th June 1943 (Airgraph)

Well, Stan, I proceeded to the confounded office, ready for the storm which I felt would start the moment I put my face in. My boss SIMPLY IGNORED ME ALL DAY!!!!! Every time I spoke he merely didn't answer. Darling, Stan, I'm in a proper pickle. Please reply immediately and let me know whether I should join the Mechanised Transport Corps. Please don't say no.

--- Well, as we know, Father did say no. So let's get back to his letters. Are you both still enjoying this?

--- Oh, yes, Mother said. We did love each other then, didn't we, Stan?

--- What do you mean by 'then'?

--- Well it all sounds so fresh. And I'm looking forward to hearing about my Scottish trip.

--- That's just coming up.

--- Keep going with Phyl's letters, Father interrupted.

25th June 1943 (Airgraph)

Last night Elsie and I went to the Empire. The (live) show was halfway through when a BBC announcer said, 'Ladies and Gentlemen, it may interest you to know that this programme is being broadcast to His Majesty's Forces serving in North Africa and India'!!! Gosh, darling, the cheers were deafening. I felt very sad and emotional and was 'itching' to shout out some little message with the hope that you would hear me.

26th June 1943

Two weeks today, Elsie and I will be in Scotland. I'm not partial to my relatives, only my grandmother's (they are the ones who reside in Scotland). The name of the place is Dalry, the nearest town being New Galloway. They have not seen me since I was 7 [in 1926], when my nannie took me. I believe then that they were raving about 'the lass with the milk and roses complexion.' They are very nice homely people, the sons and daughters were all school teachers.

Jimmy is now a Lieutenant and my cousin Albert [Precious] is in North Africa. He is terribly homesick, poor kid. His own people never write to him (because they positively cannot – so ignorant), so I drop him an airgraph about once a fortnight. He looks upon our home as HIS, and my mother and dad as HIS OWN. Jimmy has had some tough times since he has had his commission. He has had stitches in his hand caused when a 'dud' grenade went off, his ankles sprained playing football and gastritis in his tummy.

5th July 1943 (Airgraph)

My mother and dad (and Fan) are going to Yorkshire again [to stay with her cousin in Goole]. I have another week off at the end of August. I haven't decided where to go yet, but may land up there. By the way they are living in a new abode now. It sounds rather a posh affair too. Dozens of rooms, two bathrooms, plus a telephone of their own. It is a very big farmhouse-cum-manor and I believe the orchards and acres of vegetation are colossal. Darling, Jimmy has been moved to Scotland and on Saturday I got a letter from him to say he is coming to our hotel to spend a weekend leave with us!!!

10th July 1943

[Letter addressed from Lochinvar Hotel, Dalry, Castle Douglas, Kirkcudbrightshire]

We arrived here this morning at 10.30am after over ten hours travelling. Gosh what a time we had. We left Lime Street at midnight last night and had to change at Carlisle at 4.45am. It was bitterly cold on the station but we had to sit there 2 hours

Mr and Mrs Clark outside their house in Dalry.

waiting for a connection to Dumfries. The train was so packed that Elsie had to sit on a table in the dining-car while I had to <u>stand</u> in the lavatory space. I was hemmed in by kit bags, rifles, steel helmets, etc. I couldn't even move my arms to wipe my nose. Eventually we got here at 10.30am. After a wash we went out for a walk and when we got back I was handed a telegram from Jimmy asking us to meet him at 2pm on Tuesday in Ayr! It is only 90 minutes away by bus.

After that we went and saw my grannie's relatives who live around the corner. There on the door was my namesake [?] 'Clark'. They made an awful fuss of us and were thrilled to see 'the wee <u>girrrrl</u> married'!!!

12th July 1943 [Dalry]

This afternoon my auntie asked us to come to tea.

--- Mother, was this Margaret Clark?

--- Yes, that's right.

--- Nanny's youngest sister. From the family tree I've found out she was born in 1897 but I can't find when she died.

--- No. I can't remember either.

We refused at first, in a nice way, because we didn't want to use up her food when we were eating at the hotel, but there was no arguing with her. Crikey what a tea: macaroni cheese, strawberries, blancmange, jelly, raspberry pudding, scones of every description and home-made cakes. After tea they took us to Hugh Clark's up the village. He is my mother's cousin and a lieutenant in the Home Guard. Oh, Stan, I've felt much nearer to my grandmother since I've been here.

14th July 1943 (Dalry)

Yesterday morning Elsie and I got the 8.50am bus into Ayr, 34 miles away. We had a beautiful lunch with Jimmy then sat on the sea-front. He looks awfully well, very brown and healthy. We had a good laugh if nothing else.

19th July 1943

I had a hellish journey home from Scotland darling. I never got a seat until I reached Preston!!!! From New Galloway we stood in a corridor, from Dumfries to Carlisle we stood in a dining car. At Carlisle we had the devil's own job even getting into the train it was so packed. But as the train was ready to steam out somebody shouted, 'What about the Guards Van?' In it were about 30 airmen, 5 nuns, a few civilians and Elsie and me, and nobody could see a thing. Darling, Liverpool seems an awful dump after living

191

a week of luxury in Scotland. To think that the day before I was swimming in the river and getting sunburnt.

--- Who'd have thought it, Phyl, that we'd end up living in Scotland since 1965?

---- I know.

And on that happy note we called it a day.

13

17th July 1943 (Airgraph)

For the last couple of days I have been completely run off my feet with work and worry. Just before I arrived here to take over my new job (as Garrison Engineer, Wana) all the roads in my division were severely breached by the very heavy floods which have just occurred. Causeways and bridges have been washed away. As an engineer…it has been my job to build temporary diversions in order to get the traffic through as quickly as possible. This evening I crawled back to my room absolutely tired out. A few minutes later a cable arrived from you which read 'GOOD LUCK. KEEP SMILING. MY THOUGHTS ARE WITH YOU.' Wasn't it most wonderful that these words should arrive when I most wanted them!

26th July 1943 (Airgraph)

Since early this morning I have been down in the desert at a little place called Tank which is reputed to be the hottest spot in Asia. According to this afternoon's heat I can well believe it – it must have been well over 120F in the shade.

Darling whatever made you go to Dumfries from Lime Street Station? You should have got the Glasgow train from Exchange; this would have taken you all the way. [That's so typical of them both, I thought: Mother finding the most tortuous route, and Father correcting her from afar with his Bradshaw.]

At the moment I feel on top of the world because the news is so good. It certainly appears now that the Italians have thrown out Mussolini and the Fascist Party they will ask for peace in the very near future.

5th August 1943 (Airgraph)

Well, sweetheart, I have just heard on the wireless that I am entitled to one of the new war medals. At first I thought I would not be a recipient – now I understand that that this medal is to be given to men who took part in Dunkirk, Burma and the North-West Frontier. I feel rather cheered up by this because I have worked in areas where I was in very great danger of being shot by hostile tribesmen and doing work of great importance. Darling, you must continue at Napier's for a little while longer. You are very headstrong and at times vindictive and it might be better for you not to get so bad-tempered at times. By nature I am bad-tempered too but I find that sometimes a better victory is obtained by remaining dumb rather than seeing red and saying things to the person directly concerned.

--- I bet that didn't go down well, I said.

--- It didn't at all, Mother replied.

--- I know. But it had to be said.

12th August 1943 (Airgraph)

This evening I feel absolutely tired out due to playing football. Since I have been here I have been trying to get a side together. Tonight was our first match but it ended in a 6-1 defeat.

15th August 1943

Since I have been in Wana I have been able to get a beautiful wireless on hire, it is a 7 valve Marconi. I like listening to it, especially programmes from England, because I feel nearer to you. Last night I heard a Promenade Concert from the Albert Hall. Gosh I did enjoy it.

22nd August 1943 (Airgraph)

Oh sweetheart I thank God every night that I have got a wife in whom I can place all my trust. Gosh I would go completely insane if you were a woman who loved the company of men and pursued a loose life while I was away. It is absolutely wonderful to think that when I return to you I shall find you just as I left you two years ago. To be quite frank darling I am made in such a way that if you did anything to let me down, my love instead of being so devoted and loyal would instantly go as cold as ice and I would finish with you forever. I would not bother with women again and instead I would just live for my work and studies.

--- All that sounds like a threat, I interrupted, almost as if you could sense trouble ahead.

--- Not at all. Have *you* ever been in love? No, I thought not. I was just speaking the truth.

1st September 1943 (Airgraph)

Lately I have been suffering quite a good deal with pimples on my face. Actually they have been coming and going in a small way for the last 12 months or so. This morning while I was in the hospital looking at a job my men were doing I decided to see a doctor friend of mine in order to find out what was wrong. When he saw the pimples he laughed and gave me a wink: 'Well, to be quite frank with you,' he said, 'I will explain but please don't think I am joking. Without being rude I am probably quite correct in saying that you were intimate with your wife before you left. Since you left her two years ago your blood has been absorbing all your pent-up feelings.' I looked at him and knew he was quite right. So you see Phyl we are both one – part of you is throbbing through my veins and part of me is inside you.

--- I soon got rid of your pimples! Mother quipped, bursting into giggles.

[That was the most intimate thing they ever said in front of me. I was shocked.]

5th September 1943

Yesterday I returned from a rather exciting tour. I had to go out two days ago and recce a new alignment for a road in the mountains of a very dangerous hostile area. I had a big bedragga escort with me and the Political department arranged an equally big malik protection. A malik, darling, is a head man of a tribe. When such-like men accompany me the hostiles will not shoot at me in case they hit one of these men and so cause a tribal blood feud or 'Badi' as it is called in Pushto (the tribal language).

On 4th Sept I started out but we had to stop because I was told that a hostile gang was waiting for me in the hills through which I had to pass. I asked why they were waiting for me and my informer said that one of the maliks had leaked information about my trip. Apparently the tribes of this area had a 'jirga' (a tribal meeting) and had passed 19 resolutions, one of which was 'No new roads will be made by the Government in the area without terrific opposition'. I returned to Wana disappointed.

9th September 1943 (Telegram)

ITALIANS SURRENDER. GOOD NEWS DARLING. REUNION IN SIGHT.

At this point we paused for a spot of lunch, and while Mother was laying the table we noticed that the placing of the cutlery was haphazard to say the least.

--- Phyl, why have I got three forks and Tim two knives and a spoon?

--- Oh, sorry, I must have been dreaming.

Lost in our own ordered thoughts, we rearranged the table.

Once we tucked into the salad (thankfully, perfectly well prepared) I asked Father a simple question which I had been aching to ask him for some time.

--- Father, why *were* the British in North-West India?

--- What do you mean?

--- I mean, what were you doing there? Who were you protecting it from?

---'Well, it's a long story, and I may get it completely wrong, but since India was our ally in the war (and for a long time before that) we had to protect her....

---''Her'?

--- ''Mother India', as she was called. We had to protect her in the East from the Japanese, and in the North from the anti-British tribesmen within India itself...and the Germans were approaching from Russia. There'd been a history, in the part where I was, of political and religious agitation stirred up by someone called the Fakir of Opi, or was it Ipi? I can't remember now [it was actually Ipi]. Anyway, he campaigned against the Indian government in Waziristan who were on our side. Basically he wanted us out of India so we were really there to protect India from its own tribesmen.

---What happened to this Opi/Ipi chap?

--- I don't think anyone knows.

--- So, all the roads, petrol dumps and bridges you were building were for whom?

--- Us and the Indian government obviously…to help us move about this hostile country more easily.

--- Nothing much happened, though, did it?

--- No. There was quite a bit of trouble before I arrived, I think, nasty ambushes and so on, but it all died down very quickly once I was there.

--- The hero.

--- No, I didn't mean it like that.

--- I know. I was joking! Were you aware at all of the Quit India movement and the stirrings of Indian rebellion? You haven't mentioned it at all in your letters so far.

--- And I don't think I ever do. Besides, the censors would have pooh-poohed any mention of it. There were rumours of course. You must remember we were very isolated from all that talk where we were. I think most of the trouble was in the big cities.

I changed tack.

---'Here's a thing that interests me. I've been re-reading Paul Scott's Raj Quartet and last night I came across an interesting bit. I've written it down. One of his characters says, *'that the British in India were doomed because their pygmy natures couldn't cope with the vastness of the place."*

--- I'm not sure what that means.

--- He meant, I think, that, ultimately, towards the end of the Raj, the British realised their 200 year old occupation of India had failed, was rapidly coming to an end, and so they retreated into their Little Englander shells.

--- Well, I'm not sure about that. I was always aware we still had a job to do.

Another tack.

--- Scott also talks about the permanent class rift that existed between the ordinary, mainly working class soldiers and the posher officers. In other words, there was an unbridgeable divide even within the British forces.

---Yes, well, that has always been the case.

---Even today, I interrupted, you see it. When officers are interviewed on TV they invariably have public school accents.

---I don't know what you're getting at. This chat is turning into an inquisition by the look of it. [His discomfort was becoming more and more apparent].

--- All right, I said in a more placatory tone. What has always mystified me is how you, personally, rose through the ranks despite your background. You never seemed to have much of a Liverpool accent, never deliberately broke into Scouse lingo like Jimmy used to do. Dare I say it, you seem ashamed of your humble origins, your mother's illiteracy.

--- OK, stop. All that was drummed out of me in the army. I couldn't possibly 'rise through the ranks', as you put it, saying 'wack' all the time and showing off about our outside toilet. I sort of repressed all that in order to succeed…and I did.

--- Were you ever sorry about doing this?

--- Not at all, not at all. You wouldn't understand, but in those days you couldn't progress. I'd have been like a boxwallah dragging around my inheritance like a pauper in the streets. And so I cast it aside…deliberately.

I was suddenly conscious of Mother patiently sitting there, listening to all this.

--- Mother never reacted like you, did she?

--- No. She had no need to, did you, chick?

--- Except when you became middle class after the war, when your houses got bigger and bigger and you started mixing with the 'right people'.

--- Of course, but even then she never forgot her family.

--- No, I didn't. Did I, wack!

With the 'inquisition' over we cleared our respective minds with an autumnal stroll around the cricket ground.

14

We reconvened the next day with a return to Mother's letters.

22nd July 1943 (Airgraph)

Jimmy arrived home at 6.30am this morning. He knocked us up. He is home for 10 days. At the moment I am typing this on the table-shelter in the sitting-room [but] I can hardly move in here due to the valises, kitbag, steel helmet, greatcoat and even on the back of the chair I am sitting on there is a battle-dress. Mother and dad are very excited to see him home again but somehow I think it must be his embarkation leave – he doesn't say so but I am certain it is and that he is going somewhere 'hurriedly and secretly'!!! By the time you get this, darling, I will be starting my second week's holiday. It starts on August 23rd. I haven't yet decided where to go but will probably go with my mother to Yorkshire, to 'Ealand Grange' (my relatives!!).

23rd July 1943 (Airgraph)

Darling, in the post this morning was an invitation for my mother and I to a wedding on August 9th. It is to be held at the Adelphi Hotel (possibly the best hotel in Liverpool). *The bridegroom is a cousin of mine. Remember me telling you about my mother's cousin who lives in Aigburth. She has three sons and the eldest, James, is aged 30 and in the RAF. In civilian life he is a chartered accountant. The bride-to-be is the daughter of a big Liverpool ship-owner. My mother and I are worrying what we are going to wear because we will have to buy new summer afternoon dresses and the trouble is that we haven't a Clothing Coupon between us.*

Tomorrow, being my half-day, Jimmy and I are going hiking into the Wirral like we did before.

25th July 1943

Yesterday Jimmy and I...went over to Woodside Station and got the train to Chester. It was a glorious day and we got very sunburnt. We walked for miles along the famous walls and examined the old architecture in the Cathedral. We went in a very fashionable café for tea, and as I had done no paying, well it was my turn to pay!! When we came out at 7pm we went for another walk along the river but crikey darling if you had seen the troops. However, Jimmy got tired of saluting so he suggested that we get away from the public, so we went to the Gaumont Cinema. Jimmy was wanting to see the newsreel of the invasion of Sicily more than the actual film itself.

29th July 1943 (Airgraph)

Tonight I let Jimmy, mother and dad go to the Empire together because he has only one more day left before he goes back, and so far the three of them have been unable to go out together because of Fan. However, I offered to look after her, so they have just gone to the 2nd House. My dad is rather bucked at the idea of going out with Jimmy and my mother, because this is a thing of the past.

2nd August 1943

I managed to borrow a Clothing Coupon from a friend with which I was able to purchase a new silk dress for the wedding a week today. Darling I wish you could see the 'gown' – it is super! Being black it will look very smart and 'different'!!! It has a high neck and on this I will wear my pearls.

6th August 1943

IT'S COME – IT'S COME – AT LONG LAST – the inevitable parcel which you posted on the 8th April. I'll tell you all about it:

- Tonight when I arrived home...I looked on the sideboard to see if there was any mail from you. Not even a word, for which I was terribly disappointed. I then took off my hat and coat, sat down and started to eat my tea. My mother poured out my tea, and as she was doing so, Fan started tittering and looking at me with a beam all over her smiling face. I said, 'What's wrong with you?' My mother said, 'Nothing, I'm only laughing at a joke I heard on the wireless before you came in'....Then suddenly Fan couldn't hold it in any longer. She said, 'It's your parcel, it's come from Stan'.

Darling, the stockings are JUST PERFECT (and in time for the wedding), the powder is absolutely marvellous, so is the Pond's Cream, while the lipstick is 'just up my street'. Oh, thank you, sweetie.

Jimmy is in Prestwick, Scotland. He now has a 'Jeep' of his own. Incidentally, Clark Gable is there as an Air Gunnery Inspector with the American Air Force. He holds the rank of Captain!

9th August 1943

My own beloved Stan,

I have just returned from my cousin's wedding but I'm afraid there's not much to tell about it because it was <u>very</u> quiet and formal. My mother and I left the house at 10.30am and we were in Aigburth by 11.15. We went straight to my cousin's (the bridegroom) home. He was <u>terribly</u> nervous and was shaking in his shoes. We were then driven to St. Anne's Church, Aigburth Vale, where the service started at noon. My mother and I were put in the front row with the bridegroom's mother and relatives. After the ceremony we all had photographs taken outside the church (I'll send you one, darling). We were then driven to the Adelphi where the reception was held.

--- Mother, was the father the man everyone called 'Uncle Jack'? [John Johnstone Clark (1892-1959)]

--- That's right.

Gosh, it was a wonderful menu and everything was very nice, but oh! So stiff and formal. When the bride and groom left at 4pm everyone else did too. There was no music or dancing at all.

10th August 1943 (Airgraph)

Darling, I went to the Paramount Theatre straight after work tonight. I met my mother at 6.45 and we managed to get in right away, but gosh we had to pay 4/- each for a seat. However, I must say the film was well worth seeing. It was 'We Dive at Dawn'. Crikey darling it was an absolutely marvellous film. I absolutely LIVED in it!! My mother very very rarely goes to the pictures, but I could see that she too was enjoying it as much as I was.

17th August 1943 (Airgraph)

Darling, I am keeping house this week. My mother and Fan went to Lincolnshire this morning (to my auntie's) and my dad goes on Saturday, while I go the following Saturday. I have just finished cooking steak – my poor dad had the misfortune to eat it too!!

24th August 1943

[Addressed from 14, The Fairway, Blackmoor Drive, Liverpool 12]

Don't be alarmed by the address. I am staying at Elsie's for a week while my mother and dad are at my uncle Albert's in Yorkshire. Last Friday I went to the Philharmonic Hall and heard Malcolm Sergeant [sic] with the Liverpool Philharmonic Orchestra. Golly! It was wonderful.

26th August 1943

Darling, in your last letter you seemed annoyed for some reason that Elsie and I had met some people on our Scottish holiday and went swimming with them. This is frightfully selfish of you and I can't understand you taking this nasty attitude.

Last night I phoned my mother up to enquire what sort of time they were having. I believe the new farm is marvellous, very large with vast acres of land. I believe my dad opened a door in the house thinking it led into a room, but it was a cellar and he fell down 7-8 steps.

29th August 1943

[Addressed from Ealand Grange, Crowle, Nr Scunthorpe]

--- By the way, Mother, apart from at Christmas, you don't write any more airgraphs, just ordinary letters. Can you remember why?

--- No. Maybe I say why in one of my letters coming up. I could express myself in a less cramped way I think.

--- Are we nearly finished for today? asked Father, obviously becoming bored.

--- Just let me get to the end of Mother's Yorkshire trip.

My own darling,

As you will see I have at last arrived in Yorkshire. I came here by the 2.30pm Doncaster train arriving on Saturday evening at 6.30pm. My father came part of the way and met me there. There was no connection for us until 8.30pm and we arrived in Crowle at 9.10. After that it was even worse – we had no torch yet we had to walk 2-4 miles along a cinder path through fields and hedges. It was tippling down with rain too. We couldn't see a hand in front of us.

Last night I shook over a pound of real farm butter. They don't eat margarine or Danish butter here, while us poor things will be glad of it at home next week. I've got my bicycle here, the first time I've ridden it in 12 months.

1st September 1943

[Crowle]

Darling there are Italian prisoners working on this farm. They were taken at Tobruk in 1940. Don't be alarmed but I had an accident yesterday. I skidded on my bike – coming along the path there was a horse and I tried to swerve and down I came with a cropper on my BTM. I hurt myself a lot. In fact my period started a fortnight too soon!! I hurt myself so much that I sold the bike to my auntie for £7 [£225 today].

4th September 1943

[Crowle]

Yesterday morning my mother and I got the 12 noon train to Doncaster in order to spend some of our new clothing coupons. I bought a mac, in actual fact it was called a 'riding coat', then I bought shoes, had lunch in the Lyceum Restaurant and we both went to a matinee and saw Leslie Howard's production 'The Gentle Sex'.

5th September 1943

I have not long been home after my week's holiday. Darling, I am thinking of abolishing the airgraph service to you for the simple reason that it takes too long when these [letters] take only 2-3 weeks. Let me know which you prefer.

--- So there's your answer to the lack of airgraphs, I said. You must have decided on only sending letters.

--- Yes. Can we stop now?

During lunch Peter suddenly turned up unannounced.

--- Oh, that's well timed, he said, breezing in. Can I hear some more family secrets the boxwallah has been digging up?

---Aren't you working today?

--- No. It's an Aberdeen holiday. Crack on, will you?

15

1th September 1943

I know I have a jealous mind – you know too!! But it appears most strange to me that the holiday snaps of Bude should either get lost or fail to turn out and now the snaps taken on the Scottish holiday should be equally as bad. How amazing!!! Thanks for not sending the one of you taken with the couple [the MacMichaels] *you met in Dalry. I am not interested in seeing strangers with you whom I have never met, nor am I likely to meet in the future.*

--- That's you well and truly told off, Mother, Peter said. Sour and sarcastic, eh, Father?

--- Oh, just get on with it.

15th September 1943

Well, sweetheart, this week I have my Colonel with me.

--- What, what! Peter butted in with a touch of George III.

He is here on inspection and for answering any difficult questions which I may have. I had to go and meet him at a pre-arranged spot which was kept most secret. He went over some important reconnaissances and tomorrow I shall have him in my office most of the morning going through some of my files. It is quite likely that next week I shall have to do a job which may mean a trip on an aeroplane. I have never been up in the air before.

Phyl I have heard today that my friend Joe Newman may be leaving to go to another part of India. I will be sorry when he goes.

208

--- So, you actually had a friend!

--- Ignore him.

19th September 1943

Oh, Phyl, I am awfully upset over the bicycle accident you had [here we had to re-cap for Peter's benefit], *but on the other hand I am simply jubilant over the fact that you have sold it. Darling, I am glad to be back in Wana again after my very tiring three days' tour – one day I walked miles and miles up and down nullahs (dry river beds) and mountains working out a new alignment for a road.*

24th September 1943 (Airgraph)

At the moment I am writing this letter to the strains of the melodies of 'The Dancing Years' played by the BBC Midland Orchestra. Oh, sweetheart, wouldn't it be marvellous if you were now sitting on my knee in an easy chair in front of a nice rosy fire with the lights out listening to this lovely music? Do you remember how we used to do this in York, darling?

'Oh, I say! [Peter again] This is a bit risqué, isn't it?

'Look, if you're going to keep interrupting we're not going to get very far, are we?

'Sorry, Father, I'll keep quiet.

'See that you do.

Yesterday I became our Mess Secretary – what do you think of that, Phyl? I have to prepare the menu each day and give orders to the cook and inspect the food before it is cooked.

'Gosh, you're really hitting the heights.

'What did I just say?

Yet again Father realised he had two forty+ year old errant children at the table.

27th September 1943 (Airgraph)

Well Phyl I have got over my motor accident shock and I feel quite well now. On Saturday night I had a bad spell of nerves: my tummy went out of order too.

--- What happened? Peter interrupted, legitimately on this occasion.

--- I can partly answer that, I said, because you don't actually mention it again until an airgraph dated 29th October. This is what you said: *'Phyl I see that you have got a little mixed up over the motor accident I had in the middle of September. You seem to be under the impression that I was driving my station wagon when the accident occurred. I was* <u>not</u> *– I was sitting next to the driver in my big tribal escort lorry. I was awfully surprised over your attitude over my accident – you did not seem very upset'.* So, what **did** happen?

--- We skidded off the road and hit some boulders.

7th October 1943 (Airgraph)

Last night I played my Brigadier in the golf competition – gosh we had a marvellous game and he beat me on the last hole after a good two hours' battle of wits. Honestly, darling, he is one of the finest chaps I have met in such a high position.

--- Pip, pip, old chap. [Peter had now affected his monocle again, a 10p piece] I say, Wilkie, old chap, what a devil of a shot! What absolutely ripping fun!

--- Right, that's enough.

--- OK, I'm off. There's no fun here.

---- Oh, Stan, don't be so serious. For heaven's sake, cheer up

--- I will not be mocked at in my own house.

And that, regrettably, was that. We resumed our now humourless readings while Peter went to the supermarket.

11th October 1943

Last Friday, darling, was the date of a big religious Hindu festival throughout the whole of India – it is called Dussehra. I was quite surprised when I was approached and asked if I would like to witness the Worship of Fire ceremony at 900HRS the following morning and a lunch called Priti Bhojan at 1300HRS. Well I went along and this is what I witnessed. In front of the Mandir (or temple) was a round altar of fire and sitting around this were 20-30 Hindus with a Pandit (priest). The Priest was chanting away and he chanted this particular chant 108 times. Every time the chant ended everybody threw some food on the fire. When the chanting was over the fire was then lifted up to the sun and everybody started chanting all over again. Honestly, darling, I felt as if I was in the middle of a lost decade [?].

The lunch was like any other Indian meal, except that I had the roast flesh of a she-goat...which I must say was rather nice. In the evening I attended a play and between each scene there were men dressed up as dancing girls and they danced the most sexual dances I have ever seen. They were called 'The dance of the virgin before her lover' and 'The Kite dance'.

--- It's a good job Peter wasn't here to hear all that! Mother said.

--- Indeed.

13th October 1943

Gosh, your latest letter was a real shocker and certainly gave me a thorough chastisement for some remarks I made about your friendship with a Scots couple in Dalry. Please, darling, eradicate my criticism from your mind NOW, FOR EVER. I did think, though, that you were very nasty in places and did your level best to hurt me as much as possible, but I am a most peculiar chap over such silly little things. Do you remember the quarrel we had during our courtship over you walking home with a fellow one night from Unity House when there was a lot of snow on the ground? We said the most horrible things to each other at the time but soon made it up.

16th October 1943

At the moment I am on tour and many miles from Wana, in fact I am in British Territory again. I have had a terribly busy day making inspections of barracks, cookhouses, etc, of various regiments stationed in this particular place. Yesterday, darling, I was given two beautiful Pomegranets [sic] which had come from Kabul in Afghanistan. Oh Phyl I have never tasted such delicious fruit in all my life.

19th October 1943 (Airgraph)

At the moment I am in a fort right in the middle of Waziristan. This spot is in the middle of the mountains and is over 4000ft high, consequently it is extremely cold and bleak. Yesterday I walked miles and miles with my assistant engineer and bedragga escort marking out a new alignment for a road. In about one hour from now I am going through a very hostile country. Last night on this same road some hostile tribesmen blew up two small bridges. The particular tribe are called Shabi Khalo [?].

21ˢᵗ October 1943

My Dearest and Most Precious Darling,

I am going to take the whole of this airmail to describe to you a fight I had yesterday evening with a hostile Lashkar which very nearly meant the death of your hubby and his British A.G.E. whose name is Merson. I was on tour of roads and works with two big lorries and a badragga escort of 33 men. We were 12 miles from safety at a place called Sarwekai when, rounding a hairpin bend, [we] came upon a convoy lorry being looted by hostiles. They fired at my lorry and bullets went whizzing all around. Gosh darling they were terribly near. The bedraggas of my lorry quickly jumped off and engaged them with return rifle fire. My bodyguard split into three: one lot to advance up a nearby hill to dislodge the hostiles at the top; a second [lot] set off to climb hills behind the enemy; the third remained guarding the two Brits. That was the situation from 5.10pm until 5.25pm. Merson and I decided to crawl out of the lorry on to the roadside to get in some cover but we were pinned back by gunfire. Meanwhile the two other parties helped to scatter the enemy. One was found dead in a nearby drain. My guard said he was the biggest hostile in the area and was called Jalat Khan. He had five shots through his body and one through his head. As soon as we got out of range we simply flew to the next Scout Post [at] Tansi.

Darling nobody was hurt and 395 of my bullets were fired.

--- That was my hairiest moment in the war. Gosh, I wish Peter had stayed to hear that: he wouldn't be so mocking now.

--- He was just play-acting, I said.

--- I remember reading that letter in double-quick time, said Mother, to make sure you weren't hurt!

--- Perhaps we should stop now and then next time we'll let Mother catch up with her letters. I think we're coming to a robbery.

--- Oh yes. I remember that.

16

10th September 1943

Darling Stan, Isn't the news of Italy's unconditional surrender absolutely wonderful? Although we had been more or less expecting it, it came as a wonderful surprise. My mother greeted me at the door with the news! [Apparently Nanny was glued to Vatican Radio throughout the war] *I went a walk afterwards and was amazed to see the colossal number of Union Jacks hanging out of bedroom windows.*

13th September 1943

There has been an electric storm here today. I was caught in torrential rain coming off the tram in Walton Lane. I have had to change my clothes, right through to my skin it went! It is only 7pm and the sky is so overclouded that it looks like midnight. When it was like this at school, we all used to say 'the world is coming to an end'. It suddenly struck me (child that I am)!!!

19th September 1943

I have just returned from Upholland after having spent a rather nice weekend there. Your people are both well and your mother is growing quite fat! This afternoon, after dinner, your dad took me a long bus ride to St.Helens. It was the first time I had ever been. Trust your dad – he goes up to an RAF sergeant and starts carrying his kitbag for him all over St.Helens looking for a certain bus. He was terribly overloaded, though, and I even felt sorry for him. After putting him on the bus we went to do a bit of sightseeing.

20th September 1943

Darling, ever since we parted in July 1941 I have never felt any different from what I am at the present moment. I have never stopped loving and wanting you more than anything else God could give me.

I have just finished eating an orange, the first I've tasted for 2 years!!! I'm glad to see darling that you are sending some tobacco with the next issue of stockings. My dad doesn't get much money and the cost of tobacco is really disgusting. What used to be 8d an ounce is now 2/3 an ounce!!

23rd September 1943 (A letter from Elsie)

Dear Stan, Phyl is doing very nicely, doesn't say too much about the loneliness she so bravely disguises. I understand her better than she knows, and now and again she has a restless, lost soul attitude as though she is wandering around not knowing exactly what she wants. I know very well what's in her mind: things, to her, seem so much at a standstill. She is waiting for her future to move.

--- Elsie wrote very articulately, didn't she?

--- Oh yes, and with beautiful copper plate handwriting. Deep down, she understood us all.

27th September 1943

There has been rather a serious case here at work. A young married girl whose husband is in India was working on the night shift (office work) preparing wage packets for the following day. A man entered her office, masked and armed, and held her up at the point of his revolver. He then filled a suitcase full of wage packets totalling £400 [about £13,000 today]! *When Catherine intercepted he brought down the butt of his revolver full belt on her head and smashed her skull. She fainted and is now seriously ill in hospital.*

The man – who is not yet caught – absconded, and in order to get out of one of the exits without being caught by Napier's Police, he <u>shot</u> the sentry. I've never heard anything so frightening. The man is definitely one of Napier's men because one is not allowed in without a permit. We've all got the 'wind up' here, expecting hold-ups whenever we have money in the office.

--- Gosh, excitement all round: Father shot at, Mother in an armed robbery!

30th September 1943

I am going to York this Saturday afternoon until Sunday night in order to bring home our tea service, china and glassware. Crikey I am not looking forward to it one bit because I know before I get there I will be horribly 'broody' and sentimental.

9th October 1943

We had a letter from Jimmy this morning. He is coming home on 9 days leave in 3 weeks' time. He is now only 30 miles from Reading, having returned from Scotland and the East Coast.

13th October 1943

My darling Stan,

Many thanks for your wonderful parcel of stockings, silk and tablecloth which I received last night. Oh darling, the stockings are absolutely marvellous. 'Aristoc' used to be my favourite long before the shortage. The Masudi tablecloth is rather nice, the 4 yards of silk I have parcelled up and sent on to your mother, as per your instructions. I also sent her the native bedroom slippers (from your last parcel) which were too small for me.

22nd October 1943

Last night we had all just got into bed when there was a knock somewhere around 11.30pm. My mother went down and opened the door. It was Jimmy and he had come home for 10 days leave. I was going to your mother's this weekend so I will take him too. They always ask to see him as they are very fond of him.

23rd October 1943

Jimmy and I have not long been home actually [they had been to see the film 'Mr Lucky' at the Paramount]. My mother had our tea waiting for us, then when I got my typewriter out to write to you, Jimmy said, 'If I dictate a letter to Albert, will you type it?' So I have finished typing one of these to Albert who is in North Africa.

Next week Jimmy and I are going to the Playhouse to see Nora Pilbeam in 'Ah! Wilderness' [a rare comedy by Eugene O'Neill]. I believe it is absolutely marvellous. Then Elsie is going with us another night to the Royal Court to see The Man Who Came to Dinner'*.*

--- Let's quickly return to Father's letters, I said. You'd just been in that skirmish with some hostiles.

--- It was more than a mere 'skirmish'.

24th October 1943

This evening I had a very good game of golf, probably the best game I have ever played since taking up the game. I played with two other chaps and somehow fortune was on my side and I won quite comfortably. Our golf course here is rather strange and not like your conception of an English golf course. We have holes situated around the perimeter wire of the camp and we play up and down dry river beds. When I come home I will continue with my golf but it will only be on one condition– that you start also under your hubby's coaching and instruction.

Since my horrible experience of having a pitched battle against a tribal gang I have been obliged to tell the story to all sorts of people. Last night I was asked out to dinner at the Medical Mess in order to describe the show. While I was there I was talking to a colonel doctor friend of mine and lo and behold he knew Hamilton (Canada) where my family lived for a short time.

[My father and his parents emigrated to Canada at some point in the early 1920s to find work. I have found records of their return when they arrived in Liverpool from Montreal on 27th August 1927, having sailed on the 'Doric' of the White Star Line. Their address at the time was 12, Albert Road, Wavertree. He rarely spoke of this aborted emigration: all he said once was that his lifelong fear of water was due to him falling through the ice of a frozen lake in Canada (Lake Ontario?) as a child and nearly drowning].

31st October 1943

It is a beautiful morning here Phyl – a complete deep blue sky with very bright sunlight. In the sun it is quite warm but in the shade there is quite a nip in the air. I have just been sitting out on my veranda but I found the sun was too bright and hot for me to write comfortably. This afternoon I am giving my escort bedraggas a big dinner. I am doing this as an appreciation for the way they helped to save my life quite recently in my awful battle with the tribal outlaw gang. There will be about 40 people attending and I know it is going to cost me quite a packet of money but I do not mind that in the least. These men look like real brutes but inside they are grand fellows. Quite a number of them have sworn they will lay down their lives for me. My work here often reminds me of Lawrence of Arabia.

The other evening I saw a really grand film called 'Dangerous Moonlight'. Do try and watch it, darling.

2nd November 1943 (Airgraph)

I have just finished my lesson in Pushto – this is the language spoken by the tribesmen in this part of the world. It is a most strange language and seems very queer to an English mind having to read from right to left. Of course the whole construction of the sentences is entirely different to ours and they always put the verb at the end. If I ask a simple question like 'What is your name?' it has to be spoken this way 'Your name what is?'

8th November 1943

This afternoon I returned from a long tour of my division, unfortunately two and a half days of my time was spent in bed due to a slight attack of fever – malaria. However I did not get a very bad dose and made a quick recovery.

11th November 1943

Two nights ago, sweetheart, I saw one of the best films I have ever seen. Actually you recommended me to see it ages ago. The film was called 'Mrs Miniver'. Gosh darling I thought it was absolutely grand. We get some terrible films up here but this was certainly an exception.

--- We've neglected Mother's letters for a while, I said, so let's get back to hers.

28th October 1943

Here I am celebrating your birthday all on my own – in a manner which is best suited to me. I am off work and celebrating it by wearing a pair of the most recently sent stockings, also by powdering my nose with a box of powder which, until today, had not been opened. Before typing this I had a lovely bath then redressed myself in my clean undies, put on my best black dress and pearls, new stockings, then did my hair in a 'becoming' style. After this was done I felt 'just right'.

Last night Jimmy and I went to the Forum and saw 'Watch Over the Rhine'. Gosh, darling, you ought to see it because it was absolutely a tip-top performance.

This morning I got up at 11am and then I pressed Jimmy's uniform and greatcoat because he had got them creased in the pictures. Yesterday he received a telegram and was scared to open it for fear it said 'Return to unit' but instead it asked him to report to a new camp right on the South Coast.

31st October 1943

Jimmy went back to Dorset this morning via Euston. I did not see him off – he left too early and besides I was in bed!!

1st November 1943

At the same time your letter came so did one from your mother and dad. Your mother has got a 'job'. I cannot tell you more because she did not even mention WHERE or WHAT to me.

2nd November 1943

Darling, before I go, <u>don't</u> mention anything in your letters to your mother about her having a job – it struck me that maybe she did not intend telling you and I might have 'put my foot in it' by telling you myself.

--- What was so awful about her having a job anyway? I asked.

--- Well, if truth be told, Father replied, it was a bit demeaning.

--- Why?

--- I didn't want the news to get about that she, at her age, had got a menial job.

--- But…

--- Oh, just get on with it, will you?

Coming home on the tram (after shopping) 4 American soldiers got on at Unity House and one sat next to me, and the other 3 opposite. I could not help but be fascinated at the ridiculous way they were chewing their gum. I watched their jaws going up and down about 100 times a minute!!! These Americans all seem to go for the Scotland Road girls, they are seen every night heading down in that direction. You know what for don't you darling? Personally, I think they are all of a horrible type, these Americans, all long and greasy hair, with 'sideboards' [sic] half way down their faces. There is an American club in Whitechapel, this is for 'darkies' [sic] soldiers, and the Scotland Road girls are to be found there, waiting for them, in droves!! It makes me feel quite sick to pass the place.

4th November 1943

Darling, your mother is <u>not</u> working thank goodness. It seems that it was too far to go or something like that. It was canteen work in a factory. This morning I went to town in order to buy my mother her birthday present. I bought her a regimental badge of Jimmy's Regiment, the King's Regiment. I gave it to her tonight and she nearly danced for joy.

8th November 1943

I returned to work today, the first time for a fortnight, so you can imagine how 'browned off' I've felt all day [Mother had been suffering from joint pains and dizziness]. *Instead of the lovely greetings a sick person should receive on returning to her boss all I got was 'WHAT IN THE NAME OF HELL HAVE YOU GOT ON YOUR FACE?' I presumed that he was referring to the dark face powder I am now using. I then merely sulked, pulled faces* [at] *all concerned, then got on with my job.*

[Two RAF men have started working in her office at Napier's]. *One, a Sgt P____, is a navigator, and crikey darling you should see his face and hands. He was burnt in a raid over Berlin, but most of the crew were burnt to death. His hands have beastly 'grafted' skin on them while his neck and ears consist of nothing else but grafted skin. Both ears are shrivelled to nothing. He is a Liverpool boy, aged 28.*

10th November 1943

Well, sweetheart, I am typing this to you on a Wednesday afternoon because yesterday I was sent home ill again. The night I returned to work I never got a minute's sleep, first it was diarrhea [sic], then vomiting!! I saw my doctor last night and he said I have GASTRO-ENTERITIS, a new name for 'a chill on the tum'. The result is I have been signed off for another fortnight.

11th November 1943

Jimmy is down in Wimborne [Dorset]....he's on tenterhooks as regards money, because you will know darling that he doesn't get very much, and he smokes heavily, even though he doesn't touch drink. On Monday night he was drawn to play in an Officers v Sergeants football match, and the result was that the Sergeants won 11-0. He said the officers couldn't play for toffee. He is on Combined Operations and wears one of those new Combined Ops badges on his sleeve, a black and red thing comprising an anchor, a gun and a bomb.

I think it is a good thing that I am off work because yesterday my poor mother cut her finger whilst slicing bread for tea and unfortunately she did not get any sleep at all last night. I advised her to go to the doctor about it this morning. From there he transferred her to Walton Hospital. She came home to tell me she had to go back again this afternoon to have it opened as it had turned septic. She went back at 4pm (I couldn't go with her *because I was dizzy and sickly all day) and when she returned 2 hours later she looked <u>so ill</u>. She had been violently sick all over the doctor when she came out of the anaesthetic. When I opened the door she just said 'Oh, Phyl, I feel so ill' and fainted! I put her to bed, put in a H.W. bottle and made her some tea. She fell asleep for a long time and that made her feel a lot better. She said they had ripped open her finger from the nail to the wrist because the blood poisoning was gradually creeping up her arm.*

--- Poor, Nanny, I said, I seem to remember her saying the exact same words when we went to Rockley Street in the 60s. She'd caught shingles in her forehead and eye and was holding her hand to her face. I'll never forget that. [The shingles remained for the rest of her life. She never complained, but just suffered in silence.]

17ᵗʰ November 1943

My own beloved darling,

What on earth is wrong? I am nearly demented here because I have not had a line from you for almost a <u>fortnight</u>. Darling, this is terribly unusual and I am at my wit's end about you. Your mother is so worried that yesterday she paid me a visit here, the first time for 18 months!

19ᵗʰ November 1943

And still I have not heard from you – whatever is wrong, darling? If there is nothing tomorrow, well I think I will go to the nearest cliff and throw myself over.

--- There weren't any cliffs around Liverpool for you to do that, Mother!

--- You know what I mean. I was going out of my mind with worry.

--- Well, let's get back to Father's letters and find out what the problem was.

17

21st November 1943

[Letter headed 'Jandola']

As you see I am on tour again, inspecting all the numerous works which I have on hand at the moment. I arrived at Jandola Fort one hour ago. Last night I stayed in a lonely fort for the night. There were only the Fort Commander, the Assistant Political Agent and myself present. After dinner we had a nice time listening to the wonderful collection of gramophone records belonging to a previous commander who was killed. The collection was absolutely superb. We played selections from 'Pagliacci', 'Madame Butterfly', 'La Traviata' and the memorable 'Rigoletto'. During the latter my mind wandered back to the occasion when we sat hand in hand in the stalls of the Empire absolutely enwrapped in the music and in the love for each other.

24th November 1943 (Airgraph)

Through being on tour I haven't had any mail from you for a week, likewise you will have experienced a 'gap' in receiving mail from me.

25th November 1943 (Airgraph)

Today, darling, I have been inspecting picquets. In this part of the world are little tiny forts situated on the tops of high hills and passes surrounding a big fort. They protect it from large hostile outlaw gangs getting too near and sniping the officers and soldiers. All your mail is waiting back in Wana and I can't wait to get back there.

28th November 1943

Arriving back in Wana I was terribly upset to hear about your second relapse, this time Gastro-Enteritis. My poor poor darling, I wish to God I was home with you and being your nurse-cum-doctor. I asked a doctor friend about Gastro-Enteritis: he told me not to worry and that it was a severe kind of biliousness which would pass away with rest and a special diet.

3rd December 1943 (Airgraph)

Yesterday I bought a native coat called PUSHTIN – it consists of sheepskin and wool. I have never had anything so warm in my life. Without any exaggeration it is 3" thick and it's so good I have decided to use it as an eiderdown as the nights are getting very cold here.

My father, wearing his new pushtin, to the right of the sign.

--- Is that the thing you're wearing in some photos which looks like the coat some hippies wore in the 60s?

--- That's right.

5th December 1943

Darling, I was awfully pleased to receive the snaps which you enclosed with the letter. The one of you holding Timmy is lovely.

--- Timmy was your cat, wasn't it? And is Peter's rumour true that you named me after a cat?

--- Oh, don't be so ridiculous.

Darling, [the letter continued] *it seems to me that you are increasing in beauty while I'm away!*

5th December 1943 (Airgraph)

About 30 minutes ago I finished an airmail letter to you. I then had a lovely bath and sang 'I'll See You Again' while I reclined in the hot water. Now that I am out and dressed I decided to sit down and write to you again. Precious Phyl, I was awfully upset to hear about your mother's sceptic [sic] hand and it was a good job you were at home to look after her. She is a precious lady.

---*I think there is trouble brewing, I interrupted.*

---*What do you mean?*

---Well, in your next airgraph I seem to remember you going off the deep end over something very small.

---I'm puzzled. Do *you* remember, Phyl?

---No...no, I don't.

---Well, let me catch up with Mother's letters first.

21st November 1943

Yesterday I received a letter from you, the first news I have had for over a fortnight. I am still off work – it's a wangle! This is the 5th week now and my mother still has her septic hand, so I suppose it's just as well that I am off.

23rd November 1943

Well, darling, I am still off work. I absolutely adore pottering about the house, today I have made some celery soup. It's on the stove now stewing. It contains celery, onions, carrots, peas, barley, leek and Beef Extract (because we have no meat). At the moment it is absolutely tantalising my pangs of hunger.

[Later] Oh, you've never tasted anything so delicious darling – I have just been to stir up my home-made soup, and taste it, and lo and behold it is BEAUTIFUL. Wait until you come home and you will taste some first-class meals, because I have come out since you have been away, I mean in making things. I have learnt progressively and successfully.

--- That was certainly true, chick, said Father, as if to mollify Mother before the storm to come.

Darling, I have eventually obtained this long awaited book which was ordered about 10 months ago. It is 'Soldier from the Wars Returning' by Gerard Tickell – a finer story has never been written. I will keep it here in my bookcase and then you may read it when you come home.

Your dad told me that he too was in Jimmy's regiment [8th (Irish) King's] when he was 15 [in 1903] but he did not remain because they wanted to make him a Territorial and he would not be sworn in. Your mother then said that all her life she did not know that he had ever been a soldier, but he had kept it a secret all his life! Isn't your father a dark horse?

--- Here we go, I said.

--- What?

--- Listen.

Darling, do you think you would mind terribly if I went to a Dinner-Dance on Wednesday?

--- Oh, yes, it's all coming back now, Mother said.

I will only be partaking of the Dinner because I can't dance, as you know. It is a birthday celebration at the Grill Room in Reece's [one of Liverpool's best venues]. *It will look like bad manners if I refuse because the girl knows I have nothing else to do. Don't worry, I will stick with Elsie all evening because she too has been invited.*

My cousin Freddie [Jones] from Mauretania Road is a captain in the same regiment as Jimmy, but a different division, not Irish, and he has been in India for 18 months. He was in Secunderabad but he has recently been in the jungle. My mother's hand is no better, she has to have it opened again in a day or two.

--- Now straight back to Father, I said, with a hint of relish in my voice.

8th December 1943 (Airgraph)

Dear Phyl, I was really shocked to see in your latest airmail that you are going to a Dinner/Dance at Reece's Grill Room. I like your cheek in asking me if I mind very much. You know very well what my attitude is to such things – I simply hate them. I cannot understand why Elsie wants to take you there. Phyl this has hurt me terribly and I cannot understand why you want to go without me. I know what I am writing now is months too late – by this time it is all over – but this is the meanest action you could have possibly done to me.

For now. Bye bye.

Stan.

12th December 1943

One more thing I would like to bring to your attention – would you like me to go to dances? Please let me know.

Yesterday was a great day for me because His Excellency Sir George Cunningham, Governor of the North-West Province, was in Wana and he made a presentation to my bedraggas for the excellent show they put up in the defence of my life recently. I had to introduce them to him by name. He thereupon gave each of my NCOs a Certificate of Bravery and 200 rupees. All the other bedraggas received 50 rupees (£5 approximately [£175 today]).

Please forgive me for being so cold but I am afraid you have hurt me very deeply.

--- Let's hear what went on at this sordid Dinner/Dance then. Back to Mother.

--- You're enjoying this, aren't you?

--- How?

--- It makes me look very silly.

--- Is that what you think?

--- Well you *were* very silly, Mother chipped in.

25th November 1943

Well, darling, yesterday evening I went to that Birthday Party at Reece's Grill Room. I must say that I really enjoyed myself. For dinner we started with soup, then came curried chicken, sprouts and milked potatoes; after this we had trifle with fresh cream and fruit, a rarity if ever there was one! To follow we had the choice of black or white coffee, cigars, cigarettes, sweets, etc.; then, to finish, a glass of port wine to toast the birthday girl. There was dancing to Reece's own dance band. It started at 7pm and finished at 10pm. Elsie and I stuck together all evening and didn't dance at all.

14th December 1943 (Airgraph)

Dear Phyl, I see from your last airmail that you went after all to the Dinner/Dance and <u>THOROUGHLY ENJOYED</u> yourself. Well I am surprised at that remark and I honestly cannot understand some of your actions at times. Indeed I am rather suspicious....

--- I must admit that for the first time I'm getting fed up with these letters.

--- Oh, Stan, why?

--- It's like you're building a case against me.

--- Well, you were a bit ridiculous, Mother replied.

18

Next morning I turned up at the house, bright and breezy, hoping this would be the last session dealing with the 1943 letters. The day before, I'd left them hardly speaking to each other, as if this 50 year old squabble had been reignited...but all was calm when I walked in.

--- Right, the last letters of 1943.

26th November 1943

Remember me telling you about the hold-up at Napier's? Well, the raider got 20 strokes of the birch and 18 months hard labour, while the young girl was awarded £10 [£350 today] damages.

29th November 1943

Darling today I went back to work the first time for 5 weeks, and I must say it did not appeal to me at all, in fact I feel even more unsettled than ever, and the sooner I can get out of the place the better. The only 'fly in the ointment' is my boss who is the world's worst slave-driver.

8th December 1943

Your mother and dad are both keeping in really excellent health, darling, but are rather worried about you because you hardly ever seem to write to them. It used to be once a week, they said, but now it seems once a month. Darling, you will have to try better than that you know.

Last night I had quite an unusual evening. Napier's offices have 'adopted' a ward in Alder Hey Hospital, a ward of wounded soldiers, so two or three girls in the office including myself, decided to go and see the inside of the hospital and how the patients live.

We arrived at 6.30pm and were directed to E3 Ward. There are 34 men in the ward and their faces lit up when they saw that they had visitors. They were all Sappers and R.A.S.C. men and we went from bed to bed chatting with them individually and giving out books.

13th December 1943

At last, after a colossal lull of two weeks, I have received some mail from you!! Work is a little better recently for the simple reason that my boss is off with flu (there is an epidemic here). We are having peace without him, the rat! Very shortly, darling, I hope to be transferred to another office!!! I went into a certain office today and I said to the Head,'By Jove, Mr Alker, you certainly have a nice office here.' He then said, to my surprise, 'You'll be in soon enough: keep your fingers crossed, I'm trying to get you away from that Hunt.' Mr Alker has asked for my transfer!

15th December 1943

Last night on the way home from work...I was nearly killed in a tram accident. It was creeping along at tortoise rate because of fog when suddenly CRASH-BANG-WOLLOP we were all thrown off our seats. The trolley was off and we were naturally all in darkness. Right across the tram track was a 60ft RAF lorry-trailer. I was quite shaken.

17th December 1943

I have some news, darling, the best thing that has happened to me for 15 months...I have been transferred to another office!!!! This morning Mr Hunt called me to his desk and told me (with much regret) that 'something has been going on behind my back, Mrs Wilkinson, and you have been taken away from me'. On Monday morning I start in the other office as Assistant Chief Accountant's Secretary. I am awfully excited!

19th December 1943

Darling, a week today and I will be 25 – fancy, I haven't seen you since I was 22!! The 'Flu Epidemic' is at its worst here, but (touch wood!) not a member of our family has yet had it. Half of our employees are affected. Last week we received a notice asking us if we would like to be inoculated but I was 'frightened'!

21st December 1943

Well, I was expecting to be transferred to the Chief Accountant's Office today but instead I have found I have been posted to the 'Engine Drawing Office'. I am a Maintenance Costing Clerk. The office is the whole length of the block, facing the East Lancs. Road.

25th December 1943

While I was typing this my mother is serving the Christmas dinner. As soon as I smelled the turkey and 2 chickens beginning to cook I said, 'Poor Stan would give his right arm to be here.'

(Two hours later) There were 8 of us sat down for dinner and it lasted for an hour and a half, during which time there was much fun by my dad (as usual). A telegraph boy has just been with a telegram for me containing a marvellous gift of £5 from you. It will just come in handy for paying for my new Harris Tweed coat.

Jimmy is now stationed in Bournemouth in one of those promenade hotels. Yesterday morning about an hour before we were due to finish, the draughtsmen (50 of them) in my new office decided to molest us with a sprig of mistletoe. Crikey it was terrible. One fellow was apparently good with a lassoo [sic] because he managed to lassoo the 3 other girls and kiss them, but another girl and I...ran right out of the office and hid in my old office until it was time to go home.

27th December 1943

On Xmas night nobody else came so instead Elsie and Dick, Queenie and Laurie [friends] *and my mother and dad all had a little sing-song. We never laughed so much in our lives!! Next morning when I woke I had no voice through shouting. We had been singing old English songs and I took the part of 'alto' – crikey I could not sing for laughing, yet I tried to sing seriously.*

--- I wish I'd been there to witness what sounds like a real family knees-up, I said.

--- It was a hoot!

--- And now, in stark contrast, let's get back to Mr Grumpy's final messages of 1943.

17th December 1943 (Airgraph)

As you can see I am still writing to you in a very cold manner. Somehow or other I do not seem to be able to pull myself together and write in my normal style of love and affection.

22nd December 1943 (Airgraph)

Tomorrow I am going to D.I.Khan to spend Xmas with my colonel and his wife in their bungalow. Your last airgraph was quite a change from your normal style – for once you actually gave me a 'pat on the back'. This is something you never do. Probably you take all my attributes (if I had any of course!!) for granted.

26th December 1943

When we arrived at my colonel's bungalow at 6.15pm on Xmas Day his wife was patiently waiting for him on the veranda. Oh, Phyl, you can imagine how sad I felt and I could not help the tears which came into my eyes. When they were kissing I turned my head away and I thought, 'Why must Phyl and I have to suffer this terrible separation?'

31st December 1943 (Airgraph)

My Dearest Darling,

So we come to the end of the year 1943. For me it has been a very slow one, but I suppose it has been just the same for you. I sent you 153 letters in 1942; this year I have sent you a total of 214, so you can see that my love for you instead of slowing up has increased in momentum.

--- As it has continued to do so, hasn't it, chick?

--- Mmmmm.

INTERLUDE
PILGRIMAGE

Now, then, dear reader, I want to take you on a journey. Yes, a physical journey. Are you up for it? Right, up you get out of your comfy chair. That's it. That was quick, wasn't it? Well, yes, I know. Let me explain. We are at Hightown Station and you see that little serious-looking boy further down the platform? Well, Hightown is the village where he lives: he's 9 and this is 1960. I know, I know, don't worry. I'll get you back all right. We are going to follow this little chap and see where he's going. He looks very determined, doesn't he? Look, here comes the electric train. Let's get on and sit on the right hand side. That's it. Settled? Once the train gets going I will point out a house to you but we'll only get a glimpse. Right, off we go. Ready? There. See it? That snow-cemmed white house with the long garden? That's called 'White Gables' and it's where our little friend lives. And these are the last houses in the village and – do you see? – there's now nothing but sand hills stretching to the Mersey. And on the left, look, reed-beds and fields. Yes, it does look a bit like Norfolk, doesn't it? And do you see there, where I'm pointing, that look-out tower. That's the remains of Fort Crosby where there used to be huge revolving gun emplacements during the war, guarding the entrance to Liverpool Bay, and later it housed Italian prisoners of war, I believe. It is like a huge dilapidated film set and our friend further down the carriage plays there all the time with his friends. Next a golf course and here's the next station, Hall Road, where Liverpool really begins. Yes, that's right, posh houses, but mostly ugly Victorian villas because, you see, Liverpool is a very Victorian city.

Oh, you knew that, did you? Now we're going through Blundellsands and here's Crosby Station. Let me quickly tell you, while we've got the chance, about another remarkable journey. This little boy (don't worry, he can't see us), this little boy has a Corgi dog called Brandy, and one day he decided in his little doggy brain to go on the train by himself, so he followed Mr Tiffin, their neighbour, and the other commuters, to Hightown Station, got on the train, was fussed over and petted all the way...until he arrived here at Crosby Station. There he made up his mind to get off , whereupon the Station Master took him by the collar and contacted the dog's owners who came and collected him. Wasn't that funny? What's that? What was the point of the story, you ask? Well, I don't know really. I just thought it was nice. Oh, we're off again. What? I know I'm stating the obvious. Yes, less affluent houses here now, and this is Waterloo Station named after the battle. Now, don't be rude. And finally here's Bank Hall Station. This is where, during the war, this boy's mother rescued a lady when she fell getting off the train. Remember? Look, the little boy is getting off, so we'd better follow him. Up all these stairs. Managing? Yes, I know you're not 'enfeebled', as you say – I'm just being helpful. Yes, it's a big bridge, isn't it? What's all that clanking and clanging, you ask? Look over the parapet. I know. So many railway lines. The noise is of shunting trains. Now, breathe in deeply, will you? Notice the smell, yes? That's the smell of Liverpool. My friend, what bouquet do you detect? Soap? Well done. And grain? Barley? Very good. Yes, Glasgow smells the same. Tetley's beer brewing and soap factories. Well done again. Oh, look, our chum is getting ahead. Up this road here, past this grimy church. Now, what does the street sign say? Ah, Rockley Street, our journey's end. Our friend is heading for No.31, but notice he hasn't increased his pace to an unseemly run, he's just walking up to that old lady cleaning her step. She's looking up and - oh – look at the surprise on her face. Her own grandson come to visit. They're going in the house. Let's follow them, eh? Yes, that's right, that's a privet hedge, and look down there, where your feet are, see what looks like a round, metal manhole cover, that's the coal-hole down which the coalman empties sacks into the creepy coal cellar. Now into the house. No, we're not intruding. I've told you they can't see us. And, no, I haven't time to explain why. I'll just say it's a bit like 'A Christmas Carol'. What? Dickens! Read it some time. Right, mind the step. Look. On the right a rather steep staircase leading to two upstairs bedrooms. Now follow me down the hall and into the room on the left. This is the parlour, piano against the right hand wall, disabled Fan's bed against the opposite wall and, yes, you're right, that's one of those ubiquitous aspidistras on a plant stand in front of the window. Yes, I would agree with you there, a most unexciting plant. OK, back out again and down into here, the sitting room. Let me take you on a tour. Dresser on the right filled with cheap knickknacks, table against the far wall covered by a shabby, peeling oilcloth, to the left of it a large window overlooking the back yard and then there's the famous radio to which this old lady was glued during the war, and then the tiled fireplace with that Art Deco mirror above it. And there's Fan to the left propped up in her invalid 'carriage'. Now through this door and down to the right is the entrance to the coal cellar, the place which frightens our little friend so much (and his brother, Peter). Did you ever see that wonderful film 'The Night of the Hunter'? No? Oh, you should, one of the best black and white films there is. You don't 'do' black and white films, you say? What a pity! Anyway, there's a frightening cellar in that film too. Let's turn our backs on the cellar and go in here. This is the back kitchen. Yes, it's very damp and steamy, isn't it? Look, here's the gas stove on the left and a deep sink here and that window above it also overlooks the back yard. Yes, that green thing is a nasty mangle and there's a tin bath propped up against the end wall and, yes, that's a washing board for scrubbing clothes. Right, now down the step – careful – oh, sorry, I won't say it again if it bothers you, and we're into the back yard. Yes, they are nice tiles, and down here is the outside toilet, the only toilet I might add. No, it's not very salubrious. It frightens our little friend a lot, I must say, because when he sits on that wooden boarding he's afraid he might fall through the hole and never be seen again. And finally here is the door which opens onto the back alley. This separates the houses in Rockley Street from the backs of the houses in the adjacent street. Let's look down on what's going on in the house – oh look, quick, the boy is playing 'Peep' with Fan and she's giggling away. What? No, I'm not going to play 'Peep' with you. What a thought! Meanwhile the old lady is trying to slip him a half-crown ('Don't tell your father', she says). Oh, look, now she's bringing him a piece of home-made cake and a glass of his favourite drink of Dandelion and Burdock. Let's leave them to their cocoon of love and happiness and let's reflect on this little boy's journey, all by himself, just to visit his grandmother. What's that? What will happen to this place and these good people? Good question...er, Shane, is it? Right. Well, one day, when he grows up, this youngster will write a book about the people who once lived in this house. In a few years' time, in the 70s, in fact, all these houses will be no more. Liverpool City Council, in its infinite wisdom, in what it deemed its Urban Regeneration Scheme, decided to demolish the heart of the city, including 31, Rockley Street, which this old lady occupied for 64 years. But she wasn't too fussed and was moved into a brand new council flat nearby, where she lived for four months. And one day she stepped out to buy a Liverpool Echo at her local newsagent's. Outside the shop, three boys, bunking off school, made a grab for her handbag. In the ensuing struggle she fell over, broke her thigh, and died two days later in hospital. She was 88. Yes, I know, I know. Very very sad. And her daughter, disabled Fan, for whom she cared all her life, was motherless. But her future was better. The family moved her to a Disabled Unit in a hospital near Preston where she lived for another 20 years. She made friends as well as enemies, guarding her handbag for dear life because it contained, to her, a precious collection of postcards the family sent her whenever they went on holiday. She was never ever told of her mother's passing; they simply pretended she was always 'too ill' to visit. Yes, that was very thoughtful, wasn't it? But the death of his beloved grandmother weighed on the mind of our young friend and it took him a long long time to get over it, if he ever did, poor chap. Now, that's enough of all this. It's time I took you back to your comfy chair, Dwayne...sorry...Shane, my dear reader, because I think the main narrative is about to start again. I hope you didn't mind this little diversion of mine. What? Oh, yes. We must do it again some time. Bye.

--- Dear reader', my arse. Stone the crows.

1944

1

I, the 'boxwallah', as I came to be called, was feeling the end was in sight as the leather case and the rosewood box were gradually filling up again with the now scrutinised letters of 1941, 1942 and 1943. The necessity to finish the remaining year and as timeously as possible was becoming increasingly urgent, however, because of circumstances that manifested themselves in early 1999.

My annual birthday present from my parents was a season ticket to the Royal Scottish National Orchestra when they played in Aberdeen, and my father and I went there together for many years. One particular concert, the last he ever went to, remains in my memory. As we were leaving the Music Hall to walk to the car parked in Bon Accord Square he almost fell down the stairs and staggered to keep hold of the handrail. And the walk to the car, normally taking a brisk five minutes, lasted an agonising thirty minutes at least: he was breathless, he had to hold on to my arm on Union Street, stopping every few yards to regain his breath. I offered to run ahead to fetch the car and pick him up, but he stubbornly refused. He was ageing before my very eyes. I was aghast.

A little while later my parents unwisely (Peter and I were adamant that they shouldn't go) decided to go on holiday to Spain. It was to be their last. My mother, with troubles of her own, never really divulged just how disastrous the trip was but she did mention a guitar recital, or maybe a display of flamenco dancing (I can't remember which) in the middle of which my father began to shout out uncontrollably and had to be taken to his room. Or his being so feeble on the journey back that he had to be put on an electric buggy in Schiphol Airport. Then she showed me the photographs.

Now, normally, the proud showing-of-the-holiday-snaps was a family ritual when they had returned from trips abroad. These 'photographs' were only aired once (and I have since thrown them away). My father's predilection was distant views of mountains/lakes/churches: this time, sadly, irretrievably sadly, he was unable to move from the confines of the hotel garden, so these 'photos' were of a nearby wall (almost as if he was *striving* to reach the view), a plant, the ground, another wall, my mother sitting glumly on a wall, a nearby roof, another wall taken at an Expressionist angle, more ground, sandalled feet….

When I met them at Aberdeen Airport my mother was crying with relief when she saw me. He tried to sound upbeat, but this 'holiday' had taken a terrible toll on both of them and was an unmitigated disaster.

And that is why I hoped the remaining letters would serve as a balm, a medicine, a cure even, or, at least, a diversion.

My mother seemed numb for a long while after they got back, but gradually the Aberdeenshire peace began to have a beneficial effect on both of them. And so I grasped the opportunity of continuing the readings, this time frenetically preparing them weekly rather than waiting until I had completed the whole year. The end was in sight.

As we arranged ourselves around the dining-room table as of old, I noticed how shrunken my father had become: he seemed like a shrivelled little boy sitting there, engulfed by grown-up clothes.

--- Well I'm glad we're back here doing this, he said.

--- That's good. We're approaching the last lap now.

2

Well, I'm afraid my New Year's Day has not been really exciting. I always think that on New Year's Eve one is apt to become very sad, particularly when parted from those [sic] they love. I finished work at 6pm and straight from the office I went up to Elsie's house where she had a few of her friends. We all had supper, then while Dick [her husband] played cards with the others, Elsie and I went to the Watch-Night Service. My dad was supposed to be fire-watching last night, so I hurried home to be with mother and Fan, because I think the New Year's last five minutes can be terribly miserable on your own. However, when I got home my dad hadn't gone, so he let the New Year in through torrents of rain, then he got his supper together and went fire-watching at 12.30.

Work is not so bad now that I am in the Engine, Plant and Tool Drawing Office. I enjoy the work immensely. It is just up my street – maintenance costing. The boss is alright too, but the only trouble is that I can't concentrate due to the noise that these 50 draughtsmen kick up. All day long they are whistling and breaking forth in song, then they open the windows while we all shiver in our short sleeves.

2nd January 1944

I have just received your airmail letter dated 12/12/43 which was intended to be serious but I'm afraid, Stan, I laughed my blooming head off!!! It was meant to be a telling-off for going to that Dinner/Dance at Reece's Grill Room.

--- 'Oh, not this *again*.

--- 'Yes, but let Mother get it off her chest. It's quite spikey.

I'm afraid I can never forgive you for writing to me in this tone, Stan. Don't you think you are worse than ridiculous? Anyway I won't tolerate this anymore. What is the use telling you the truth? Just because you get no snaps in the summer YOU THINK I HAVE BEEN SNAPPED WITH MEN -- Just because I go to a Birthday Dinner YOU THINK I HAVE BEEN DANCING -- Just because I go out with my brother on leave (of whom I think the world) – YOU THINK I AM SEEN WITH AN ARMY OFFICER.

I think the quicker you come home the better, because your mind is going rotten the longer you stay there. Cease poking your nose into my quite innocent behaviour and stop 'making a mountain out of a molehill'. If this goes on again, I'm afraid I will be impelled to ask my mother to write to you to give an account of my 'nightly frolics' – which, believe me, are all spent in this chair, by the typewriter night after night writing to you. This is New Year's Day. I am making a resolution:- NOT TO BE SO DAMNED SOFT IN FUTURE.

--- What a brilliant letter, Mother!

--- Please – this was Father – if there's any more of this nonsense in the next letter, can you omit it?

--- It's all right. By the time the next letter comes along Mother has gone soft again! As if nothing had happened.

I looked at Mother but she was staring vacantly into the garden. Even now, was she regretting her strong words?

3rd January 1944

We had a letter from Jimmy today to say he is now in Scotland again on another course and has been forbidden to write for 10 days. He is well and looking forward to his leave at the end of January, if the invasion hasn't started by then.

6th January 1944

You have no need to worry over your books darling because from what I see, and what I remember of them, there are none missing in the Blitz in 1941. They are either here in Jimmy's room or at your parents' at Upholland. I have checked.

[This comment puts paid to one family myth: that the friction between my father and Jimmy was due to the fact that the latter had 'lost' some of my father's books and drawings. Not true.]

7th January 1944

When I got home from the office last night there awaiting me was a telegram which reads: 'Wives now permitted to come to India darling, will apply if you wish.' I am so excited over the prospects that tomorrow I will send a cable which will read: 'By any means darling – am desperate.' If your application is turned down I'll die of a disappointed, broken heart. Gosh!! I'm EXCITED.

8th January 1944

--- What did you think of that news, Mother, by the way? [I was desperate to keep her flagging attention going].

--- For a while I just couldn't get it out of my mind. It was all I thought about. I remember thinking about all the clothes I would have to buy.

---You'd have enjoyed that!

Well, darling, today I went to the Cable and Wireless Co. in Castle Street and sent a reply to your cable. My mother is sick of hearing me talking all day about going to India. The £5 you sent me (with which I thought of buying a pedigree Wire-Haired Terrier) has been spent on something else, a grey worsted flannel divided skirt for hiking in the Lakes on our 2nd honeymoon!!

10th January 1944

Sweetheart, I went to Upholland early yesterday morning. Your dad is in your mother's bad books because the morning prior to me going he had disgraced himself by wheeling his bike through the kitchen on his way to work, and the table-cloth got caught in the wheel and dragged off the entire breakfast setting; dishes were smashed and sugar spilled everywhere. The milk jug also overflowed onto the settee. Then, to make things worse, the same day, your mother had prunes to soak in a dish. Your dad went into the back-kitchen in the dark to wash his hands. Instead of putting the soap in the soap-dish he goes and puts the whole tablet into the prunes. Next morning they had to be thrown out.

13th January 1944

Last night we had just finished dinner at 7pm when Jimmy came walking in!! Honestly we hardly recognised him because he was so 'dressed up' and filthy. He had been on a course – a Battle School – up in Scotland, and the convoy of Combined Operations were returning back to their units and camps down South, but as the journey was so long, they had to 'put up' at a town not far from here just for the night. He had to leave at midnight in order to rejoin the convoy. Honestly, darling, he looked like a tramp. He was wearing battledress which was absolutely saturated and sodden with mud, also there were no buttons on his trousers, he wore broken boots which were stuck to his leggings in mud that had dried. On his hands he wore 3 pairs of gloves and 2 pairs of mittens (with the trigger finger missing). Over his battledress he wore his greatcoat which was also wet. He had been 'fighting' in rivers and mountains. That was all he would tell us, nothing more!!!!!! He told us to make a note of the Rgt who [sic] plays a prominent part in the invasion!

18th January 1944

I don't feel much like typing tonight because everything you touch here seems horribly icy and cold, and I'm much too comfortable sitting by the fire here with this resting on a magazine than to bring in my 'word machine' (as my dad calls it!) which will definitely be cold! Well, sweetheart, I have not heard from you this week at all and I can't think of anything else but what preparations I will make for going out to India. Oh Stan, surely God will bring us together soon.

22nd January 1944

I notice darling that in your letter you mentioned the fact that you would prefer me to stay in England just now due to the present situation, as though the war will soon end. Maybe it will, darling, but you should realise that you will not be sent home from India immediately it does so, so wouldn't it be nice for me to travel all that way home with you? Darling whatever you do don't fail me. We simply have to be together soon.

--- I sense, Father, that you were beginning to cool to the idea of Mother joining you. Stalling, even.

--- Well, yes. We now know that the war would drag on for another year but there was a sense, a feeling, then that it might end much sooner. Things were coming to a head. Besides, we haven't heard my side of things yet.

--- We're coming to that. I just want to go a tiny bit further with Mother's letters because we're coming to an interesting development. OK?

--- I suppose so.

--- Carrying on, then, with that letter of January 22nd....

When I got home from town at 1.45pm to my surprise I found Jimmy sitting having his dinner. He has come home on 9 days' leave. He is expecting a 're-call' any time during the week though. I asked why, but he refused to tell me!! I wish to goodness he wasn't in this confounded Infantry, sitting in flat-bottomed barges, waiting to be landed on some hostile shore. He tells me that he is <u>first out</u> of the so-and-so barge when the end drops down too. He has had to 'muck in' with all the platoon, eating and sleeping on mountain tops in Scotland.

Yesterday I tried to obtain my release from Napier's, just for the fun of it. Today I was interviewed. I merely told them that my mother's domestic duties were too much for her and that I preferred to be at home. I must say they were very sympathetic and to my amazement said my release will probably be through in a week's time. ISN'T THAT MARVELLOUS? Now I <u>will</u> be able to come to India without a hitch.

23rd January 1944

Darling, what do you think of me getting my release from Napier's? Are you in favour? To think that this time next week I may be a FREE woman at last!!! I will be able to wander round the shops to my heart's content!!

24th January 1944

In your last letter you don't mention me coming to India at all. Are you cooling to the idea? Jimmy is out to supper with a schoolfriend. They are going to watch Liverpool v Everton on Saturday. [At Goodison Park: Everton 2 Liverpool 3 in the North Region War League (Second Championship). Attendance 45,820]

26th January 1944

My darling Stan, I think this letter will be the most interesting I have written to you for many, many months. I am no longer in the employ of Messrs D. Napier and Son Ltd!!!!! Yesterday I obtained my release.

My father groaned at this bombshell as if he was hearing it for the first time after a fifty five year gap.

--- That was the thing I feared most would happen. Phyl has always been so impulsive, haven't you, chick? I should never have raised your hopes of going to India, should I?

--- No you shouldn't have, Mother replied, the argument as fresh as ever.

--- The consequences were bad, too. The Labour Exchange encouraged you to go in to part-time work and that was disastrous, wasn't it?

--- Yes, mumbled Mother.

--- In what way?

--- Well, you'll see....but, never mind. Can we start seeing my side of things after we have a bite to eat?

--- Your wish is my command.

3

1st January 1944

The other day Phyl there was a Special India Army Order which has raised the embargo on the wives of officers serving in India proceeding to India from the United Kingdom. Applications must be sent to G.H.Q. Simla by the 15th February. Do you want me to apply for you? Please let me know by cable immediately you receive this letter. [This last sentence is underlined in red crayon]. *Personally Phyl I think it is better if you stay in England now that the end of the war is so near. On the other hand if you would like to come it will give me the greatest pleasure in the world to apply for you.*

--- It seems like you are dangling a reluctant carrot in front of Mother.

--- I know. It was such a difficult dilemma.

8th January 1944

Last night, darling, we had a heavy fall of snow in Wana. When I got up this morning I was really surprised to see a lovely white carpet about 4" thick. This is the first real snowfall Wana has had for five years. Tomorrow I am making a trip down the most dangerous tribal road in my area: dangerous, because it is the 'no man's land' for the hostile tribesmen.

12th January 1944

A year or so ago I never thought for one minute that I would be capable of running a big officers' mess. But I have become

Mess Secretary. Let me explain what I do. Each day I plan the menu for the following day – breakfast, lunch and dinner. The mess clerk then passes this on to the Khansama (cook) so he can tell him the kinds and quantities of foodstuffs he will require. I then write out orders for the food. The mess servants then go to R.I.A.S.C. and get the food. At the end of the month all these orders are consolidated and sent to me for paying the bills. From these bills and the number of days the officers have dined in the Mess during that month I am able to work out their Mess bills for the month.

Drinks are arranged on another system. Each officer has a 'drink book'. When he calls the Mess Abdar (butler) for a drink, say Lemon Squash, the Abdar brings the drink and that particular officer's 'drink book'. The officer then writes in the book what he has ordered. At the end of the month these books are collected and the amounts are totalled up. On top of this there are monthly mess subscriptions (which cover the paying of the servants, the upkeep of the gardens, sporting facilities, etc).

In order to give you an idea of the kind of menus I prepare here is today's:-

BREAKFAST	LUNCH	DINNER
1. Porridge or corn flakes	1. Grilled steak, onions and chips	1. Vegetable soup
2. Eggs, bacon and sausage	2. Plums and cream	2. Salmon cutlets
3. Toast and marmalade	3. Cheese and biscuits	3. Roast mutton, mashed potatoes, cauliflower
4. Tea or coffee	4. Dessert	4. Coconut pudding
		5. Sardines on toast
		6. Tea or coffee

What do you think of your hubby now? I do this work in my spare time and do not receive one single penny for it.

--- Sardines on toast after coconut pudding?! groaned Mother. How revolting!

14th January 1944

I have just received your cable agreeing to me applying for you to come here. I will fill in application form tomorrow. I am listening to the news on my radio but the only interesting thing was a statement by Lord Woolton in Liverpool yesterday that one of the first major tasks after the war will be building houses for the men returning from the war. I hope this means that architects like me will be demobilised very quickly.

19th January 1944 (Airgraph)

I am writing this letter to you from Jandola. I have been staying here for the last two or three days. Yesterday I met my Colonel and we have been inspecting works. This evening I was informed that there is a hostile gang near the area I was shot at last October. I will be going down the road tomorrow with my Colonel to Wana so I had to make quick arrangements with the Scouts at Tanai Fort by wireless so that they can go out early tomorrow and piquet the area while I go through.

22nd January 1944 (Airgraph)

I told my Colonel about your spontaneous reply by cable: he was all in favour of it and that if I send the application in he would most certainly recommend it to the higher authorities.

29th January 1944

In the very near future I think I will take ten days' leave and go to Quetta for a little holiday. The last time I went down to the Baluchistan border I met an officer of the Zhob Militia who I know very well. He promised to escort me from the border to Fort Sandeman (the railhead for Quetta) any time I went.

10th February 1944 (Airgraph)

Phyl darling I hope you get your release from Napier's – I absolutely dislike you having to work. I have never wanted my wife to do anything like that. [This comment seemed somewhat ironic to me...but I didn't raise the matter, feeling that I had riled him enough.] I heard today, darling, that the Colonel <u>has</u> recommended my application for you to join me.

4

Our next session, a few days later, was preceded by my mother ushering me urgently into the kitchen.

--- Father's in the toilet. Ever since he came back from that holiday he's been having terrible cramps in his legs, waking up in the middle of the night in agony. He's been to the doctor but he won't tell me what's wrong.

--- Well, he certainly won't tell **me.** Sounds as if he's having circulation problems.

While she was speaking to me I noticed with horror how old and sunken her face was becoming, how almost senile she was beginning to look.

--- I'm sure the doctor will have got to the bottom of it, I lamely attempted to say to her.

--- He's now got some mysterious pills to take.

--- Well, that's good, isn't it?

And, of course, I couldn't say to her what was rattling around in my brain: that this is the beginning of the end, that he is dying, that the ambulance is being readied.

Just then Father shambled in and sat down.

--- How are you today, Father? I asked in an artificially cheery tone.

--- Not too bad. Can we get on?

--- Oh, right.

Gradually, as I resumed the readings, I began to realise how radically the atmosphere had changed around the table, the erstwhile jolliness had been replaced by sombreness as if these letters were the only things in their lives that they genuinely looked forward to.

1st February 1944
___

This morning has been a rather busy one for me. I was in Bold Street at 9am to have my hair shampooed and cut. I decided to have the new 'Liberty Cut'. It is rather short, and, instead of being combed from the top downwards, I comb from underneath upwards. It is terribly smart. [At this point Mother began rearranging her hair in an attempt to duplicate this 'new' style and the three of us subsided into giggles.] *It cost me 9/-* [about £15 today].

2nd February 1944
___

Darling, the menus which you have to prepare for the mess make my mouth water. At the moment we are preparing <u>our</u> dinner which consists of sausages alone because there is a great shortage of meat and fish now in Liverpool. Yet I feel the war will soon be over...I only wish Jimmy was not in this Commando business, first out of the barge and so forth. Once he has 'gone over' we will not know any more about him until these occupied countries are permanently liberated.

5th February 1944
___

No post from you today, only a letter from Jimmy to say that he has left Bournemouth for a week's 'Hygiene Course' at Keogh Barracks in Aldershot. By the way, all the barrage balloons have gone from our towns and cities. They are all down on the South Coast I believe. It seems so strange not seeing any more after having seen them for nearly 5 years!

7th February 1944

There was only one letter today and that was from Jimmy. He said that just before leaving Bournemouth he had to attend the Odeon Cinema there with 300 of the unit to witness a special film show. When it was over, much to his amazement, his name was called out from the stalls (where his C.O. was sitting) asking Jimmy to get up on the stage and lecture the men about the similar battle (as that filmed) in which Jimmy scored top marks. He said he felt as though the floor might open up and swallow him. He lectures daily, sometimes twice a day, but not in the loudspeaker [?] of a cinema, on a colossal stage. He said that he seems to consider himself now as a 'Celebrity'.

[At this point I sensed that Father would be quietly seething at all this unwonted praise of his brother-in-law, but he just sat there, tight-lipped and ashen.]

8th February 1944

Yesterday I stood in a queue at a greengrocer's for 90 minutes in an orange queue. I was only about 3 yards from the counter when the confounded assistant shouted out: 'No oranges left, that is all'. Fancy standing there for all that time for nothing. We have not tasted an orange or an apple, nor any kind of fruit for that matter, since last July. The only fruit we taste is in jam and that is made with turnips and all sorts of unknown rubbish, and even sweetened with saccharine.

Darling, I am still a 'free agent' where work is concerned, but I am going to volunteer for a Part Time job tomorrow [here Father gave out a long groan] *just for a couple of hours in the morning.*

--- 'Notice Mother didn't tell me what the job was.

Last night I went to the pictures in town. If you were there you'd have been sickened by what I witnessed: an American officer was *leaning up against a cheap girl, in public – even though it was dark you could see the outline of <u>what</u> they were doing. He was not the only one. All the way down William Brown Street couples were leaning and being mauled about by these American soldiers. They drive along Walton Road in convoys of 'jeeps' wearing the most ridiculous tam o'shanters or zipped lumber jackets. The officers go about wearing fancy brown boots, hair soaked in brilliantine and a colossal cigar in their mouths.*

<u>I'd</u> never enjoy myself with anybody else for the simple reason that I love you too much, Stan.

--- And still do, chick.

[Once again, the warmth of these memories was having an enervating effect on us all – even me – and I could sense their love, buried like a secret power, or a stale perfume, in these letters. Mother often scoffed at Father's occasional public expressions of love as if he was a child seeking comfort, but it was there. It was there.]

10th February 1944

This morning I went to the Labour Exchange for my interview. I went to some place near the Dock Road where I was medically examined as A1....and taken on 8-1 weekdays only.

--- Mother, I said, I think you were hiding something. You don't tell Father what the job was, and 'somewhere on the Dock Road' is very vague considering you lived only ten minutes away and knew the streets like the back of your hand.

--- Exactly.

Mother was squirming in her chair as if all the pent-up guilt, buried for 50 years, was surfacing again.

--- Let's get to the next letter, then we can stop for a well-earned break; either that or a punch-up in the garden.

No-one said anything.

14th February 1944

Never in all my life have I known such double-crossers as the Labour Exchange in Liverpool. I left one bad job at Napier's which I loathed, but this confounded one is fifty times worse. They said I would have clerical work but if I gave you a hundred guesses you'd never know what I really am doing – <u>making cigarettes</u>. When I arrived at the place near the Dock Road I was given a CAP and OVERALLS. We [the new arrivals] were marched into the 'Churchman's' room on the fourth floor and were distributed to various machines. Mine was up a 10ft ladder and that's where I stood from 8am to 1pm. At the top of this ladder there is a large wooden bath affair which contains tobacco that is continually being filled through a belt in the ceiling. What I have to do is flake the tobacco with my fingers and pick out any stalks or hard dry leaves. When I have 'sorted' the contents of this container I lift it out and slide it down a tube which passes to three girls at the bottom of my ladder who then make up the cigarettes!! Then there is the loudspeaker about 2ft from my ear which continually blasts out Dance Music all day long, until my head swirls with swing music and tobacco fumes.

--- Well, Father, how did you react to this wonderful change in Mother's circumstances?

He took a long time to reply.

--- Humiliated. Cheated. Angry.

--- Why 'angry'?

--- That a wife of mine would stoop so low, an officer's wife I might add, and accept such a demeaning job.

--- But I didn't know it was going to be like that.

--- So you say.

--- God strike me dead if I deceived you.

At this rather fraught juncture I called it a day. Driving home, I imagined them going into garden and having a Monty Python-type brawl for all the neighbours to see. But, then, the poor man could hardly walk and my mother would worry about her hair going 'frizzy'.

5

The following morning I was greeted by the usual fug of kipper fumes, but we soon got down to the day's reading with no little keenness on their part. And there seemed to be calmness about them as if yesterday's anger was a thing of the past.

17th February 1944 (Airgraph)

Sweetheart...I am absolutely delighted at your wonderful release from Napier's. But darling I want to give you a warning. Please do not abuse it by going to shows and town every day because the Ministry of Labour have people who make a report on these sort of things – and you may be watched. Help your mother and do other domestic duties and look after Fan because she is a great tie on your mother and dad.

20th February 1944 (Airgraph)

At the moment I am sitting in the garden because it is much warmer in the sun than inside. I honestly feel, Phyl, that I shall make a good gardener when we have our own garden. I shall potter about either weeding, digging or planting.

--- What are you both laughing at? he asked, interrupting our giggles.

--- Nothing, I said....apart from the fact that neither of us has ever witnessed you taking part in any of these activities.

--- Oh, do get on.

23rd February 1944 (Airgraph)

Darling, what kind of part-time work are you going to do that you mention in your last letter? Please select something which will not cause you any worry. Well, Phyl, we most certainly seem to be giving Germany a really good plastering by our night and day fighters. I somehow feel that this bombing will go a long way towards shortening the war. I am awfully pleased at the sound of your new part-time job. Please let me know more details at a later date if it is not terribly, terribly secret.

4th March 1944

Oh! My dear dear darling I am awfully upset to hear about the kind of part-time work which you have got to do. Phyl, you must not remain in a factory with a lot of low-living women who think of nothing else but lasciviousness and 'Yankee' soldiers. I never thought my wife would ever have to do such horrible work – gosh it is most repelling and humiliating. Sometimes I cannot quite understand your moves. You had a good job in Reading then you decided to change. You then were transferred to Napier's and became most unhappy because of your boss. Then you were moved to another dept. and you felt ever so much brighter and cheerful. Phyl, this is the second time you have jumped from the frying pan into the fire. Now I shall worry myself silly and anxiously await every one of your letters to find out if your status has changed.

--- Before both of you start arguing again, let's cut the suspense and jump to Mother's next letters.

15th February 1944

It is really marvellous darling to be free like this afternoon. I don't honestly know what I'd do if I had to do this terrible Dickensian factory work all day. It nearly killed me again this morning. I am still at the top of the ladder, sorting the stalks from the tobacco and sending the 'good stuff' down the chute, or conveyer belt to the girls below who make 'Churchman' cigarettes of it! I feel an absolutely dirty sight when I reach home at 1.20pm. Firstly I stink from head to foot of tobacco, secondly my fingernails are like nothing on earth, and thirdly my skin is yellow, also my hair and clothes, due to the nicotine and tobacco dust. I am more than ashamed of all this!! I am too proud, and I am telling a deliberate lie to your people and mine that I have been put on clerical work. I am just about to go up to Elsie's once I've got the tobacco out of my ears!

16th February 1944

Today I was put on two machines, not one, which means scurrying up and down two ladders. I am with all the Scotland Road 'buckoes' too. To beat it all, as I was coming out at 1pm the foreman called me back with another couple and had us searched for pilfering!! Darling, I could have smacked his face for daring to insinuate that I might steal cigarettes. As I walked along Lambeth Road homewards, I saw a queue for Jaffa Oranges. I stood in it for 20 minutes but didn't eat them until I got home.

I had a letter from your dad today. He surprised me by saying that he has written or is going to write to Mr Grieve to ask him to get you out of the army. What an odd thing to do!

--- Surely a nice thing to do, wasn't it?

--- Well, yes, in a way, but I hadn't told them that I actually wanted to leave the army. Besides, this Mr Grieve was in the Housing Dept. and had no influence whatsoever. Quite honestly, I thought it was an ignorant thing to do and I was very annoyed.

18th February 1944

I am afraid I am feeling a lot happier tonight, darling, for the simple reason that I have no more fears of having to work in that terrible factory – instead I have been transferred to the office!! Darling, isn't that good news?

--- Gosh, Father, you must have breathed a sigh of relief when you read that!

--- I should say so.

I had it out with the foreman who was very sympathetic and said that they had clearly made a mistake in employing me in this way. There and then he phoned up to the Manager of the Administration Block and fixed up a part-time clerical job for me.

25th February 1944

This is the first time I have written to you for a week but it has been impossible for me to write. Today is my first day downstairs. It started last Monday with a <u>very</u> sore throat and on seeing the doctor he told me that I had Tonsillitis and that I must go straight home to bed and keep myself isolated for at least 48 hours. However yours truly is now well again.

Jimmy and I have been invited to a very posh wedding at the Adelphi on Wednesday. You know the Unwin boys, who are Jimmy's best friends, well their sister Maud is marrying an American Army Officer. Jimmy has been asked to represent the boys, one [Frank] is a P.O.W. and the other is in India.

'Now back to Father.

10th March 1944 (Airgraph)

For nearly one week now I haven't had any word from you. This evening I have been out to the new site of work in order to select a suitable place for the coolies to live. When doing

My father proudly showing off his new armoured vanette.

work in Tribal country even the coolies have to be protected against being shot by hostiles. I am also having an armed car made (it will be ready in 14 days). Gosh I will feel safer while travelling on these dangerous roads with a little steel around me.

13th March 1944 (Airgraph)

This evening I received a wonderful batch of mail filled with good and bad news. Your transfer to the office was the most cheering information you could have given a very worried and anxious hubby. Then I read about your tonsillitis. I do wish I could have been at your side to nurse yourself back to health.

13th March 1944

Sweetheart I am afraid I have some very disappointing news for you. Yes, you have guessed correctly – you cannot come to India. A new Indian Army order has just been issued saying that British Service Officers attached to the Indian Army are not allowed to return home. Unfortunately I fall into that category. Well, my dear darling, there it is and nothing can alter it. I, like you, am terribly, terribly disappointed. Last night I played a grand game of football with the South Waziristan Scouts but unfortunately the ball while travelling quite fast [here I adopted a high, squeaky voice] *hit 'Little Stan' very hard and he is terribly sore. If only you were here to make him better!*

--- I told my mother and dad about that and we had a good laugh at your expense. Even Fan had a giggle about it.

--- What did you tell them that for? How humiliating!

18th March 1944

Your dear hubby has been very busy. This new piece of work I am starting requires a tremendous amount of organisation for just one man. To give you an idea of its size, it will employ 600 men for about 7 months. In another couple of days' time I am going a hike across Waziristan into a very unknown part. I believe I shall be spending the night in a native Malik's house – this will be a very strange experience.

19th March 1944

In Jandola there are a tremendous number of sparrows and yesterday morning I was watching some of them collecting pieces of dried grass etc for building up their nests. As I watched them I wondered when the time will come when we shall start collecting furniture, carpets, curtains etc for our *home. Gosh when I looked at those sparrows I thought how ridiculous human life can be. Simple birds can mate and live together while we – the highest form of life – cannot do what we wish. Isn't it pitiful. No matter what we possess in this life there is nothing equal to love and happiness. At the moment I am earning marvellous money -- £775 per year or very nearly £15 per week – I have the most interesting and creative engineering job a young man of 26 years could possibly wish for and I am very fit and healthy. I have a lovely quarter and plenty of food….<u>Yet I am not happy</u> because you are not in my daily life.*

There seemed to be a stunned silence around the table after this (even for me) moving passage.

''Yet I am not happy' was written in a reddish-orange crayon, I added. That was very nice, Father. From the heart.

--- A rare compliment from my boxwallah! he mumbled.

--- I'll just finish this letter and then we'll stop.

My new big road job has started and everything so far seems to be going exceptionally well. So far no tribal trouble, thank heavens! Quite recently the biggest hostile leader, Faqir of Ipi, has written an order that any new work will be opposed in every possible way, but I have tried to get the work started on a good footing. So far so good.

6

Well darling I am glad to be able to say that I am feeling heaps better now. My tonsillitis has almost gone. At the moment I am listening to the new General Forces Programme which started operating on Sunday last. It is meant to bring the men overseas more in touch with their relatives and friends at home, by listening to the same programme. So, darling, I have been wondering if you too are listening to this programme, Evensong from Oxford Cathedral. I still have an awful cough. My mother bought me a colossal jar of Cod Liver Oil and Virol (malt). I adore it because it tastes like toffee!

--- You gave me Virol as a child to build me up, I interrupted. It was wonderful!

Do you remember telling me once that you would send Elsie a pair of stockings? Well, I told Elsie and now, every time I go up to their house, Dick [her husband] *will say to me, 'Elsie hasn't had her stockings from Stan yet; he didn't send them to your house did he?' Honestly, if he says this to me once more I will smack his face. He is insinuating that you have sent them here and I have kept them for myself. He is an awful man, a bad-minded devil.*

2nd March 1944

I am still off work due to my tonsillitis but this morning I went to see my doctor with the object of being 'signed off' but when he examined my throat he said I am suffering from yet another complaint – Pharyngitis. He advised plenty of fresh air so today I walked as far as the Pier Head and as I was waiting for the tram back I suddenly got the desire to go over the water for a sail. Gosh, darling, it was lovely. It was marvellous to feel the keen air in my hair. New Brighton looked lovely in the sunshine. When I got home my face was the colour of a turkey cock and I had the appetite of a horse. My mother had managed to get me a New Laid Egg from some kind neighbour and I really enjoyed my tea.

4th March 1944

Today I saw the doctor (after sitting for over 2 hours in a cold surgery) and he has signed me off for another week. Darling, I am fed up as it is too cold to go anywhere. To tell you the truth I am merely 'existing' and that is all I can call it, because I am not living in the true sense of the word with you as far away as you are.

Jimmy wrote home to say that 'Monty' inspected their battalion one day this week, and shook hands with all the officers, which of course included Jimmy. He spoke to the officers for half an hour and seemed most confident that this forthcoming invasion would bring an immediate victory. Jimmy also said that he has made a friend called Lang who is also a Liverpool University fellow and is in the same regiment. He is a woman-hater too.

I was just about to query Mother about this last, very odd statement (Jimmy never showed any misogynistic traits when I knew him) when the phone rang. Father shuffled off to answer it and we heard, 'Yes....yes...oh dear...I'll put her on. It's Liz, Phyl.'

--- Bad news, I'm afraid, Father mumbled to me.

It certainly was. According to my cousin, Liz, Jimmy had collapsed and died of a brain haemorrhage as he was leaving a restaurant with the family. There were no tears, not in my presence anyway, only a stunned silence as Mother slowly absorbed the fact that her much-loved brother was gone, the last of her siblings. Ironically, Jimmy had recently been showing signs of the dementia that was beginning to afflict his sister, too. Sadly, the last time I saw Jimmy at Liz and her husband Paul's house in Clapham, he barely knew me.

Anyway, the four of us planned to drive down to Liverpool for the funeral (Mother, Father, Peter and myself) but when Peter and I turned up at the house for the journey south Father was crying on the doorstep.

--- I can't go. I have this terrible cough.

Now I knew Father never really saw eye to eye with Jimmy, but this was, to me, an insufferable insult to Auntie Muriel, Liz and John. Couldn't he just suffer his cough for just a few days for the sake of family unity? But, no, he was adamant. With time ticking by we had to come to a rapid decision, so the three of us left in a flurry of incriminations and smouldering resentment. Maybe, just maybe, he **was** quite ill, and maybe I have done him an immense disservice, but as we left him, still lingering on the doorstep, I felt he had crossed one particular Rubicon.

To keep Mother's mind occupied on the journey down, Peter and I had gathered together cassettes of 30s and 40s dance band music (featuring such singers as The Andrews Sisters and Al Bowlly) so the six hour trip seemed to fly by and the three of us were amazingly happy. The funeral itself was both humorous and dignified, and at least Father had the decency and courtesy, to phone Muriel to express his sympathies....or perhaps his conscience was playing him up.

Less than a week later we were back at the dining-room table and the routine resumed. But things weren't the same: having recently witnessed a physical manifestation of Father's animosity towards Jimmy (or so I thought) I was determined to find out its source, hopefully buried in the remaining letters.

7th March 1944

Darling, I still haven't heard from you for almost a fortnight now. Last night my mother, Elsie and I were invited to my Auntie Gert's in Mauretania Road and we thoroughly enjoyed ourselves. My cousin Beryl, the ATS, is home on 7 days' leave, that was the reason for us going. They showed me a letter card from cousin Freddy who is, at present, fighting in Burma. He spoke of his jungle experiences such as going out after dark to hunt for such things as jackals, snakes, bittern, peacocks etc then coming home and cooking them. He said that roast snake and peacock are, to them, the grandest of luxuries. Roast jackal is vile apparently!

I am a lot better now. Am still off [work] but most definitely will return to my part-time job on Monday next – typing the labels for the Duty Free Cigarettes for the Servicemen and P.O.W.s overseas.

16th March 1944

I arrived home from work at 1.15pm to find a nice little wad of mail from you waiting for me. Darling, you seem <u>terribly</u> annoyed with me for having left Napier's but you have no more cause to worry about me because I am working with a nice set of girls and like it more than any other place I've worked in. We haven't heard from Jimmy for a fortnight now. My mother and dad are very upset because he usually writes twice a week. I simply dread the thought of him taking part in this forthcoming invasion.

Jimmy, quite rightly, was immensely proud of his war-time experiences, and I remember a visit to his house in Ormskirk with my mother when, over two carafes of Californian white wine, he told me his fascinating story way into the small hours. Just me and him. And I was so hung over (I must have been in my twenties) the next morning that, much to Mother's embarrassment, I had to pull the car over on to the side of the sliproad to the M6... to be violently sick. As we are about to find out, Jimmy saw action in one of the greatest theatres of war ever experienced – unlike my father, stuck uneventfully in the wings.

--- Right, I said, bucking us all up. Let's hear about this wonderful trek of yours, Father.

--- Oh, yes, I'd forgotten about that.

27th March 1944

I wonder what you really like in me, more than any other men you have met? You are differently placed than me – you mix with and meet men, while I am in a land where no women are allowed to live.

--- What do you mean by that? I asked.

--- I meant that they were not allowed to live like Western women.

I have only seen a couple of white women in the last 8 months. Of course this suits me admirably because I do not wish to see any. Other men are different, especially the bachelors. When they go on leave to hill-stations they all flock around all the women they find. Because of this I am afraid the morals of the Indian Summer hill-stations are very loose.

Darling I am getting a dog. Some time ago the Wana Brigade Major told me that he had a high class Airedale bitch with his wife in Quetta. He was about to cross her [the dog, not the wife, presumably] with another Airedale. As soon as I heard this I asked him to keep a puppy for me. Four days ago he told me his dog had given birth to eight pups and he had reserved one for me. It is going to cost me 100 rupees

(£7.10.0) [about £250 today]. *Well, darling, I want you to give him his name.*

Now I want to tell you the story of my recent trek. On Tuesday morning the A.P.A. [Assistant Political Agent] *John Dent and I started off from Sarwekai on a journey of 28 miles through the most dangerous Mahsud country. We had a large collection of head villagers called Maliks and Khassadars for my personal protection. In the afternoon we arrived at our first destination, a big malik's house for lunch. It was a first class meal called 'pilau'. This consisted of sweet rice boiled in fat and covered with meat and curry. After this dish came meat ribs and flavoured potatoes. As soon as lunch was over I visited a large native irrigation work nearby. Gosh it was the most impracticable thing I had seen and I told them they were throwing money away as it would never work. At 5pm we climbed from the mullah bed over a very steep valley called Narai to a lovely native village called NANU.*

The house we stayed in [he provides a tiny sketch] *is constructed of mud with a tower at one end, this for protection from murderers and thieves. There are no windows on the outside and no lavatories or baths – for every No1 or No2 I had to do I had to go down the hillside and crouch behind a tree. After another meal of 'pilau' Dent and I slept in the same room on native beds called charpoys. They were absolutely clean beds too.*

Next morning we followed the river until we reached a narrow ravine called Tangi Toi. Gosh this was terrific, just like a chimney cut in the hillside. At 4pm we reached Tiarza. Journey's end!

8th April 1944

This evening I received a letter from your Auntie and Uncle and I am sure that it is one of the nicest letters I have ever had from anybody apart from you. It was full of sincere affection. Here is what Auntie Gert says about you: '....you will be pleased to hear that Phyl hasn't changed in any way, still remains very girlish and is very much in love with you.'

11th April 1944 (Airgraph)

Yesterday I sat for my Pushto examination. Before I went into the room I knew that I hadn't a chance of getting through. I am just no good at languages.

14th April 1944

Yesterday I wrote a letter to my colonel asking him if I could go on ten days' leave at the end of this month as I feel like a change and a rest. Another major in my mess and myself decided to go to Quetta together. I wanted to go for three reasons: (1) to get two of my teeth filled by a really good dentist (2) to see the Quetta reconstruction and new concrete architecture (3) to bring my Airedale puppy back to Wana. Today, however, I received a reply to say that I couldn't be spared.

22nd April 1944

Yesterday I went on a trip on an aeroplane. Gosh it was absolutely marvellous. It was part and parcel of a reconnaissance of a big new job which I am surveying and planning. The aircraft was a beautiful two-seater Harvard, something like a Spitfire in shape and size. Gosh we simply roared up the landing ground and before I knew it we were off the ground and climbing steeply. It was a marvellous experience altogether.

26th April 1944 (Airgraph)

So you wish to call my new dog 'Chips'....well, darling, your choice is selected and he will be called this from the day I get him. It is very strange about the way in which Jimmy has to leave all his clothes behind, it certainly looks as if the invasion is near. I hope he comes through it all right.

30th April 1944 (Airgraph)

Oh, Phyl, whatever our forces may do I hope God will guide them so that the greatest military invasion of history will be successful. At this point our thoughts also turn to Jimmy, may God bless him and keep him safe from all harm and danger.

--- Right, coffee time I think. Big things ahead: D-Day and the arrival of Chips. But we must get back to Mother's letters since we've fallen behind somewhat.

7

22nd March 1944

Darling, do you know we haven't a scrap of coal in the house? Due to the strike there is very little coal at all and now that it is rationed to 5 bags a month per house, well it makes things pretty desperate. My dad has been bringing wood home from work every night. We have been going to bed very, very early because it has been too cold to sit around a low fire. My mother has just been brushing the cellar and she is now throwing on what coal dust she managed to scrape together.

24th March 1944

About our lack of coal – well a kindly neighbour gave us about 6 shovels full [sic] today and, what is more, she does not want it back from our ration because she has a ton or more in her cellar. Naturally we had to pay for it. However, we are, at the present moment, enjoying a couple of hours before a rosy fire. My Auntie Gert has just come here, darling, as her husband is fire-watching at his office. He is a 'big chief' at Ellerman's Shipping Company. She sleeps here every time he does this as she is nervous on her own.

28th March 1944

Today I received your Letter Card containing the horribly disappointing news that wives are not allowed to go to India. My mother was just about to serve dinner but I'm afraid I was too overwhelmed to eat, instead I merely sat down by the fire and broke my heart crying. But, darling, the shock soon passed.

It is Jimmy's birthday on Friday, 1st of April. He will be 23. Yesterday afternoon I went to town and bought him a beautiful *khaki officer's Van Heusen shirt and two collars, rubenised. We heard from him today. He sent my mother a cheque for £10. It was such a pathetic letter, as though like a 'farewell' before he goes. Lately he has been doing a lot of this invasion practice, sailing up and down the Channel, with Combined Ops, in Landing Craft.*

Mother seemed to be flagging a bit, so, in order to grab her attention I interrupted the letter-reading.

--- Mother, can you remember why you decided to call Father's dog 'Chips'?

--- Well, when we were in York your father and I went to see the film *'Goodbye, Mr Chips'* and it made a big impression on us.

--- What a nice idea! OK, let's move on.

30th March 1944

I got quite a surprise yesterday: I was transferred to a new branch of the British American Tobacco Co. This place is in town, in Stafford Street off London Road, and is a lovely big office, very new and sunny. I have just finished washing my hair. Have just rubbed it dry and am listening to the Thursday night programme 'Itma' with Tommy Handley. All our friends here love it. I think it has something so original and different from the other ridiculous radio entertainments.

Remember me telling you that Frank Unwin, Jimmy's friend, was a P.O.W. in Italy? Well today his father received word that he has been transferred to Germany. We were very pleased here because he is such a nice boy.

7th April 1944

I had just finished typing one of these to you last night when there was a knock at the front door. I got up and opened it....and Jimmy walked in! It was a terrible surprise because his leave is not due for another 3 weeks. He had come all the way from the South Coast and his advanced leave is for 10 days. The reason for the leave is 'secret'. There was a shuffle around looking for food for him. As my mother fried fish and scallops I made myself busy preparing the bed. Now that I am on part-time work I suppose I will be going out every afternoon with Jimmy.

As I was reading out this last letter I began to notice a sea-change in my parents' concentration: while my mother palpably perked up at any mention of Jimmy's name, my father, on the other hand, seemed less – shall we say – enamoured of the subject. He became fidgety as if ill at ease. This was somewhat concerning to me (and, at the same time, faintly exciting) since I knew Jimmy was going to figure prominently in the forthcoming letters. Perhaps Father anticipated that too.

9th April 1944

My own darling Stan, I have just finished giving my mother a hand with the cooking of the dinner and also making of the three beds, and while we are waiting for the chicken to roast, I have taken the opportunity to write this to you. It's a beautiful day and the only sign of war is a close-by droning of a few fighter aircraft going overhead. This afternoon Jimmy and I are going up to Elsie's for tea. At the moment he is busy cleaning his gear. He has his Sam Browne belt the full length of the table, polishing it away there, and cleaning pips and buttons, while my mother is complaining that she wants the table for the dinner to be set.

14th April 1944

By Jove, your trip into the native quarters sounded awfully exciting. We are rather depressed tonight, this being the last night, or rather last few hours, at home for Jimmy. At the moment he is pressing his battledress and cleaning his brown boots, ready to catch the 8.05am train to London in the morning. I know something is afoot...

--- That's a great word, Mother, 'afoot'.

--- I'm not just a pretty face, you know.

--- I know that.

--- I may be thick and uneducated, but I can write a good letter.

--- Oh, Phyl, don't talk like that. Whoever said you were 'thick', as you call it?

[That was one of my mother's finest, and, in many ways, strangest attributes: that in the august company of visiting lecturers, professors and writers who visited their house when my father was a professor himself, my mother was able to hold her own both as a hostess and, bizarrely, as a conversationalist. Her down-to-earth warmth and humour obliterated any intellectual deficiencies she might have had.]

I know something is afoot. For one thing, Jimmy has to report back to camp in only what he stands up in. He has no baggage, only a haversack containing a change of socks and some eatables for the journey. He has enjoyed his leave very much: we have been to several shows. This afternoon he took my mother and I [sic] to the Forum to see the American, all male show, 'This Is The Army'. Jimmy has been home 9 days but tonight the house seems awfully quiet because we have all our own thoughts while we watch him press his battledress. Tomorrow I am going to see him off at Lime Street Station.

Darling I got weighed today. I am 8st 8lbs and I still take size 5 shoes and 9 and a half in stockings!!

16th April 1944

Jimmy went back to camp yesterday morning. He wouldn't let mother or me see him off. I wonder when we'll see him again.

18th April 1944

Today I took a parcel to the G.P.O. which contained a cake for Jimmy from my mother. Unfortunately, I had to bring it home again because the latest news now is 'No foodstuffs must be sent'!!!

21st April 1944

Yesterday afternoon I took a little Persian kitten for your mother. Crikey, I <u>did</u> enjoy myself on the way. Passengers on the train made such a fuss of him, but I had to nurse him in my arms, just like a baby, to keep him warm. Your mother and dad nearly ate him – he's such a bundle of fluff. Your father roared his head off laughing when I left last night on the 9pm bus. He seemed so happy.

23rd April 1944

I have not long been in, having just returned from my Sunday visit to your parents. Your mother was absolutely going mad with neuralgia all the time I was there. She had been crying when I got there due to the pain. She told me, to my amazement, she had taken nothing for the pain and there was nothing in the house. I knew the real reason: because she didn't want to purchase anything on a Sunday because of her religion [she was a devout Methodist]. *I then put my hat and coat on and dashed out to a little shop nearby and came back with a good stock for her. Gradually during the afternoon her pain ceased but I suggested she had her teeth out. She lifted up her top lip for me to reveal gums which were terribly inflamed and – crikey – she could certainly do with such decayed teeth being out, but she said she hasn't the courage to go to the dentist because of her weak heart.*

By the way, the kitten now sleeps in bed between your mother and dad. Your father told me today that I am getting fatter each time he sees me. He thought this a compliment but to me it was a terrible shock because I don't want to get fat <u>ever</u>. There was an aeroplane in my teacup tonight (tea-leaves) so your mother said that it means 'Speedy News'. I said, 'Perhaps it is something better such as Stan coming back to us'.

--- What a load of nonsense, my mother and her tealeaf reading! Father said. She was very religious yet superstitious at the same time.

--- Yes, but hold on a minute, I said. Neither of you mention this in your letters, but this letter of Mother's is dated 23rd April, right?

--- So?

--- Well, don't you see? Your ride in the aeroplane took place on the 22nd! One day earlier.

--- Gosh, I never twigged.

--- There *must* be something in tea-leaf divining after all. Both Nanny and your mother believed in it.

--- Well I never. Coincidence?

Mother smiled and said nothing.

--- One final letter and then we'll have a breather.

25th April 1944

This afternoon I went to Bon Marche, saw a queue for <u>stockings</u>, got in it and after standing for three quarters of an hour the person in front of me explained that they were not pure silk at all only Utility. So I stepped out of the queue, walked up to the 3rd floor and bought myself a summer dress made of a flimsy silk. It cost

£3.7.6 and 7 coupons! It is pink and blue floral, piped with dusky pink round neck and sleeves.

8

When I arrived the following day I was more than surprised at how unusually jolly they both seemed. Father was dressed in a new and, for him, uncharacteristically jazzy green jumper (which, I'm afraid, didn't really suit him) and they were both beaming from ear to ear.

--- We've been having a good giggle over the recent letters, Mother said. And Father has had a bath.

--- Well, that *is* a surprise. Let's crack on then.

3rd May 1944 (Airgraph)

Two days ago my Brigadier left. From outside the camp we all lined the route and saluted as his car went by. I stood in front of my men and saluted. As I did so Brig. Campbell leant out and shouted, 'Goodbye, Wilkie, and good luck to you.' Gosh I thought that was awfully nice of him. Somehow or other he seemed to like me very much.

5th May 1944

I am excitedly awaiting the arrival of my Airedale puppy 'Chips' which is due to arrive on 9th May if everything goes all right. This puppy is coming to me all the way from Karachi via Quetta.

10th May 1944 (Airgraph)

My dog 'Chips' arrived yesterday.

---Ah, lovely Chips, Father said, with real affection and love in his voice.

Chips as a puppy.

A more mature Chips.

He had travelled 800 miles in 5 days. Gosh, I am absolutely delighted with him. At the moment he is quite small, born only on 4th March. Already he has gained a little place in my heart. At the first opportunity I will send you a snap of him.

21st May 1944

Well, darling, today I was presented with the India Service Medal. Only two people in my mess were eligible – perhaps because I am liked or popular the other people decided to stage a little presentation and pin the ribbon on my tunic one night in the mess. Wasn't that nice? In actual fact not many officers or men have received it because they have not taken part in an actual operation on the Frontier.

28th May 1944

Recently my own Colonel has had to furnish a confidential report on my capabilities and character. While I was in Brigade HQ I was told most secretly that my C.R.E. had said that I was very efficient and strongly recommended me for the post of a Major. Gosh I was most pleasantly surprised when I heard that.

Chips now knows his name and answers it whenever I use it to call him. He is so awfully good and a grand little fellow. At the moment the heat is getting him down a little – while I am writing this he is lying underneath my bath in order to remain cool. He follows me to the Mess when I go for breakfast and he remains in the cool of my office while I am working there. Two days ago I went on a most marvellous aeroplane flight. For the first time I was able to see into Afghanistan and, gosh, Waziristan looked most wonderful from the air.

6th June 1944 (Airgraph)

So the <u>invasion</u> has started. What wonderful news that is!! I heard the Indian News at 1.30pm. In your last letter you said how much sisterly love you had for Jimmy – let us hope he comes through safely.

--- At this point, I said, I think we should return to Mother's letters so she can catch up.

8th May 1944

The weather here is topping, very sunny and unbearably hot for May. Yesterday my mother and I went to Longmoor Lane Cemetery. I bought some lovely tulips for my nanny's grave. My mother cut the grass around the stone while I arranged the flowers. [This was the grave of my great-grandmother, Agnes Clark (nee Smart) (1865-1938), a person my mother revered.]

12th May 1944

I have just this minute returned from town and am more than thrilled and delighted over the cable that was awaiting me. It reads 'Parcel received darling, Chips also arrived'. I am very happy for your sake. Did you know that when you bring Chips home he will have to remain in quarantine for a few months before you can bring him into England? Jimmy is somewhere in England, where we do not know. We had a letter today to say that he's got a 24 hour pass but is not allowed beyond a 20 mile distance.

17th May 1944

Elsie and I are planning to go to Scotland again in July or August. That is of course if we are not held back by the forthcoming invasion.

20th May 1944

This morning I queued outside Saxone for 2 hours to buy a pair of shoes. Luckily I found a pair of 'Joyce' shoes with a wedge heel. Elsie arranged to meet me outside the shop at 9.30 and then we went into the Kardomah Café for a morning coffee and a bite to eat. We discussed our summer holidays and thought about Shropshire (Church Stretton), Llandudno, Anglesey or Prestatyn. We did prefer Scotland but there is a lot of talk by the railway companies that trains must not be relied upon due to the invasion.

As I write my dad is in the yard taking his bike to pieces and Mother is out at a Whist Drive with Fan. Fan minds all the women's gloves and handbags and they always give her a few coppers. My dad says she'll have to be paying Income Tax if this goes on much longer!!!

--- Dear Fan! I said. (She was one of the most abiding creatures of my childhood.)

My mother friend's son is somewhere down south waiting to take part in the invasion and one day he saw Jimmy walking along. This chap didn't like approaching him so he asked one of Jimmy's men if that was Lt. Jimmy Moore. The man said, 'Yes, that's the boss, the best officer in the mob. On the parade ground he's an officer but off he's one of the men.' Darling, wasn't that a wonderful thing to say?

24th May 1944

This morning I received a large parcel from Jimmy. It was a box containing 8 bars of Cadbury's Plain Motoring, 2 Chocolate Crème bars, 11 bars of Cadbury's assorted centres and about half a pound of assorted sweets. In a heavily censored letter he says he thinks he will be away by this time next week!!!! Oh darling Stan I'm so upset and scared. I do think the world of Jimmy and there is no *denying it. He once told me he would willingly exchange places with you just to get you back to England.*

29th May 1944

Elsie and I have finally booked our summer holidays. It is to an hotel in Church Stretton in Shropshire. The proprietor is charging us 11/- per day each full board. Yesterday we all went up to my auntie's in Mauretania Road. Unlike you, my cousin Freddie is not too frequent with his mail because he is in the jungle fighting in Burma. He's Transport Officer in charge of mules. Before he was called up he was a chemist in Dunlop's laboratory.

31st May 1944

No news of Jimmy for about 10 days now. My mother feels it very badly. All my dad looks for when he gets home is a letter from Jimmy and I feel so dreadfully for him when he finds there is nothing at all. He wears such a haunted look lately, I think. On every church around here there is a notice, 'This church will be opened daily for private prayer the moment the opening of the second front starts.' Darling, that positively gives me the jitters!! And all the hospitals here are being cleared of minor cases to make room for casualties.

6th June 1944

Well, darling, as you will see from the date at the top of the letter, today is the longed for D-Day for which the whole world has been waiting. So far all seems to be going well and the Allied and British troops are making rapid headway. Naturally our thoughts turn to Jimmy and hope and pray that God will bring him safely through. His last words written in a letter a fortnight ago were, 'I shan't be able to write for a while now, but remember, that if the Canadian troops are all right in the Second Front, then I shall be.'

My mother is terribly worried but I'm doing my best to console her. All that worries her is whether he will be hungry or whether he'll be cold or have wet feet. Please forgive me, darling, for devoting most of this letter to Jimmy and not you but I'm sure you'll understand.

I must admit that I was finding it difficult to concentrate on this most recent session, and, while I was reading aloud, my inner self seemed, for the first time, to be really questioning what I was doing. My original purpose was two-fold: – (1) by revivifying their past I could divert my parents' minds from their obvious decline – that side of things seemed to be working; (2) to find out why my father suffered this lifelong animosity towards Jimmy – **that** remained unclear, yet I sensed the truth was approaching.

The previous night, though, I'd been reading J. B. Priestley's '*Time and the Conways*', a play which investigates the roles of precognition and fate in the lives of a family. At the end of Act I, Kay Conway is speaking to her brother Alan, bemoaning the fact that a family reunion has turned a bit sour.

Alan explains that at any point in time we are only cross-sections of who we really are. And it's only at the end of our lives that we become our real selves.

Last night I'd suddenly thought about these readings and I said to myself: 'It's all shit, this. It's the individual moments that matter. I'm simply reigniting a short cross-section of my parents' lives and trying to make some kind of sense out of it.' What they were **then** is not how they are **now**; it's only a cross-section of their lives at one particular point in time.

More and more, then, I was becoming aware that the past **is** a foreign country and that the only valid reasoning for continuing the readings was as a diversionary tactic. But continue we did.

9

Well, Phyl, I have got some bad news for you – I got rather badly hurt at football the other day. During a tackle my opponent hit me right under my balls: as a result I just doubled up in absolute agony. Pain in a man's balls is the worst possible – it is about 20 times worse than toothache. However, I eventually played on but had to give up because of the pain. When I got home I got an awful shock – my right-hand ball had swollen up to about the size of a cricket ball. Phyl, I was really scared, so I went to the doctor who said everything would be all right after rest and hot linseed poultices had been applied over four or five days. Luckily, now, the swelling has gone down. Darling, please don't mention this to my parents because they write the most worried letters.

--- A pity Peter wasn't here to hear all this, I quipped.

--- Quite. But, gosh, it was incredibly sore. And there's worse to come I think.

--- Indeed.

13th June 1944

Yesterday morning I left my office at 5.15pm and just as I got into my room a most frightful pain started in my injured ball and up my right groin. For five minutes I was in absolute agony and the ball swelled to the size of a cricket ball again. The doctor was worried when he saw it and said only rest would cure it – so I have been sent to bed for 4 days! When he saw that my ball had also turned black he said to me,

'Wilkie, with your ball being that colour you will have a nigger offspring.' Gosh, I did laugh over this.

--- Hilarious, Mother said sarcastically.

21st June 1944

I have been on tour since last Sunday morning and I have only just returned to my beloved Wana and my little room, your photos and Chips. Well, my love, I am glad you have finally settled your holiday programme in Shropshire. Somehow I agree with Mother and consider you should not in future bother with Elsie. I think she is most fickle and unreliable at times. Sweetheart all your last five letters consisted of nothing else but Jimmy. Never mind. I can forgive you because I can appreciate just how anxious you are over him – I am anxious too.

23rd June 1944 (Airgraph)

Sweetheart I played a quiet game of golf last night and I got a slight pain in the injured place. Chips went with me around the course: whenever I went to putt he always stopped the ball, much to my annoyance.

25th June 1944

Darling, today I went to the hospital for my final examination. The doctor told me I had nothing to worry about and an operation would not now be necessary, but I couldn't play football for another two months!

28th June 1944 (Airgraph)

I am most relieved that you have had a line from Jimmy to say that he is quite safe and sound. I suppose this news has cheered up your parents terrifically.

2nd July 1944 (Airgraph)

I haven't heard from you for some time now and as a result I do not feel just like my 'normal' self.

Right on cue, as if sensing what was coming, Father asked for a break, so I suggested we all went out for a breath of fresh air with a slow shuffle around the cricket ground. It was a glorious day with the birds and the trees clearly sensing spring was just around the corner. During the walk I tried to reflect on what my father had brought to my life: this ground was where I had played cricket for decades and it was he who arranged that my friend Charles and I had cricket coaching from Len Adams, once of Lancashire C.C., when I was a youngster at Hightown C.C. It was he who bought me a season ticket every year at Anfield in the early 60s. It was he who took us on fabulous summer car tours of Europe ranging from Scandinavia to distant Corsica taking in the architectural highlights of the Continent. I had to be grateful. But, was I, **really**?

After a quick bite to eat we resumed.

10

My mother has not eaten a bite since yesterday, since the invasion started. I suppose she will soon get used to it, but probably it has upset her rather badly. I've just been reading an old letter of Jimmy's. He said that his platoon, as they advance, are to blow up all obstacles such as bridges, buildings and houses which might have booby traps in them. It was my mother's 39th Wedding Anniversary yesterday [6th June 1905]. Elsie has finally agreed to the dates so by the time you get this I will be in Church Stretton!

10th June 1944

I can honestly say that my mother has neither eaten nor slept since 6th June. It is awful to see her. She is sick quite a lot for the want of something in her inside. My dad was left alone here last night while I went to the Forum with a friend to see 'Madame Curie'. When I came back he was crouched over the wireless listening to a news flash from Richard Dimbleby. I could tell that he had been crying while we were all out. My aunt has written a nice letter to my mum and dad saying "I am thinking of 'Dinty' all the time." ['Dinty' was Jimmy's nickname, given to him by his fellow officers.] *Wasn't that nice?*

14th June 1944

Today we received a good piece of news, a Field Card from Jimmy to say that he is safe and well but in France (somewhere) and has got over the initial landing on 6th June. I wept for joy. I wish you could see the change in my mother, she is singing and laughing again, and I'm longing for my dad to come home in an hour's time, just to see how happy he can look again.

17th June 1944

(Written from Church Stretton)

We left Lime Street at 7.05pm having to change once only, at Shrewsbury. The place where we are staying is a tiny hotel. When we arrived late last night we had a lovely supper waiting for us, shrimp salad! And this morning at 9am breakfast was served, and gosh what a meal. Egg and bacon each. I couldn't believe my eyes when I saw a whole egg on each plate.

Church Stretton is a lovely place, rather like Keswick, and this morning we climbed a mountain called Caradoc. It is 2120ft high. St. Dunstan's School for the Blind is here, situated on the mountainside with special transport to bring them into the little town. Darling, it's awfully pathetic to see the young boys, all ex-servicemen, in khaki, walking about with white sticks and wearing dark glasses. One Canadian staff-sergeant we saw today had been shot between the eyes at Dieppe. Tomorrow we are going to climb a mountain called 'Long Mynd'. There goes the dinner gong! All my love.

19th June 1944

(Church Stretton)

This morning a letter came from my mother....

At this point we were interrupted by a car zooming into the drive.

--- It's Peter, Mother said with obvious pleasure in her voice.

--- Evening all! I was passing, so I thought I'd drop in. How is everyone?

--- Fine, was Father's somewhat curt reply. Sit down and join us.

---'Mother's on holiday with Elsie in Church Stretton, I explained.

This morning a letter came from my mother. It felt rather thick when I lifted it from my plate. It contained a letter written to us all from Jimmy. It was written a week after D-Day and he told us that he was one of the first infantrymen to reach the beaches and famous West Wall. He implied that he was in the thick of the fighting and that he'd just had his first wash and shave for 5 days. He says there is no shortage of food but they are lacking cigarettes so Elsie and I each bought a few hundred this morning and sent them off along with Brylcreem, HP Sauce, Horlicks and shaving soaps. Today we climbed Long Mynd, a height of 2,230 ft.

21st June 1944

(Church Stretton)

Elsie and I have just returned from Ludlow which is a most awful place. In 10 minutes we had seen everything including an old castle, a bridge and a few second-rate shops. The day before we went to Shrewsbury which is much nicer. All over Church Stretton there are notices to visitors asking us that if we care to take [the blinded soldiers] walks, picnics or dancing we have to apply to the matron of the V.A.D. {Volunteer Air Defence} or W.V.S. Elsie and I are going to volunteer. {Here Mother explained all about St. Dunstan's for Peter's benefit.}

24th June 1944

(Church Stretton)

Yesterday Elsie and I took some St. Dunstan's boys out for a walk through Carding Mill Valley. It's a beautiful place with no traffic which is the main reason why we took them there. We had to call for the three men at the workshops and we saw what marvellous work they were doing: one showed me an electric clock he'd made

298

out of Meccano; another boy made leather boots and children's toys from leather (he gave me a pair of kiddy's reins he'd made which I've kept for my bottom drawer!!).

--- I remember those! Peter interrupted.

Then another boy was typewriting in Braille. Two were wounded in Algiers, the third was a riding instructor in the Bengal Lancers. Oh, and Jimmy is now Captain Moore!!!! So you're not the only captain in the family.

By the way, Mother sent me your letter card in which you describe the accident which occurred to L.S. during football.

--- What accident? Peter asked. And what is L.S.?

--- I was hit in a vulnerable spot…quite badly.

--- L.S. is Little Stan, said Mother, who then dissolved into giggles.

--- Oh…I see. And what happened?

--- It swelled up to the size of a cricket ball.

--- What did? Little Stan? (Repressed giggles from most of us.)

--- Yes…no….well, my right….testicle.

--- Ooooh, nasty.

---I was in great pain for 4 days.

--- I bet.

--- Now, can we *please* get on?

26th June 1944
___

Elsie and I arrived home safely yesterday afternoon and I must say Liverpool seems absolutely foul. Today it is POURING and *everywhere is grey, miserable and colourless. I have just been writing to Captain Moore who says he is now having his rest time from fighting. He says 'I've been made captain for managing to survive on 6 cigarettes for 8 days!!!!' He says we are <u>not</u> to read the papers as they are a lot of bunk! One paper he read said that all the invasion troops ate a hearty meal on the way across. It was the complete opposite. All his men, as well as himself, were all either sea-sick or sitting on the WC (with fear).*

29th June 1944

I had an accident today darling while my mother was out. I don't want to tell her otherwise she will be annoyed at my carelessness, for I might have set the house on fire. You remember the two blue undersets you sent me? Well! Today I was having a bath in our bath in the back, when Fan suddenly shouted, 'Phyl, I've just noticed your underwear, come and look.' Before I have a bath I usually leave my underwear over the rail by the fire to air before I put the cool silk next to my body. At one end I put my blue vest, then in the middle the knickers, then the slip at the other end. However, when I dashed in (in the nude!) there, to my astonishment, was the pair of knickers absolutely in flames in the hearth ash-pan. I got quite a fright. There was nothing I could do, so I just had to let them burn out.

The only letter today, darling, was from Jimmy. I think it is so interesting, and you might be interested, that I have decided to copy it word for word. Here it is:

Dear All,

At the moment I am quite comfortably set up in a dugout with another captain who used to go to the Collegiate [Jimmy's old school]. Well, I think I can describe to you a bit about what happened on and around D-Day. From the boat I was on I had a remarkably good view of what was happening. As we drew towards the coast shortly after dawn, at 4am, I watched the terrific barrage that was put down by the navy: battleships, cruisers, destroyers and various other craft. I had an 'Orchestral Stall' seat for this, and saw hundreds of shells go tearing into German defence posts along the beach. [Four men of Jimmy's regiment were each placed in the landing craft of the Canadian battalions about to storm Omaha Beach]. It was queer how little opposition was encountered by the ships from the enemy shore batteries. I watched one battery from a pillbox very foolishly turn its small gun on to a naval ship which was very close to shore. The ship simply turned round and blasted the pillbox into rubble and powder. The air cover was as complete as possible. I didn't see an enemy aircraft until the evening of D-Day while thousands of our fellows flew over.

Then I watched the assault troops go in and then the silent enemy machine-gun nests and mortars opened up. I've never seen such indescribable courage and determination as on the part of those fellows. Naturally I can't disclose their units but I'll remember who they were forever: men storming pillboxes single-handed after their parties had been mown down. Slowly and surely they fought their way in until they were past the hard crust of enemy resistance, and the much heralded Western Wall was gone. Mines were one of the biggest problems then and I got my party dealing with them, making gaps through the mine-belt etc, and although several people lost their lives, my platoon never lost a man. Soon the chaotic disorganisation which was inevitable at the start began to work out according to plan. It was in the late afternoon that I saw the first visitor from the Luftwaffe. He dived out of cloud and swept the beach with machine-gun fire and then I found myself looking at two black objects wobbling down to earth.

I stood there like a soft fool watching them until it occurred to me what they were, so down I went face first. They landed only about 60 yards away but did no damage. During the night we got little rest through enemy aircraft. They only dared to come during the hours of darkness and they took a rare old battering from the AA fire. I lost one or two friends here just at dawn the next day from a bomb hit! As time went by it became much quieter, apart from the occasional ping of a bullet over your shoulder as a sniper potted away. The French people were very queer. At first none were to be seen; they had probably buried themselves well under as the battle raged, and then appeared gradually. It was remarkable walking through a French village, French people giving the Victory sign with one hand and throwing flowers around our necks with the other, while farther up the village French snipers were giving us their own particular welcome by an occasional bullet.

Now we are quite comfortable, in fact very comfortable, in German dugouts. My French, though not so hot as in 1938, is still quite workable. I managed to buy a couple of eggs this morning from an old French farmer, and I even managed to win an argument over my change, of which he tried to diddle me!! I've got my old camp bed to sleep on and the food is good and requires only a tin opener and a fire to cook it. Today's (dehydrated) dinner for instance was some very good steak and kidney pudding and potatoes, followed by treacle pudding and tea.

Well, I don't think the war will last very long; this may seem very slow at first but there'll be a terrific push on before long I'm sure. All I can say about their Western Wall is that it wasn't nearly so good as made out to be, but even as it was, if they'd had British or Canadian forces to man it, they'd have held out for weeks against all comers. Man for man they're not a patch on the Allied troops.

Don't worry over me,

Love, Jimmy.

There was an appreciative silence throughout the reading of this letter apart from some noises of approbation from Peter who always seems to be stimulated by military stories. I shuddered to think, though, what Father made of all this.

--- While Peter's here, I said, can I go on a bit further?

They all agreed, Father somewhat gruffly.

6th July 1944

Darling, I'm sorry that 5 of my 8 letters contain nothing else but Jimmy, but I'm sure you forgive me due to the present circumstances. If you had a brother or sister perhaps you would have understood. Never mind, darling, if you received 8 letters from me, well the other 3 would surely give you some recompense, eh?

--- Unlike you to be sarcastic, Mother! Peter said sarcastically.

--- A tiny bit further and then we'll stop. I want Peter to hear some of Father's letters.

--- As far as I can see, these letters are so typical of those who wrote them, Peter continued. Jimmy, modest, and immersed in the war; Mother, exaggerating stories, obsessed with clothes and the family. Now, what about Father?

4th July 1944 (Airgraph)

I am glad you enjoyed your holiday in Church Stretton but I'm sure it can't equal lovely Keswick with me. Sweetheart, what is Elsie like to go on holiday with? Does she ever talk about sex with you? What is her opinion? – I have often wondered this.

--- What a strange question! Peter butted in.

5th July 1944

Last night I looked up Church Stretton on the large atlas we have in the mess. Gosh you did make me feel terribly Phylsick when you described your little bed and how you cuddled up to Elsie one night. Darling, how different it would have been if I had been Elsie. What is Elsie like to go on holiday with?

---There you go again!

Is she cheerful and happy? Does she ever speak to you about her married life? Phyl, does she ever talk about sex? What is her opinion? Darling please let me know all the answers to these questions.

--- You're curiously persistent, aren't you?

11th July 1944

Darling I wonder how much longer God is going to keep us separated in this way. For three years now I have managed to stick it but honestly Phyl I cannot hold on much longer. I simply adore you and judging from your recent photograph you were never lovelier. Sweetheart I get really browned off when I think that I am losing your precious companionship and the sight of your present beauty.

Chips is a grand dog and I am really pleased with him. At first he was a bit of a nuisance because he did his No1 and

No2 on my carpet. Now he is a perfectly trained house dog. At the moment I am trying to teach him a few tricks. Already he is quite proficient at one of them, carrying his lead and my swagger stick behind me when we go a walk together.

12th July 1944

The best bit of news in your letter was the promotion of Jimmy to Captain. I am delighted he has got to the three star stage – anyway he fully deserves it for what he has gone through. I will write a few lines to congratulate him.

16th July 1944

Dear Phyl, This afternoon I sent Jimmy a letter congratulating him on his promotion and also for coming through the first invasion fighting safely. I suppose you now look upon me stuck on the NW Frontier of India as a pretty poor fish.

Here I paused and, mischievously perhaps, asked Peter, as a relative outsider to our readings, what these brief extracts revealed about Father.

--- Well, I would say cantankerous, lonely (why else would you get a dog?), jealous of Jimmy, obsessed with sex and still deeply in love…and frustrated.

At this, Father hit the roof.

--- There are two things I want to say about this (during the following harangue a pendulous drop appeared at the end of Father's nose which increased in pendulosity as time wore on. I couldn't take my eyes off it. He was totally unaware of it until the very end). First of all, I think Tim has deliberately yet subtly edited or manipulated what's in these letters to put me in a bad light. Why he has done this I don't know.

--- Don't be daft, I said. All I've done is miss out the daily repetitious litany of expressions of love for Mother and vice-versa. We'd be here till Doomsday if I'd kept them in. Although I **have** included some, to give a sense of all this.

--- Let me continue. Secondly, I also think you timed it so that you could read out these particular extracts at exactly the time Peter was here, again to show me up.

--- Nonsense. I didn't know he was going to turn up today any more than you did. Peter, did you tell anyone you were coming?

--- No.

--- And why would I want to show you in a bad light anyway?

--- Thirdly....

--- I thought you were only going to say two things.

--- Thirdly (now it was turning into a Monty Python sketch) none of you has any idea what it was like being stuck at the end of the world, isolated from the ones you love, reading about what a wonderful war Jimmy was having.

--- But we're not condemning you. It was you who called yourself 'a pretty poor fish', remember.

--- Well, I've had enough of these readings, so the boxwallah can damn well put the letters back where they came from.

--- Oh, Stan, don't be so childish.

--- This is just a cross-section of your life a long time ago, I added. It's not you **now**. It's what you **were** and we understand why. Father, you don't mean it...

--- I do.

And with that the drop at the end of his nose splashed onto the dining-room table.

We dispersed. Later, at home in my bachelor flat, I reflected that, yes, Father, footling around in the foothills of the war, **was** jealous of the role Jimmy played in the vanguard of action. But what I realised even more was that, for the first time, Father could **share** his anger with us, rather than bottling it up in the wastes of India, alone with a dog. And that's what we had just witnessed. The letters had seen to that.

'I was angry with my friend,

I told my wrath, the wrath did end.'

How would Father react now?

11

I didn't have long to wait. A few days later I got a phone call from Mother – this was a rare event indeed since she had become incapable of using a phone at all, so Father must have done the dialling.

---'Father is very sorry for what happened last week, she said, and wants you to go on with the readings. We both miss your visits.

She then said that they had been in to Aberdeen on the bus (previously Father wouldn't have been seen dead using public transport in this way), had shopped in Marks and Spencer's and had even bought a two-seater settee which they wanted me to see.

Certainly when I went to their home there seemed to be a rejuvenated atmosphere: the settee was a welcome addition to the lounge, a vase of daffodils was in the centre of the dining-room table and Dvorak's New World Symphony was playing in the background, my father's favourite symphony. And so the ritual recommenced. However, I also knew one major crisis was looming in the letters.

18th July 1944

[Father is reminiscing about their honeymoon in Keswick. He has sent Mother a picture of Millbeck Farm, Great Langdale, which his parents had come across in the Liverpool Echo]. *Sweetheart we actually walked through the farm after we had spent a most beautiful day walking from Grasmere to the Langdale Pikes and then into the village of Langdale for the bus. Let me remind you:*

1. *We took the bus from Keswick to the little village of Grasmere. From there we climbed the hills overlooking it. When we got to the top we could see Lake Windermere in the distance.*

2. *On and on we walked along the ridge which brought us to the magnificent Langdale Pikes. It was a very hot day and after much huffing and puffing we reached point 'X' (marked on the picture). There you stopped and said you could not go any further but I could go on to the top of the highest peak called Sugar Loaf if I wanted. Darling, I was afraid of leaving your side in case some bad man came along and ran off with you. And so we took a little rest and started to descend.*

3. *When we got to the bottom we walked through this lovely farm via a stile and caught the little bus.*

4. *Then came 82 Main Street Keswick – a lovely dinner and then to round off the day a beautiful cuddle in the arms of each other. When this ghastly war is over we must return to dear old Keswick.*

---'And we did, didn't we, chick? (There were now tears in his eyes) Remember? Just after the war. In June 1945, I think.

Mother smiled back, the warm glow of memory suffusing her eyes.

22nd July 1944

I am writing this letter from Razmak, here to discuss certain matters with my colonel such as aerodromes and contractor's rates. Oh, Phyl, isn't the war news wonderful? Gosh, wasn't it a shock to learn that some Germans had the courage to try and take Hitler's life? I think you can start preparing for my homecoming in 1945. One of the first things we shall do will be to go on a long holiday into the Lake District. Chips has accompanied me here. I have taken some photographs of the little fellow and I will forward them to you soon.

28th July 1944

I am awfully sorry that Freddie [Jones, Mother's cousin] has been seriously injured in Burma and the news has greatly affected Auntie Gert. For the last two days I have been taking Chips to the Veterinary Hospital to get him inoculated against Rabies. He is awfully good and doesn't even flinch.

--- Let's get back to Mother, I then suggested.

10th July 1944

My auntie (Gert) in Mauretania Road has had a heart attack and my mother has been up there all afternoon helping with the housework. She has been ordered to bed for rest. Lately she has been terribly run down, worrying over Freddie and not hearing from him and now Beryl is in the heart of London and has already been bombed twice since these Buzz-Bombs have been coming over. Meanwhile I have been busy baking a few scones and open jam tarts.

12th July 1944

Your mother was here yesterday morning for news of you. You are a one you know darling. Why can't you write to her more often? We had a letter this morning from Jimmy. He said his men had discovered an old water trough in a village and they dragged it along the lane, one and a half miles long, to their camp for the officers to get bathed in!! Jimmy added that it must weigh 2 TONS, being made of granite!!!

Yesterday I visited Elsie. Coming home I had just missed a No 19 tram in Breckfield Road so I decided to cut along Premier St. and get a 25 in Heyworth St. [Premier St. was where my father lived as a boy]. *Darling this was the <u>first</u> I'd been there since May 1941 when you and I were helping to salvage some of your belongings from the debris!!!* [The street had been bombed]. *Up to about 20 yards from the Unitarian Church there is nothing but a massive wasteground of rubble. Dirty children were playing in a sand-pit on which had once stood 'dear old 67'. I cried all the way home. Aren't I soft?*

14th July 1944

I have not been very long home from Upholland where I spent a very enjoyable day with your people. Your dad was saying that your Uncle Edgar has been decorated, but he was also torpedoed, having been wounded in chest and ankles. He is in a hospital in Bradford. Their eldest son is in the Parachute Regiment. Tomorrow my mother and I are going over to the Wirral to look for holiday accommodation for her and Fan. She (mother) has come in now with bad news that my cousin Freddie has been seriously wounded in Burma and when the telegram arrived Auntie Gert took another heart attack.

16th July 1944

Yesterday my mother and I rushed up to Mauretania Road. Gert was in bed looking absolutely ghastly, her face a purply colour. We stayed there a long time but she began to improve knowing that Freddie was at least still alive. This morning my mother and I went over the water to Moreton where we found a nice house in the new part. The lady whose house it is, is taking my mother, Fan and dad for a fortnight starting next Saturday while I go and live up at Elsie's.

19th July 1944

No, darling, Elsie never talks to me about Dick or herself of a sexual nature. We did speak of it once when she told me that she and Dick never have any sexual relationship because he was once rather 'fly' with women and she refused there and then to have anything to do with him. They have no love for one another I don't think, but all the same Elsie won't have a wrong word said against him.

My auntie is much better. She's had a telegram from Freddie himself to say he is now back at Assam and that his wound was only a broken wrist, but I think he's covering up something more serious.

24th July 1944

I'm so sorry that my letters regarding my worry for Jimmy have obviously bored you, Stan, but I think the world of him. You really are terribly absurd at times darling. Your very jealous mind gets the better of you at times. You shock me with your jealousy.

--- Oh, not this again! Father moaned.

--- This is the last of it I think, I reassured him.

REALLY, DARLING, YOU ARE AWFUL. Soon you will be jealous of Jimmy and I [sic] exchanging letters. I get so tired of the old routine here. You do go away on tours etc and have your own professional work which must be a godsend at a time like this. If you go on like this I'll do something desperate such as going to the pictures with an American one night!!!!!!!

29th July 1944

I am now back at dear old '31' darling after my stay with Elsie. I am going to look after Dad for a week until Mother and Fan finish their holiday. Elsie and I walked to the Pier Head yesterday. Darling I was disgusted to see the young flappers of girls hanging

312

around, dressed up in the most terrible clothes and cosmetics, waiting for Yanks to 'pick them up'. Two girls were lolling on the side of the Liver Buildings. They had large, terrific pink ribbons through their hair. Then two Yankee soldiers, both sergeants, came along, stopped, gave them some money (it looked like 5/- each!) then all four of them walked to a No 13 tram and got on. It made me terribly depressed somehow [to me, at this point, Mother sounded strangely like Holden Caulfield].

1st August 1944

My day here has been rather heavy. First of all I had to come home from work, dash out to the shops for meat, bread and milk, then come home again and cook myself something for dinner before making my way to the hairdresser's for 2.30. I also had to make the two beds, my dad's and my own, then feed the chickens and cat. When I cooked my dad's steak and fried tomatoes at 6pm I then decided to wash my undies and blouses for the coming weekend. Anyway, I was busily hanging them on the clothes line when one of the darned cockerels started chasing me all over the yard trying to get a bite out of my legs. I ran around screaming with fright. My dad rushed out and saved me by throwing a bucket of water over it.

Later when my dad finished his steak he said, 'Well, Phyl, I've been in the Adelphi for lunch but never in all my life have I ever tasted such a beautiful steak'!!!! This was only sarcasm, darling, because he hardly touched it really. I gave it to the cat, and he wouldn't eat it, so you can imagine how tender it was!!

7th August 1944

When I got off the 19 tram this afternoon I saw a soldier wearing exactly the same uniform as Jimmy, so I approached him and – yes – he was actually in Jimmy's platoon. When I mentioned 'Captain Moore' he raved on and on about what a fine chap he is.

He also told {me} something Jimmy has never told us, that he had been 'mentioned' for clearing mine-fields on D-Day. He said that Jimmy had been transferred to an Anti-Tank platoon only recently. This soldier had had a hand injury and was in Liverpool hospital.

8th August 1944

Darling, I'm afraid the talk about a decoration being awarded to your uncle is only a pack of lies from your auntie. Your mother says she is noted for telling lies. He was torpedoed definitely but there's no decoration....and she told your mother that her son, aged 18, who is in the Parachute Regiment, had landed in France on D-Day, yet your mother called there on June 7th and he was sitting there having his dinner!

Jimmy said in a letter today that he had been to supper to a French farmer's home, he and another officer. They had a hearty supper and wine, then the farmer's wife sewed a rip in Jimmy's shirt on a Singer sewing machine. Then she asked if he would like to bath their baby girl because the child herself would think it an honour to be bathed by a Tommy. Jimmy naturally refused because he is so shy, but his friend, who is a married man, carried out the good work!

10th August 1944

---

*Last night, darling, I was feeling pretty fed up and lonely here so I went to the pictures in town to the Trocadero to see a Noel Coward production called 'This Happy Breed'. It is magnificent, a truly British production portraying an ordinary middle class English home from 1919 to the present. The trouble started when I came out as all the trams were full so after much swearing (" / £ _ & (=) + *) I walked to the Landing Stage and took my place in the queue which must have been 2 miles long for a No 22 tram. Suddenly a*

314

cheer went up and people started running to the wall and peering over. There was that Mercy Ship, the 'Drottningholm'. People, I presumed the civilian internees who had got away, were waving frantically. The Drottningholm is a repatriation ship from Lisbon and it was being towed in. It was all white with terrific red crosses on her sides, but the bridge was painted yellow with the name of the ship in colossal letters painted from one end to the other.

It was Fan's birthday yesterday. She was 36!! I gave her half-a-crown, and she bought a N/Savings stamp with it today, 'towards Christmas'!! Darling, the news of the war is awfully encouraging, isn't it? 'Monty' reckons that 18 days will see the European War over.

13th August 1944

With your last letter, darling, came the snaps of you and Chips, also of your armoured car. Chips looks a grand little chap. When I saw his snaps I let out such cooing 'Ahs' and 'Goshes' and 'Ooohs'!!

15th August 1944

I am sorry to read that you had developed a chill through your servant neglecting your bath-water after a game of tennis. Darling, the worst thing you could ever do was to get into a cold bath after a hot game. Crikey, what a crazy thing to do.

17th August 1944

Sweetheart, I am glad to know that your trek was successful and that you did the distance of 22 miles without anything eventful happening.

--- Can we hear about my trek? Father asked.

--- Certainly, Father.

3rd August 1944

On Saturday I have to do a lot of climbing. The Political Agent has got a scheme whereby he wants to irrigate a large part of the tribal territory. It will require the blocking up of some mountain streams and blasting a tunnel through some rocks. As Engineer advisor I have to do a survey of the scheme. He and I are to go on horseback but we shall have a lot of protection with us.

7th August 1944

Well, my love, last Saturday I went a journey of 16 miles on horseback. When the Political Agent suggested horses I nearly fainted because even though I have done about 8 lessons I am no real expert and never done more than about a mile or so. Anyway at 8am we started out, protected by mounted Khassadars. After we had gone about 8 miles we were overtaken by a tribal informer to say that where we were going was very dangerous because there was a hostile gang in the neighbourhood. Very wisely the P.A. decided to turn back and travel right across the Wana Plain to a place called Shin Warsak near the Afghan border. This was a distance of another 14 miles. Gosh I feel like a cowboy now but the next day I was so stiff I could hardly walk!

12th August 1944

Once or twice I remember you pulling my leg over my football side always losing. Well, the Wana league finished the other day and my side finished fourth with 16 points from 15 games. {Insert photo of football team} I think that is a grand achievement and I think that if I hadn't been injured we would have won even more matches. So there!

17th August 1944

Your last letter was most interesting, especially the copy of Jimmy's description of D-Day. Somehow I wish I had been there also instead of staying up here dodging hostile tribesmen's bullets. One day last week Chips walked ten miles with me in order to inspect some landslips caused by recent flooding. Gosh! He was absolutely tired out. When we got back my badragga bodyguard said, 'Spay der takra' which means 'The dog is a very tough fellow'. The local tribesmen never touch dogs and whenever Chips goes near one of them, they move away in disgust.

I was noticing that Father was looking more and more pensive, so I asked him the reason.

--- If a total stranger was reading these letters (not that they will) what would they think of me as a person? I don't come across very well, do I? Phyl, there, is exactly the same as she ever was, just as nice, aren't you, chick? But **me**, I don't know.

He was looking for some kind of comfort, so I made a feeble attempt to placate him.

--- I read somewhere about a character in a novel or a short story, I can't remember which, who was said to be 'imprisoned within the limits of his own nature'. We're all like that, aren't we? It's a bit like a boxwallah, I suppose (here I began straining for metaphors to explain what I **think** I mean), dragging around throughout life all the quirks and qualms, the prejudices and phobias, we picked up in childhood. Or are we sailing ships (I'm beginning to get carried away), launched pristine, yet gradually gathering barnacles which accumulate through time and begin to weigh us down? Or like a....

--- So, you're saying it's to do with childhood then?

--- Isn't it true of all of us?

--- I see. So, you had a happy childhood, didn't you, Phyl?

--- Oh, I did. Happy, happy, happy.

--- And I couldn't escape it quickly enough. And I suppose my isolation in India didn't help.

--- Well, no, that's more than obvious. But that's war for you, I said, somewhat lamely.

12

When we resumed next day I sensed an almost palpable keenness on my parents' part to finish the readings as quickly as possible – not that they were bored, far from it – but because the end was in sight. Their reunion was fast approaching.

--- You do realise, of course, that the worst crisis in all these letters is nearly upon us?

--- Oh, yes, I know, and I was very silly, wasn't I, Phyl?

--- You can say that again!

I looked at Mother and smiled. Her mental deterioration had slowed, certainly, but there were signs recently of emerging problems: she was beginning to lose things (the front door key, for example, and only last week she had lost her beret in Sainsbury's) and their house, normally so tidy and dust-free, was beginning to feel a bit neglected as far as housework was concerned. Perhaps more seriously, Father told me on the quiet that she was now unable to write, so **he** had to pen all their Christmas cards. So, yes, for all these reasons, I was very keen to crack on.

20th August 1944

We are expecting Auntie Gert and Uncle Fred at any moment now. She wrote yesterday to say that she is much, much better and would like to come down to stretch her legs after being in bed so long. She said that she had just heard from Freddie that he is now in hospital in Northern India, suffering from malaria.

Jimmy is now attached to the 1ˢᵗ Oxford and Bucks Light Infantry. He has sent home for his pipe because, he says, 'tobacco is now issued to us free of charge', so I have sent him 200 Senior Service cigarettes through our firm.

21ˢᵗ August 1944

This afternoon I have been exceptionally busy bottling 7lbs of greengages and egg plums. I now have 16lbs of plums, greengages and raspberries stored away for the winter. This is the first time I have done anything like this. While I was hanging out my undies one of the cockerels got out of its cage and followed me all over the yard flying at my legs and pecking them. This is the second time it's done this. I was terrified and ran across the yard screaming, but it flew and pecked me all the more.

23ʳᵈ August 1944

Well, sweetheart, the news today is really absolutely wonderful. Today, the Americans took Paris. We are not able to forget it because the wireless has done nothing but play French music all day long, with shouts of 'Vive La France' down the microphone. Darling, hold on just for a few weeks (yes! I say 'weeks') longer now. I'll lay a bet that we shall see each other in another 6 months! Sweetheart, your letters have been the making of me during the past 3 years and 1 month! Without so many, and such encouraging ones at that, I would not have the spirit I have today. I'll save your letters till I die, darling. We'll read them all some time when we are old.

--- And that's exactly what we are doing! she added.

I'm going to Elsie's in Maghull tomorrow [this was her friend, Elsie Metzler]. *She is teaching me to make biscuits! Last week it was bottling fruit.*

25th August 1944

We had a letter from Jimmy this morning. He was telling us that he is in the front line 'good and proper' and has been transferred permanently to the 1st Battalion Oxf & Bucks Light Infantry. He has the same sort of platoon, an 'S. P. Coy', and the work is the same. When he left his previous regiment all the men lined up and shook hands with him and every man made a little speech of his own, thanking him for his help, etc. Then the band came out, playing Irish jigs on the pipes, and then the C.O. shook hands thanking him for the excellent work he did on D-Day.

28th August 1944

I went to Upholland yesterday and spent the day with your mum and dad. Your mother tells me, darling, that she has not heard from you for 4 or 5 weeks. This is awful of you.

4th September 1944

Sweetheart, the present news is simply amazing. At the moment we are liberating Brussels and making for Holland and the Siegfried Line. On Sunday my mother and I went to her cousin's in Aigburth where we went to the National Day of Prayer special service in which my cousins, who were home on leave, were partaking in the choir! After that we all went back for dinner after which we came home. They are lovely people, very refined and their home is beautiful. Their mother and my nanny were sisters, so you can imagine how Scotch they were.

8th September 1944

In your last letter you mentioned the letter you'd had from me telling you about the soldier of Jimmy's I'd met. Well, darling, all I can say to your idiotic opinion is that you are terribly 'narrow-minded'. I thought that I had got you out of that awful complex; when I met you, you were terribly so but now, however, after being away from me for nearly 4 years, I fear, darling, that you are going back to your old 'family' way. Yes! Just like your mother!

Yes, I agree about your relatives being a quarrelsome lot and inclined to make trouble with one another. I've never had anything to do with them because I've noticed what mischief-makers they are, so I've steered clear, so to speak. I don't think there is one of your relatives I'd be bothered with, only your dad's cousin in Lea. By the way, darling, your cousin Mildred [this is Mildred Sandison (1927-2001)] *sent me her photo this week so I sent her one of mine.*

--- Let's nip back to Father's letters now, I suggested, and see what stirred up Mother's anger yet again.

--- Oh, Lord.

23rd August 1944

At 5.10pm I went into the Sararogha Mess and turned on the wireless. I had settled down to hear a good orchestral concert when it was suddenly interrupted by the wonderful news that 'Paris had fallen'. Oh, darling, that is marvellous news – each little victory is bringing you and me nearer and nearer together.

26th August 1944

Darling I was most amazed at your brazenness and affrontery [sic] in approaching a totally strange soldier who was dressed in the clothes of Jimmy's regiment and asking him if he knew your brother. Gosh, Phyl, I was completely taken aback. I never thought you were capable of such an action. If I had been in that fellow's shoes I would have taken you for a 'street walker' preparing to open the way to tender your goods for 'half a crown' or 'five bob'. Darling, don't do anything like this again.

Fancy Uncle Edgar's decoration being only a pack of lies from Becca. Becca has always been a bit of a fibber. I am afraid I do not like my father's relations – there is nothing genuine in any of them and they are all inclined to be over-loquacious and unintentionally cause family quarrels. I like my mother's relations and I think the absolute world of my mother's sister Dolly [born 1895] *and her children even though they may be rather poor.*

28th August 1944 (Airgraph)

This evening I played the most strenuous game of football of my life. My side was playing against a Battalion side in the Wana Knock-Out Cup Competition. After a very hectic game when the final whistle blew it was nil-nil so we decided to play extra time. One minute from the end your hubby ran right down the wing and scored the winning goal! All the supporters went mad and everybody started shaking me by the hand. Now we are in the semi-final.

31st August 1944

Darling, please don't criticise my English. Please bear in mind that I passed my degree in Structural Engineering and not in English. Darling, why did you suddenly decide to have this outburst? I have never once criticised your English, but while we are on the subject I would like to point out to you that it is about time you learnt how to spell the word 'BELIEVE'. You also say that one should never start a sentence with the words 'So, if, then, and, but, etc' but I think you should try reading a novel more carefully in future! Incidentally you finished your last airmail letter card like this 'So, darling, I will have to close now...'

---*Gosh, we are getting tetchy, aren't we?*

---As usual, Mother said. I was only having fun criticising him, but, **AS USUAL**, he took it as a personal slight.

--- OK, point taken. Let's not dwell on this trivial argument. Carry on.

3rd September 1944

Today is the 5th anniversary of the present war. Gosh when I look back over those years I recall the beautiful times and the sad times which we have jointly enjoyed. Dearest, do you remember Sunday 3rd September 1939 in Keswick – the evening news about the declaration of war – our stroll through the Keswick Square at the end of Main Street and the low chatter of the people as they bought the newspaper. From then nothing happened until I received my calling up papers at the end of April 1940. On 1st May 1940 we became engaged and on the very next day I left Central Station for the A.M.P.C. training camp at Skegness. The parting on 2nd May was terrible. We tried to console each other but it was all in vain.

Then came my move to Bradford and the numerous weekends I was able to take. Sweetheart I don't suppose you will ever forget the weekends of that awful winter – the bombing of Merseyside – our return from Thurstaston to find Liverpool ablaze – our stay in the Birkenhead air-raid shelter. Then came your visit to York for Xmas which resulted in my proposal to get married the following spring. I will never forget 12th April 1941 when you became my wife and after that our honeymoon in dear old Keswick, the place of our first love.

Leaving them blubbing, I got up and went into the garden for a cigarette or two. I reflected that the letters now seemed to yo-yo between extreme emotions: deep love, obviously, contrasting with an increasing irritation with each other. With my admittedly scant experience of human emotions I concluded that this must have had something to do with the approaching end of hostilities and the inevitable reunion. Clearly they weren't the same personas any more: Mother, now a mature young woman, was confidently giving as good as she got; Father, I'm sure, must have found that quite unnerving.

Anyway, after a quick lunch, the sparring continued.

9th September 1944

I am writing this letter from Jandola because I am here for a very special occasion, the farewell party of the Commandant of the South Waziristan Scouts. Colonel Wood is a grand fellow and he has done a lot for the Scouts. Actually I was rather surprised when I received an official invitation. The Scouts have a wonderful reputation and they can be more or less classed with the men of Lawrence of Arabia and Wingate's Chindits. We had a firework display and native dancing. Eventually the night ended up with the officers (including your humble) firing Vernier Light Pistols at floating fire balloons.

22nd September 1944

My darling Phyl,

I am writing this letter solely with the intention of replying fully to your letter dated 8th September in which you question my sanity and then accuse me of narrow-mindedness. Thanks awfully for the compliments.

--- Gosh. Both formal and sarcastic at the same time!

And I repudiate the statement, or the implication, that the so-called narrow-mindedness comes from my mother. Never once have I criticised a single member of your family. [I didn't say anything because it would have felt like stoking the fire, but his less than kind words about Elsie in earlier letters sprung to mind]. *You also seem to think that a period of nearly 4 years away from you in India should make me 'broadminded'. For once you are correct. I have a code of principles I would never break especially having witnessed some of the loose morals exhibited out here.*

Goodnight and God bless, from your 'narrow-minded' hubby.

The atmosphere around the table was becoming icy, to say the least.

24th September 1944

I wrote a long airmail on Friday telling you off. Look upon it seriously – it is definitely not written as a joke. Remember, --- You have been warned

--- Blimey! I interjected.

--- Oh, pooh, was Mother's response.

25th September 1944

A few hours ago you nearly lost your hubby. I was involved in a major road accident two miles outside of Wana on my return from a tour. I was sitting in the front seat next to the driver of my escort bedragga lorry. Suddenly on rounding a bend we came upon a native riding a horse on the wrong side of the road. The driver did the very natural thing and swung to the right across the road, but as he did so a tribal Mahsud lorry travelling in the opposite direction dashed around the corner. Well, darling, the crash was inevitable. We collided and I could see our lorry's engine double up like a concertina. Luckily I got off without a scratch but three of the bedraggas ended up with some nasty cuts.

1st October 1944

I am afraid your last letter has rather upset me. It seems awfully strange to me that a fellow's parents (meaning the parents of a young chap called Basil with whom you used to work at Napier's) should write from St Helens to you asking you to do some typing for the father.

--- Oh no, Father groaned. Here it comes.

How very odd. I just cannot understand such an invitation. Also the offer to keep you for a full weekend in their home. Until I receive some kind of explanation I cannot make myself believe that there is something more in this than I have been told. In your airmail letter card dated 12th Sept. you went to some considerable length to describe a costume which you bought in Southport for £4.10.0. Then you made the following remark, 'You'll love it. You always did like green. This is going to be my 'Victory' suit for when you come home.' You are a hypocrite. {Here I glanced at the two of them: Father, head bent, scrutinising his hands as if he'd only just discovered them; Mother, tearful, looking at him with barely disguised animosity.} You are a hypocrite because in this recent letter you state that since Basil's home is a first class house, specially designed etc etc (how do you know?) you will wear your new costume to look your best on this occasion. I THOUGHT IT WAS TO BE WORN FOR THE FIRST TIME ON MY RETURN. Soon changed your mind, didn't you!!!!!!

Until I get a satisfactory reply to this letter I will only write to you formally once per week.

Yours most sincerely,

Stan

--- I think, I said, that we should leave it there…

--- No! No. You can't leave it hanging until tomorrow. You must hear my side of things.

She said this as if she was using me as her judge and jury. Had they ever discussed this before, together, face to face?

--- Well, if you want. There's a bit of a preamble though.

--- Just get on with it, Father said, no longer interested in his hands.

12th September 1944

On Saturday morning I got up early, about 9am, and caught an early train to Southport in order to buy myself some clothes!! I got a 'Hebe Sports' suit in an emerald green. After I'd finished shopping I went to Southport's new cinema, The Regal, where I saw 'Fanny By Gaslight' which was an excellent thriller. I then got the train home to Bank Hall. Albert Metzler came with the news tonight that Gaumont-British (where he works) has ordered Bunting and Flags to be at hand immediately in the Hippodrome and Troc for fear they shall be needed soon!!

14th September 1944

Elsie wants me to go with her to Church Stretton this weekend. We'll have two full days there.

20th September 1944

I've been back from Church Stretton two days now but I am still unable to settle down here in this dirty foggy city. Unfortunately I sprained my ankle doing a spot of climbing in order to reach a peak where a USA 'Lightning' had crashed, but I didn't make it. However, the ankle is getting along nicely now.

I should have been going to Wigan this weekend to see your mum and dad but I have just written to them to call it off, because today there was a strange letter in the mail for me bearing the St Helens postmark. It was a letter from Basil's parents. Basil, if you remember, darling, was the young boy who I worked with at Napier's. I used to say what a funny boy he was. He is an only child, 18, and has recently been called up in the RAF as a pilot in training. His parents have written to me asking if I would do them an extreme favour by doing some private typing for Basil's father. They have asked me to stay at their home this weekend and to bring my portable typewriter. Anyway, I've decided to go. I think I'll wear my new suit.

21st September 1944

I went up to Elsie's last night to see how she is [she had flu], *but, unfortunately, she was looking very ill. I felt like smacking Dick's face when he got home from work because the moment he got in he wanted to know, 'What's the delay with my dinner?'*

Darling, I wish you could see Liverpool now that the lights are all on. There seems to be more life about the place now. I'm just going to wash my hair tonight. It hasn't been washed for a fortnight. Darling, I'm thinking of bleaching it a little at the front, but I don't want to do it without asking your advice first. Several girls in the office have [had] *theirs done and it looks awfully smart and modern.*

--- That didn't go down well either, Mother added.

24th September 1944

(Written from 17 Cecil Drive, Eccleston, St Helens)

The Blackburns are awfully sweet people. Mr Blackburn is 42 and she is 38. They brought me home to their bungalow last night, had tea, then we went to the pictures in St Helens to see 'Rose Marie.'

Their home, darling, is absolutely first class. I had Basil's bedroom last night and everything was arranged for my comfort. Soon after a sumptuous breakfast (eggs and bacon galore), Mr Blackburn brought my typewriter in and we got started before a nice big fire in the dining room while Mrs B prepared the dinner. Mr B is the Chief Fire Officer for the Trafford Park area, but he has not been content with his position, so he's been writing to posts abroad for a position there. I've just finished typing to Newfoundland and Indianapolis.

We've just finished dinner now, and I've been told to get ready for a 'drive' through the country!! Yes, in a car. Mr B has his own car and is allowed petrol for his work.

We had a letter from Jimmy yesterday and he is in Brussels (or he was!).

26th September 1944

My mother and I have been very busy tonight taking down the Morrison indoor shelter in the sitting-room – it's been there for three and a half years!

27th September 1944

We had a letter from Jimmy today, the first for 10 days. He says he can't write much, nor has he the time, being in the Light Infantry. One sentence has worried my mother: he said, 'Yesterday was a hectic day for me and A VERY LUCKY ONE.' Apparently something happened whereby he was lucky to be alive. I've written to him to clarify what took place.

30th September 1944

We had two letters from Jimmy this morning to say that he is 'somewhere in Holland.' We think he is near Arnhem. He said that he rode through a village in Holland in a Bren Carrier and people were pitching fruit and cigars in to him until he was absolutely covered with the stuff.

2nd October 1944

This afternoon, darling, I got a terrible fright again. I was on our W.C. {in the back yard} when suddenly one of the cockerels dashed in to the lav with me. Not only did it walk in but it flew at me on the seat. I quickly shot up and kicked it, but it only went for me all the more. My mother came dashing out hearing my screams. She said that she'll get my dad to kill it tonight.

Tomorrow, darling, I am having my hair shampooed and set at Bon Marche hairdressing saloon [sic]. As you know I very rarely have my hair touched by anybody but myself but I think it does it good to occasionally have a shampoo by a professional. The Beauty Parlour at Bon Marche is called 'The Rose Room', being decorated in rose pink.

4th October 1944

I can't understand it at all. I have not heard from you for about 8 days.

--- 'And we know why, don't we? I said. I must say, Father, that this Blackburn affair seems very innocuous.

--- Oh you do, do you?

--- I'm just saying.

Yesterday afternoon I had my hair shampooed and set and also 'curly cut.' I couldn't get a tram at Whitechapel so I jumped on one to the Pier Head and joined the No 22 queue there. The rain came down in torrents then and the wind was so strong it blew men's hats right over the Pier and onto the Landing Stage. Yours truly's curly cut, shampoo and set got a bit saturated and sticky through *the salt air and the rain belting down on it so I had to <u>wash</u> it when I got home, fancy after paying 5/6 too!!!!*

11th October 1944

Very many loving thanks for your numerous air letters which arrived here this morning. They were terribly overdue. I can't think where they have been all this time. I've been away again this weekend to Eccleston where I went a couple of weeks ago. They were so grateful for the work I had done that they asked me back!

16th October 1944

On Saturday afternoon I was just about to write to you when lo and behold who should arrive here but Mr and Mrs Blackburn. They were desperate for me to type some more letters so for the next 3 hours I tip-tapped away while they went in to town to buy me a 'REWARD' for my work. It was a bouquet of flowers!!!!

18th October 1944

Dear Stanley,

I have just finished typing a short note to you to go by airmail, accompanying two letters which you 'requested' I should send to you <u>FOR PROOF</u> that the Blackburns invited me there for the weekend a few weeks ago. I am glad to be able to send them to you to ease that polluted mind of yours. Apparently you are not satisfied with my word but you want other people's side of it too. However, if you want to find out more about this 'indiscreet weekend' with the Blackburns perhaps you should write to them and hear their story.

In future I will write only once a week and in these letters I will give you only a weather report, but please do not expect anything about my personal life. Even when you come home, I will always hold this against you.

--- Did you? I asked Mother.

--- No. You know me. I exaggerate. But I meant it at the time. I even told my mother.

--- I know. We're just coming to that.

--- This is like a war all of your own, isn't it? I said, leaning back in my chair feeling a pontificating mood coming on. What should we call it? The War of the Letters? The Typewriter War? It's very odd, isn't it? Your only weapons were the written word: you could use sarcasm, anger and wit; you could both get hostile, hurling all those exclamation marks you're so fond of; you could become ultra-formal to remove all emotion; you could threaten; you could call each other names, like 'hypocrite'.....But thrown into this mix is the time element....

--- Who are you talking to? Father interrupted.

--- Myself, probably. The world at large. But let me finish. The extraordinary thing for me is the delay in time between writing and receiving these letters, so the anger and the passion are like time bombs waiting to go off. And – yes! – this is a war enacted from a distance, and this is the first time you've encountered this face-to-face. How do you both feel?

--- This sounds like a television interview.

--- Well, we're different people now, Mother began. I don't think we even spoke about it when he came home.

--- It was the war. I was an idiot. A jealous idiot.

And so we progressed.

I was so upset on reading your letter, that I had to tell my mother and she is certainly going to tell you something in her next letter.

--- Did she?

--- No.

I will write weekly UNTIL YOU CAN FIND TIME TO APOLOGISE TO ME IN A CORRECT MANNER.

Yours truly,

Phyllis.

28th October 1944

I'm writing today, condescendingly, because it happens to be your birthday. I hope you spend it happily and that you are very well. I am very fit.

30th October 1944

No news from you. Probably you are still on your leave. I certainly hope you enjoy yourself on your own. Your cousin Winnie was married Saturday. Grieves me having to write in this manner darling.

--- Ah, you're wilting already, Mother.

6th November 1944

I often think of you, but not as much as I used to, I'm afraid. The 'spark' is gone!!!

--- This rumbles on for another month. I think we'll stop there, and tomorrow we'll see if there's an armistice in your particular war. And we'll read about Father's leave.... on his own.

13

This protracted 'battle of wits' continued the following morning.

4th October 1944

Fancy asking me if I will allow you to bleach the front portion of your hair because the girls in your office do it. I think I shall now ask you if I can drink like a fish....because the other officers in my mess do. I suppose you want to do this so it goes well with your new suit <u>when you go to the Blackburns</u>. Honestly, Phyl, I am absolutely ashamed of you. When I return my affection will not be the same.

In a few days I am going on leave – the C.R.E. has at last decided to let me leave Wana for a few days.

9th October 1944

I am going away on leave tomorrow to a faraway place called Katrain at the head of the famous Kulu valley in the Himalayas. I am going with the sole intention of trekking over the gigantic Rothang Pass which is 13,500 ft high. Dear old Chips will go with me as far as Katrain but I don't think I shall take him further as I may have to climb through snow.

The other evening I saw a wonderful film called 'Casablanca', one of the best films I have ever seen.

15th October 1944

(Written from Tysonia Hotel, Katrain)

--- Your threatened formality didn't last long, did it? I asked.

--- No. Well, I was going on a unique journey and I didn't want to spoil the account with petty blandness.

--- Good for you!

I started my very long journey to Katrain on the 11th. I crossed the River Indus to Darya Khan where I got the train to Lahore and arrived there at 9.30am. As my other train was not until 6.35pm I had plenty of time to do some shopping and look around Lahore properly. I made a mental note of some presents I would buy for you on the way back. The train left at 7.35pm, one hour late. At 1.30am it reached a place called Pathan Kote where I got on a narrow gauge railway and reached a tiny place called Nagrota. Then I got a country bus at 8am. The scenery during this bus journey was absolutely wonderful. After spending 7.5 hours on this bus a place called Mandi (the capital of Mandi State) was reached. There I got another bus to Kulu where I stayed the night and then travelled on another bus to Katrain. When I arrived at 10.30am the lady of the Tysonia Hotel, Mrs Tyson, was there to meet me which I thought was awfully nice.

All today I have been making elaborate preparations of supplies, pack mules etc to take me on my adventurous expedition tomorrow.

20th October 1944

(Written from Kyelang, British Lahore)

I left civilisation last Monday and went over the Rothang Pass amongst the snow. I reached the top at 12.30am after climbing about 5000ft in 4 hours. The first halting place called Kokar was reached at 5.30pm. Gosh, the last 2 mile climb to the top was simply terrible. I could only go about 100 yards before I had to stop and take five minutes rest.

Breathing at that height was difficult – I think after about twenty breaths I had to take one very deep one like a gasp. The views were breathtaking (!) and I had my camera with me so I took many snaps.

In the Kokar Dak Bungalow I stayed the night and went on up the Chandra River Valley as far as a little village called Sissu. Next day I trekked from Sissu to Kyelang, a walk of 18 miles. Kyelang is a lovely little place on the Bhaga River amongst the gigantic Himalayas. While taking pictures of a Tibetan monastery some girls came around and started laughing. After much chatting I managed to get over their embarrassment and take some photos of them.

24th October 1944

(Written from Manali, Kulu Valley)

I am back again in the Kulu Valley. Manali, darling, is a wonderful place, very like the Lake District from a scenic point of view. It is the most beautiful place in the world but for one thing which it lacks – YOU. The people here seem very happy with their simple life of looking after their crops and attending their cattle and sheep. I spoke to many of them in Urdu.

This morning I went sight-seeing and visited the hot springs. Here water comes out of the hillside boiling hot and contains a large proportion of sulphur. The Hindus have made it a sacred place and have built a temple there and four tanks in which people can bathe.

Darling, if you're wondering, I did not take Chips with me to Kyelang because I thought the climb over the pass and through the snow would be too much for him. I will see him again in two hours' time when I get to Katrain.

26th October 1944

(Written from 'Tysonia Hotel', Katrain, Kulu Valley)

This morning I went for a beautiful walk with Chips along the bank of the River Beas.

---That must have been quite a reunion, seeing Chips again.

---Oh, yes, Father replied, his eyes welling up with tears. He was so pleased to see me. Where I went to was like Shangri-La, you know.

---Sounds it.

31st October 1944

Well once again I am back again in D.I.Khan after my leave. When I was in Lahore yesterday morning I spent quite a lot of time shopping and, believe it or not, darling – hold your breath and don't get excited – I managed to buy for you 3 pairs of pure silk stockings. I also bought a brown suede handbag for Elsie, said to be the latest fashion in America!

5th November 1944

--- Now for more fireworks! I said. Brace yourself, Father, you're in for a bumpy ride.

--- Oh, I know.

When I got back to Wana there were five letters waiting for me containing your reactions to my letter asking for proof of your invitation to the Blackburns. I knew that your first reaction would be to accuse me of having mistrusted you, but your second took me completely by surprise – namely telling your mother, which was understandable, but I cannot see the point of including my people also. In fact, Phyl, I think it is quite childish of you. Also, your sarcasm about my parents praising me all the time is hurtful: my parents are not rich and such a blessing (to have a well-educated son who didn't cost them a penny) was beyond their wildest dreams.

15th November 1944

Regarding this Blackburns business – not for a moment did I think that you had spent the weekend with another man, please never think that. I only thought perhaps your friendship with the RAF chappie in Napier's was a little more than you had told me in your letters.

19th November 1944

I just cannot write any more formal letters to you – it is absolutely against the feelings of one's mind and soul. During the past week I haven't received a single letter from you and this has naturally made me depressed and 'down in the dumps'.

Chips has a lovely nature. At the moment he is fast asleep under my bed with his little woollen jacket neatly wrapped around his body.

25th November 1944

My Dearest Beloved Darling, I am absolutely fed up writing to you in a formal way and I am here and now going to stop.

26th November 1944

Somehow I have reached the end of my patience with this separation and I am becoming very curt and sharp with everybody. In medical language I suppose we would call it 'sexual repression'.

Darling, sometimes I write and say some very nasty things. The Blackburns episode was one of them. For a peculiar reason which I cannot explain I allowed my jealousy to get the better of me. I am very foolish.

--- Well, I said, without actually writing the words 'I am sorry' this seems to be an apology, doesn't it?

--- Yes...oh yes. You see, I think in my isolation Mother's 'punishment' had worked and brought home what an idiot I was. I am sorry, chick.

--- Oh, don't be daft! Mother replied. It was so long ago.

--- Well, anyway, you seemed to have won your war of attrition. Father's letters now get back to normal, thank goodness, but I'm afraid your letters, Mother, continue the pain for quite a bit further....but we'll leave that till next time.

---And there's the 'death' of Chips, too, he added.

14

10th November 1944

I wish I hadn't to write in this strain. It bores me. I long to be able to write as we normally did. Perhaps after you have apologised to me in a correct manner, then I shall go on telling you how much I really love and miss you.

11th November 1944

Jimmy is still in Holland by the way. He has recently spent 48 hours in Antwerp. He was staying in an excellent hotel and met some Dutch people who took him to their home and made him one of the family. When they learnt he was a student of architecture they took him out in their car touring all the famous cathedrals, churches and castles. The lady of the house even cleaned his battledress for him, the first time it had been done since D-Day.

22nd November 1944

We had a letter from Jimmy this morning to say that he had a very close shave, nearly losing his life. He was sheltering in a slit trench in Holland and had been hiding there for the whole of the night when he decided to get up and have a look around. He had only walked about 5 yards when a whistle came overhead. It happened to be a mortar bomb and he quickly threw himself into the nearest slit trench (which he thought was the one he'd vacated) but when the thing had dropped he got up and did some exploring and found that the bomb had dropped where he had just been. There wasn't a fragment of it left!!!

26th November 1944

Yesterday morning, Saturday, Elsie and I met in town and went with my mother to buy her a tweed suit (for which Jimmy sent her a £5 cheque recently). She chose a beautiful tan tweed one. She looks grand in it, very well turned out and 'most out-doorish'. Elsie and I then walked to Exchange Station where we got the train to Southport. It teemed with rain all the time we were out. It was noon when we got there, so we went straight into Marshall & Snelgrove and had a beautiful dinner. We had fowl!!!!! I bought a few things which are very, very scarce in Liverpool. After shopping we had tea in Woodhead's on Lord Street where we had hot buttered crumpets, little open jam tartlets and coffee. We got home at 7pm.

29th November 1944

I felt very miserable all day today so I decided to dress up and go to the Forum alone to see what was on. Gosh! I was certainly glad that I went alright because I really did love the film. Irene Dunne in 'White Cliffs of Dover'. DON'T MISS THIS FILM!!! There is a most wonderful love story attached to it. I cried an awful lot, but almost everyone did.

6th December 1944

We've just had a letter from Jimmy. He says he's still in action and absolutely up to his eyes in mud and snow. Mother and dad are as thrilled as anything over the news that the D-Day men are getting 7 days' leave shortly after New Year. It's being drawn by ballot, but every man will have been home by March so we are all looking forward to seeing him again.

8th December 1944

We had a letter from Jimmy today saying that he's in hospital in Holland suffering from kidney trouble and enteritis!!! He says it's grand to be between sheets again and pyjamas on instead of sleeping in slip trenches in mud-caked battledress and boots.

11th December 1944

Darling, I hope you remembered to send your dad a birthday card {his birthday was December 9th}. Your mother was saying the last time I was there that, all the three and a half years you have been abroad, you have not remembered either of their birthdays. This is rather awful of you, darling.

15th December 1944

I am glad you got Mrs Blackburn's letters. I don't feel a bit inclined, nor am I in favour of answering the questions you ask. The fact is I absolutely resent being 'cross-examined' like that, darling. You think you are being funny by asking me all these damn silly questions, yet if you could only see Basil, the child he is, you'd laugh at the fool you're making of yourself. I am warning you that if there is no apology here by, say, January 15th, I will cease all correspondence with you.

--- Your final warning, Father. Did you actually apologise?

--- Wait and see [a favourite saying of his].

--- So, I continued, with this ultimatum hanging over you, both wars are approaching their endgame.

--- I suppose so.

I was about to go on tour with the cricket club – to Mevagissey in Cornwall – and the next day I was faced with a 666 mile trip, driving all that way in one go. While I was there I received a phone call from Peter, saying that Father had collapsed in the bathroom, that he'd been seen by the doctor and was OK and that it was a 'circulatory' problem. I wasn't to worry. But I did.

15

A week later, when I returned, Father didn't seem to be any different. I asked about the collapse.

--- He's been getting cramp in bed lately, Mother said. On this occasion he'd been trying to walk about the bedroom to ease the pain, he went in to the bathroom to go to the toilet, there was a loud thump and I found him collapsed on the floor.

--- It was nothing, he said. I felt dizzy. The next thing I knew I had my face on the weighing scales.

--- What did the doctor say?

--- He said I had to have more exercise.

--- And?

--- Well, Hugh {an old friend from Rotary} has agreed to pick me up each morning at 10 and we both hirple around the cricket ground every day.

--- Has it helped?

--- Oh, yes, I think so. How was the tour?

I gave them both a brief resume, dwelling on the superb glass-like, clay wickets, the cream teas, the friendliness of our Cornish opposition, omitting to mention the drunken high-jinks, the fights, the attempted suicide of our hostess on our last day....

--- Right, I said finally, let's get rid of 1944.

Once again I am food Secretary of our Mess. While I was away on tour last week the other members had a Mess Meeting and they decided to elect me as the best connoisseur the Mess has had for a long time! Chips and I are great pals. He has grown into a marvellous dog. Last night he suddenly woke me barking at the top of his voice. The time was 1.30am. I put on the light and called him to my bedside. He just wouldn't stop his terrific barking. I tried to work out what all the fuss was about. Just then I heard the leaves of a tree rustling in my front garden. Old Chips went off the deep end again. Curiosity eventually got the better of me and I put on my dressing gown and went to the door. There standing in the middle of my garden was a huge camel and it was enjoying itself eating my precious rose bushes. I let Chips out and he went for the camel. The old camel went lumbering around my garden. Finally it decided to jump my fence, but it became rather entangled, much to Chips's delight. Eventually it ran away. Chips came back as proud as proud could be over his accomplishment. Every morning he stands on the side of my bed and licks my face.

Once again, I saw my father's eyes filling with tears.

--- He meant a lot to you, didn't he, Chips?

--- Oh, the world. I never realised how much one can love an animal. That's why as a family we've always had dogs.... Brandy and both Utsis. And what was about to happen broke my heart. I never recovered from that, you know.

--- No. I bet.

This was the first time Father had ever expressed such strong emotion in my presence, or Peter's. I decided to bite the bullet.

--- What did Chips mean to you?

--- Oh, gosh. Gosh. I suppose you have to say that....well, he was some kind of substitute for Phyl there. I needed something to love. He provided that.

I filled up. In an emotionless life, dogs had filled my days in the same way, too. Immediately I understood his every thought. What was to come must have been truly appalling. He was **my** father now.

1st December 1944

Today I had a very interesting experience. I flew in a large Dakota Troop Carrying Plane from Wana to Jandola and back. I made this journey with a Squadron Leader from Delhi in order to inspect the Jandola landing ground and the new alignment for it. Somehow I can hardly believe that I have been responsible for the building of the airstrip and runways at Jandola and Wana and also the grand experience of landing on them.

For the last two days we have had His Excellency Sir Claude Auchinleck {1884-1951, Commander-in-Chief, India, from 1943} paying old Wana a visit. This was a very great occasion for us. This afternoon he gave a talk to all the officers and he told us that schemes were now being prepared in Delhi to reduce the period of service down to 3 years for officers. If this comes off I shall be in the very front line to return to you immediately.

3rd December 1944

Your most recent letter contained the two letters written by Mrs Blackburn inviting you to her home in order to do some typing work for her husband. One question I need to ask is why did Basil have your address in his possession?

9th December 1944

Chips is getting a villain. He has now reached his period of adolescence with the result that now he is running after all the lady dogs he can find. In a short time he will grow out of this though. He is an awfully good dog and I like him a lot. I am sure you will love him.

--- What a shame you never got to meet him, Phyl.

10th December 1944

(Written from Sararogha Scout Post)

Today (Sunday) has been a very strenuous one for me. From 10am until 2pm I walked over the work for my new road. Of course the road isn't built yet so I had to climb over boulders and all sorts of things. Now that the road is beginning to take shape it is beginning to look something of an achievement.

20th December 1944

I am looking forward to having Xmas in my Mess this year, especially when all the food arrangements are in my hands. At the moment I am rather anxious because so far I haven't been able to get any Xmas puddings. Today one of my lorries went up into the mountains and brought back 6 Xmas trees for me.

24th December 1944

At last things are beginning to move for the forgotten British Service personnel attached to the Indian army. People at home are suddenly realising that we exist out here in a country which is unsuitable for Europeans. Also and above that the Indian people I feel definitely do not want us.

26th December 1944

So Xmas is passed for 1944. Last night we had a good party in our mess. We played the usual parlour games and tried out various tricks on the Brigade Sergeants who came to our mess after dinner. For dinner we had Roast Turkey, Sausage, Xmas Pudding and brandy sauce.

28th December 1944

My father seemed to be delighted by the present you bought him for his birthday. I know it is an awful thing to admit but I always forget my parents' birthdays. It isn't as if I don't think of them – that is certainly not the case. But I have never made a point of buying presents for them.

31st December 1944

During the last three days I have had a worry on my shoulders. On Thursday I sent a 15 cwt lorry with a works foreman and an escort of some bedraggas to a road work job on a dangerous road 7 miles from Wana. On Thursday night I received a telephone message to the effect that my lorry had fallen over one of the cliffs and was smashed up. So I decided to send my armed lorry out to bring back the hurt men. At 10.30pm it returned. Inside were lying two bedraggas – one looked as if he was going to die at any moment. A doctor looked at him and said he had two broken ribs and the other a very nasty cut at the bottom of his stomach. Apparently the accident happened like this: when the driver stopped the lorry at the site of the work, he put on his hand brake and got out in order to urinate. The bedraggas on jumping off the back of the lorry started {it} free-wheeling down the slope – unfortunately the two injured men weren't able to get off in time and they went over the cliff with it. Well darling such is life!

--- We're nearly at the end of 1944 now except for Mother's account of *her* Christmas.

18th December 1944

I went to Upholland yesterday where your mother let me read your Air Letter Card (her first one, ever!). They are both terribly thrilled to know of your repatriation in March. We could do nothing else but talk of you coming home and what we'll do!

22nd December 1944

Xmas cards are arriving here every few hours right now being only a few days from Xmas Day. I received a lovely present from the Blackburns. It is a stainless steel saw-edged cheese knife – and a card with it saying 'Just towards that bottom drawer, Phyl.' Tomorrow we go up to Elsie's for the holiday – all of us!!

28th December 1944

This morning I received a letter from your dad saying that your grandfather died on Xmas Eve. [David Wilkinson (1864-1944)] *He was suddenly taken ill and your mother was sent for. She didn't say what he suffered with, only that he died quickly and free from pain.*

We had quite a lovely time at Elsie's. There was quite a crowd of us staying there: Mum, Dad, Fan and me, Auntie Gert and Uncle Fred, Bobby (Elsie's 15 year old office-boy), Marjorie (Elsie's friend) and Elsie and Dick. We all slept too, about 3 or 4 in each bed, but we certainly had some fun alright. We seemed to do nothing but laugh all night long. We did awfully well for food too: hams, turkeys, our own chickens, and pork and lamb.

Jimmy is still in hospital but is able to get up and about now. Well, darling, the Flying Bombs have reached us after all. On Xmas Eve night (6am) we were awakened by the sirens howling away. I shot up out of bed and ran in to Elsie and my mother. Then we heard three of the most terrible thuds and the house rocked on its foundations. The warning lasted for a whole hour. Later we learned that the bombs had reached Chester and Manchester.

--- Well, that was quite a year! I said. And a lot to look forward to: the January 15th deadline, Chips, and the happy reunion.

--- Thank you, Boxwallah, for everything. Your boxes must be nearly empty now.

--- **Your** boxes. I'm just the messenger.

--- Just 3 months to go.

--- I don't honestly know how we'll spend our days once you finish.

--- You'll soon get back to doing what you did before, the old routine.

1945

1

This year Chips let in my New Year. At 12.30am last night I let him out and he returned in about five minutes which he spent in chasing a jackal around my garden. I hope dear old Chips will make 1945 the greatest of my life. I have not long returned from our local cinema where I saw the film 'Now, Voyager' with Bette Davis and Paul Henreid. It was a wonderful story, full of real love and pathos, more than I have ever seen in a film before.

4th January 1945

Your last letter made me smile, especially over the way you replied to the cross-examination I gave you over your Blackburns. In the third paragraph you said, 'I don't feel a bit inclined nor am in favour of answering the questions you asked.' Then in the fourth paragraph you answered all my questions. Why did you suddenly change your mind? Perhaps you thought better. So you want me to go humbly on my knees and say I am sorry. An Indian, especially a Mohammedan, can do nothing less humble than to take off his turban and place it upon the feet of the man he has hurt. His gesture means 'I am more humble than the dirt under your feet. I place myself at your feet for you to do what you like with – such is the depth of my sorrow that I have offended you.' Darling, if you were here I would take off my hat and place it upon your feet as a sign that I am sorry for what I have done.

--- Well done, Father. Nobly said and nicely put. Personally, I never thought you would apologise. Did *you*, Mother?

--- I had my doubts. But it seemed sincere.

--- Very.

--- To continue the letter....

Well, Phyl, last night we had quite a heavy fall of snow in Wana. It lasted from 5pm last night and continued until daybreak this morning. Chips, who has never seen snow before, went 'crackers'. He rolled in it, rubbed his face in it and even went so far as to eat some of it.

9th January 1945

Poor Chips has met with a bit of an accident. Either he has had a fight with another dog or else some soldiers threw a stone at him. He was rather badly wounded at the top of his right leg. He cannot put his leg on the ground.

11th January 1945

Last night I received a letter from my people telling me about Grandfather's death. This news upset me quite a lot because he was a very good man although I always thought he favoured the children of his second marriage – Becca [b 1903], Hetty [b 1905] and Willie [b 1908] – rather than my father and his two sisters, Susannah [b 1891] and Ann [b 1893].

Well, Phyl, I have been worrying about my child quite a lot... .I mean Chips. Due to his leg wound and a sprained shoulder I have had to take him to the vet every day for treatment. I have since found out that he was in a fight with an Alsatian.

13th January 1945

For the first time Chips had his bandages removed today. Gosh he went wild when he found his leg no longer hurt him when he put his weight on it. He ran round and round, rolled in the snow and almost tried to run up a tree.

--- Right, let's see how Mother's New Year went.

31ˢᵗ December 1944 / 1ˢᵗ January 1945

At the moment the house seems to be overflowing with relatives and friends, so that I came into this sitting-room to obtain a little peace and quiet and I don't care a hang what sort of awful manners they must now think I have. We were all up at Elsie's for the Xmas holidays but they are here tonight, also Auntie Gert and Uncle Fred, Esther and ourselves. The supper has just been completed so I suppose I had better go in and have my share of the chicken which has been reared and killed for the occasion!!!

Well, darling, I am resuming the letter but this time it is now another year!! There was the usual banging on doors when midnight came and my dad going out with salt, bread and a potato, then the usual handshaking and kissing and gradual tears. I hate this part of it. Darling, this year is going to be ours.

8ᵗʰ January 1945

Yesterday I was up bright and early for my trip to see your folks at Upholland. They are perfectly well, darling, but I think they are unhappy living there. They are keen to get back to Liverpool, so in the meantime, while waiting for a house, they are looking for an unfurnished flat. When your mother went upstairs your dad made me smile to myself; yet I kept a straight face for his sake. He went on to tell me that, in years to come when they have gone, I must remember that if any of his sisters (Becca or Hetty) want any good deed doing for them, we've to ignore them. They are not worth bothering with. It seems that your dad was mad with them because they didn't invite ME to your grandfather's funeral.

Well, you'll be disappointed to hear that Jimmy is back to Lieutenant again due to being in hospital for 4 weeks. He says he's disappointed but really rank doesn't bother him in the slightest, so long as he gets through well.

10th January 1945

Jimmy has drawn his leave from the ballot for the second week of February. My dad wrote back to him and told him he's going to take some leave from work for then, and will tell his boss that 'his wife is coming home from the ATS'!!! Trust my dad.

11th January 1945

So you've all had orders to hand in your name, etc, for those who have done 3 years 8 months. Well, never mind, darling, yours will be in the next lot, March. Once March comes, I, too, will be excited. I'll be doing such silly things as washing all my undies and getting them all nice and I'll be buying new clothes so that I'll be ready for you when you come.

15th January 1945

--- This was 'Deadline Day', remember. Let's see how Mother reacted to your apology.

I had to smile at some parts of your letters, particularly the paragraph where you 'apologised' for all the Blackburn business. At long last you have 'condescended' to apologise to me. Well, well, well I am certainly flattered that you did finally get round to it. I take it we are now 'good friends' again!!!!!! I hereby swear that your apology is accepted, but it must never occur again!!! If it does, we're through.

--- So ends the storm in a teacup, I said.

--- Well, no, Father interrupted. It was deadly serious at the time and even threatened our whole relationship. I've

355

admitted I was foolish and I think Mother's whole reaction to my idiocy chastened me.

--- You became more humble, maybe, I added.

--- I suppose so.

--- I won the war! Mother cried out.

I continued....

It's snowing here tonight and it's bitterly cold. At night when I go to bed I wear bed socks, pyjamas, night jacket and two bottles, one at my feet and the other at my back.

--- How do you 'wear' a hot water bottle, Mother?

--- You know what I mean.

17th January 1945

Going to work this morning up Heyworth Street, I happened to look towards the docks and I got the biggest shock for some time. As you'll realise it was pitch dark at 7.30am and I was amazed to see a long line of buildings on fire somewhere in the dock region. Crikey it was awful. They blazed fiercely and furiously just like that night when the Custom House blazed. From the tram I could clearly see the girders and 6 or 7 storeys with flames licking out of each space which was once a brick wall between the girders. Against the black sky, the red flames looked absolutely marvellous, just like fire does in a technicolour film. Have just finished listening to the news and it said they were Flour Mills (two of them) storing flour, wheat and corn.

19th January 1945

Jimmy is in Holland back with the fighting again. He says he is up to his eyes in ice and snow. He got a jeep stuck in a field of snow, thinking it was a road, and had to dig it out with his hands and feet and he's now suffering from frostbite.

21st January 1945

I've never seen a storm as bad as this. There is a terrific blizzard and everything is under 2 feet of snow.

--- Were you exaggerating, Phyl?

--- God strike me dead if I was telling a lie. It was awful.

It's been going on like this now for three days. I like to see it – I think it hides a lot of that dirty old bomb damage. We were all supposed to be going up to Auntie Gert's today, but mother was too ill to go (I think it's a touch of the flu) so my dad and I will have to go without her and Fan I think. We tried ordering a taxi but they won't turn out on a Sunday which means poor old Fan will be disappointed – she's been excited for days now and we have still to break it to her that she will have to stay home!!!

25th January 1945

Well, darling, at the moment we are experiencing the coldest winter for 50 years according to the BBC.

--- See, I wasn't telling fibs, Mother burst in.

There's been a foot of frozen snow for over a week now. Every window cannot be seen through because of Jack Frost's patterns!! The snow outside the doors is so hard that it has to be struck with a heavy hammer and then it merely chips off in tiny fragments. Horses are falling over and breaking their legs, so that many in Liverpool have had to be shot. To make things worse, there is a great coal shortage right now but, fortunately, we have enough to last another week, but I pity the poor people I saw today, in throngs queuing up at coal-sheds with bags, just waiting for a bit to be going on with. Potatoes are scarce too. We've had to have 'stew' consisting of meat and bread!!!!

29th January 1945

I can't remember a winter like this. There's no coal to be had. Everybody seems to be burning old chairs, potato peelings, old books and anything they can get their hands on. Our outside WC is frozen, and to tell you how many degrees it is below zero I'll explain how my dad's teeth were frozen in the cup which he soaks them in overnight. He went to get them this morning and they were 'set', so that he had to scald them out!!!! At work we sit typing with our coats and scarves on.

4th February 1945

Well, darling, we are all terribly disappointed. We were expecting Jimmy home yesterday for his leave but we got a letter saying that leave was cancelled and that only one officer could go, and as the other officer has a baby boy whom he has not yet seen, Jimmy gave up his leave for him.....instead, he'll be here in a fortnight.

6th February 1945

[A letter from Auntie Gert and Uncle Fred]

We received mail from Freddie a couple of weeks ago. He has been downgraded to B2 and has a staff job. He simply detests his work (administration officer), being surrounded by books, ledgers, etc which doesn't suit him one bit. I sincerely hope your reunion with Phyl will be very soon.

--- After coffee, Mother, I said, dropping a large hint, after **coffee** we will get back to Father in India.

2

18th January 1945
___

Sweetheart we haven't very long to wait now for each other. My present excitement reminds me quite a lot of the time when I was counting the days towards the approach of our wedding.

23rd January 1945
___

Darling, I think my father was right you should have been invited to my grandfather's funeral as my representative. I know it doesn't matter a 'damn' to you and me but I think my dad was looking at the principle of the affair. Honestly, Phyl, my father's relations are awful people and we shall have absolutely nothing to do with them when we have a home of our own [they didn't!].

31st January 1945
___

Isn't the news marvellous at the moment? The terrific Russian advance is certainly going to bring about a quick German collapse.

4th February 1945
___

Sweetheart, at the moment I am 'lazying' [sic] *in an easy chair in the garden of my bungalow in the lovely warm sun, while Chips is quite close to fast asleep. Oh, what a different man I would be if the whole situation could be transformed to England, and the garden was our garden, and the veranda the veranda of our home.*

15th February 1945

Oh, sweetheart, we haven't very long to wait now. In another month's time my 3 years 8 months will be up. Darling, it will be wonderful to hold you in my arms again and put my lips on the coolness of yours.

18th February 1945

Phyl, I have been thinking about where we should live when I return home for the first two months which will consist of leave. The first month will I hope be spent in Keswick or somewhere in our dear old Lake District. But what about the second month? This afternoon I thought of two likely solutions: (a) live with Elsie Metzler [Mother's friend] *(b) live with Elsie. What are your reactions?* [They ended up living with Elsie and Dick]. *One thing I am set upon is that we <u>must</u> not live with our respective parents.*

I have just had a hectic time washing Chips. Gosh he is funny inside the bath. He remains perfectly stiff like a wooden doll. As soon as he has had a good swill in the warm water he jumps out of the bath and shakes himself. The water just flies everywhere. Immediately after a little rub-down he rushes everywhere rubbing himself on the carpets and mats.

23rd February 1945

I was most delighted to hear the grand news that you had received my parcel, but I recoiled at your remarks over the silk stockings I sent you [Mother had revealed that they were not silk and had a 'Made in England' label]. *I am as wild as wild can be <u>because some damned thief has taken out my stockings and substituted them with English utility ones</u>. I am absolutely livid.*

1st March 1945

I am glad you liked the snaps of Chips – he certainly was most excited over the poor cat up a tree just watching him. The other day he had a most awful fight with a bull terrier which resulted in a slightly ripped ear.

Gosh! I wish I was your brother just for the period he is home and going everywhere with you. So Elsie liked her handbag and your dad his tobacco – everybody pleased except you, the most important person of all.

In order to make the time go quicker I am contemplating going on ten days leave next month with the intention of going to Peshawar and up the Khyber Pass.

---'Let's switch now and hear about Jimmy's leave.

6th February 1945

Jimmy wrote today saying that he will be home in 10 days' time, on the 15th or 16th February. Mother has gone to the Royal Court to see the pantomime with her friend, using the two tickets for her and Jimmy. OH I'M FED UP – it's too cold to go out and it's too cold to stay in!

8th February 1945

Elsie was here last night for tea. She brought me my belated Xmas-cum-Birthday present combined in the form of a green Hungarian peasant-style skirt, most suitable for the Lake District, darling.

16th February 1945

On Wednesday I went to Upholland to see your mother and dad, but I was terribly sick on the bus from Ormskirk to Upholland. In fact, I felt so awful that I had to get off half way and walk the remainder of the distance. I had to go down a country lane to be sick. When I got to your mother's I was green. Dad is pleased with his tobacco, darling, and Elsie simply shouted with joy when she saw her bag.

19th February 1945

Well, as you know, we were expecting Jimmy last Friday on 7 days 'Blighty Leave'. We all sat in all over the weekend waiting, waiting and waiting for him, all dressed up in our Sunday best and quite excited. My mother invited all the family for a 'reunion party' on Sunday (yesterday), but we were still without news of him, so there was no way of letting them know on Sunday that they were not to come as Jimmy hadn't turned up.

However, at 3 o'clock yesterday afternoon the first of the guests started to arrive till the house was almost to over-crowded point. We sat round the table and had a lovely supper which my mother had prepared for some months now. I hadn't seen such a 'spread' for years in fact. Elsie had a beautiful cake made and iced with his nickname {Dinty} on the top and we were all just about to start on the feast when a Priority Telegram arrived. My Uncle Fred opened it and it was to say that Jimmy would arrive home at 2am so we had only 3 hours to wait. So we covered up the food and sat around the fire and waited. Then we heard the taxi arrive at the door and you'll imagine how surprised Jimmy was to see every one of us still there at that hour of the morning. When he saw the food his eyes nearly popped out. Nobody went to work this morning because it was 5 or 6 when we finally got to bed and stopped talking.

He's come right from Germany itself and he looks a lot older. He brought home a German pistol and all sorts of souvenirs. He won't tell us anything about the fighting or where he is. At the moment he's got the wireless to pieces – I can't think why because there was nothing wrong with it – but it's just what we knew he'd do. He wants to go to the pictures in town tonight. He made us laugh last night telling us one tale which occurred in Antwerp when they first got there: there was hardly any food so a few of the men from the platoon went along the road where they knew a few pigs were handy in a nearby farm. One soldier was a butcher before the war, so he did his job well and they were just about to carry it off quickly and quietly when they heard some people coming, civilians. They were scared of being caught out so the first thing they spotted was a stretcher with a blanket on it, so they put the pig on the stretcher and completely covered it with the blanket and marched away quite mournfully. When the civilians saw the stretcher-bearers with their 'charge' they took off their caps and crossed themselves while some children even came up to the 'corpse' and threw wild flowers on top of the blanket. Eventually when the men reached a trench and their camp, they did the necessary and pork chops were had by all for tea!!

Jimmy has come from that 'something' Forest on the inside of Germany. I forget the name but there's been big infantry fighting there recently and it's still going on, then before that he was in that something-or-other Bosch. He smokes an awful lot of cigarettes, one after another, but fortunately he doesn't drink.

--- That must have been a fantastic reunion, Mother.

--- Oh, it was. But I was a bit taken aback by how Jimmy looked. He was a boy when he left for the war but now he was a man, a rather care-worn one. And the whole reunion thing took a lot out of Nanny who became quite ill I remember.

--- As we shall see.

22nd February 1945

Jimmy is still enjoying his leave. Yesterday we went to Southport for the day and it was lovely there, a warm sun and a blue sky. After lunch we went to a show then came home because Jimmy was going out to dinner at the Officers' Club in the Adelphi with two wounded officers who went across with him on D-Day. Tomorrow,

Jimmy, Elsie and I are going to do some shopping and on Saturday we are spending the day in Chester. Monday afternoon he goes back.

26th February 1945

Mother is ill in bed with Sciatica and I am absolutely run off my feet. She took bad a few nights ago and I had to call a doctor. She isn't allowed out of bed so I have a full-time job just looking after her – apart from shopping, cooking and keeping house for Fan and my dad too. Jimmy went back to his unit this afternoon. My dad took the day off work and we both went and saw him off on the London Paddington train. He definitely didn't want to go back, and during the past couple of days he grew quieter and quieter.

28th February 1945

At last you have mentioned where we intend to live once you come home. I have asked you dozens of times but only to be ignored!!!! Your 'only alternative' doesn't strike me as being wonderful: to live with Elsie would be ideal because they are both out at work all day and their home is modern and lovely, <u>BUT, I could not live under the same roof as her husband Dick</u>!!! I can't stand him – never could –so that's out eh?

Mother is very ill. She is still in bed and can't move a limb. I had to smile at your description of washing Chips. Darling, what will happen to him when you come home?

--- Well, we're coming to that, I said. Mother, can you believe that there are only about 10 letters of yours left? The marathon is nearly over.

--- We've had Jimmy's reunion, soon it will be ours.

And the look in her eyes made me believe that she was almost experiencing the very same anticipation as she did fifty-odd years earlier.

--- Ironically, I added, Father is about to undergo a separation, aren't you?

--- I'm afraid so. The moment I'm dreading.

3

11th March 1945

Darling, I am very upset to hear about your mother's illness. Sciatica must be really awful. I do hope and trust she fully recovers by the time this letter reaches your hand. Like all mothers I suppose she got all keyed up and excited over Jimmy's leave and then the reaction set in.

13th March 1945

At the moment I am on tour. I left Wana last Monday and stayed the night at Jandola. As soon as I returned here for lunch I was told the most wonderful news imaginable. Oh, Phyl, I have never felt so wonderfully happy in all my life. In fact it is so marvellous I haven't recovered from the shock yet. One of my officer friends, immediately he set eyes on me in the mess, shook me by the hand. Naturally I cannot tell you what it is all about until I hear officially from my colonel and through my own department. But I have been assured by at least six people that the news is perfectly true. Can you guess what it is? Well, I can only say that it is what <u>we</u> have dreamed about for so long!!!

17th March 1945

This morning I sent you a cable giving you the wonderful news. My fellow officers said that they have never seen me look so happy.

--- Unfortunately, nobody seems to have kept this telegram, I interrupted. Can you remember what it said?

'Gosh, I can't exactly. Something like CEASE ALL CORRESPONDENCE. HOME IN APRIL.

20th March 1945

I have offered Chips to the people from whom I originally got him. Some time ago I heard that Major Sparrow's dog Moses (the brother of Chips) had been put down due to Rabies and his wife's dog (the mother of Chips) had died of old age. Mrs Sparrow loves Airedales and the loss of Moses and Belinda was a bitter blow for her. So I know if he goes to her he will receive a wonderful home.

23rd March 1945

I feel very annoyed at the moment because the Wana Postmaster told me that a telegram which I sent to you on 17th March has been returned from Liverpool with the remarks that the address is unknown, so I told him to send it again.

--- Oh, right, I said. I've got it here. It says: CEASE ALL CORRESPONDENCE MAKE KESWICK ARRANGEMENTS.

--- You know, I'd forgotten all about that.

--- Me, too, Mother added.

Today I received a reply from Major Sparrow to say that he will be most delighted to take Chips. This is a wonderful piece of news because now I know that dear old Chips will get a really good home. At the moment he is barking his head off at a crow which is sitting on my roof. I am going to miss him terribly.

At this point my father uttered a kind of stifled sobbing noise and I could see that this business with Chips was very difficult for him.

--- Father, I know that this is going to be quite a strain for you. Do you want me to go on?

--- Yes, yes. Don't worry. I'll face it again.

--- Happy for me to carry on then?

--- Go ahead.

25th March 1945

Darling, I think it is very silly for my people and also yours to arrange a reunion party or anything of that nature. Do try your best to put them off such a scheme because it is really not warranted.

27th March 1945

I am taking the opportunity to let you know that I have received my orders for Repatriation and that I am expected to sail sometime in April with the probability of arriving in England about the end of May.

29th March 1945

Today my relief arrived. Chips is leaving me on Saturday much to my sorrow. Just because I am going to part with him I naturally appear to love him more and more. Gosh I wish I could take him with me.

Last night I received a wonderful letter from the Political Agent thanking me for all I had done. This is what he said:

--- My Dear Wilkie,

I am very sorry indeed to hear we may be losing you at any moment. It is bad news for us. We shall be very lucky indeed to have another Garrison Engineer as good-humoured, cooperative and enthusiastic as you. The Mahsuds and Wazirs will all regret your departure as they all vouchsafe that a fairer and more equable tempered G.E. has never been seen in these parts. Have a safe trip home.

Yours sincerely

Gerald Curtis.'

Don't you think that was lovely?

31st March 1945

As I look from my writing desk across my room I see nothing else but trunks and packing cases. Sweetheart, in this part of the world they would call me a 'boxwallah'. I've certainly collected a lot of baggage since I've been here. Do you know, darling, I am one of those awful people who simply hates parting with a single thing...each article holds some sentimental value. I only wish one of my dearest treasures could have accompanied me....you guess to what I refer.... Chips [muffled sobs in the background]. *He is leaving me on Monday to make a journey to Fort Sandeman in order to become the pet of a friend of mine. Oh, Chips.*

Well, this was too much for all of us, even me, so I left them to console each other while I took a turn around the garden. There I stopped at the grave of Utsi, our last beloved pet, and wept for all the pets we have ever known and loved.

--- One last thing in this letter was complete news to me, I said, once we'd reconvened. And it's this.

Sweetheart, believe it or not just as I am ready to leave I have been promoted to Major, but of course I have had to turn down the appointment.

--- Right, I said. I will finish the letters tomorrow, so brace yourselves for the reunion. Oh, and I've asked Peter to join us if that's OK.

4

When I arrived next day Peter was already there.

--- They've been filling me in with everything that's happened, like the typing controversy, Jimmy's reunion, Chips.

--- That's good, I replied. Let's get started then.

--- Tim, interrupted Father, because it's the last reading, let's break with tradition and sit here in the lounge. It's more comfortable.

--- Fine by me.

Mother and Father were already settled, sitting side by side on the new settee. Unusually, with Peter present, I felt slightly self-conscious, almost as if he was intruding on a private ritual. But that soon wore off.

--- Let's have a glass of wine, Peter said, since this is a special occasion.

Mother, who abhorred wine, suffered a sweet sherry instead.

--- Right. I want to start with Mother's letters first.

--- Off you go then, old chap.

1st March 1945
_____

My mother had a terrible night again last night with the sciatica in her legs. She rolled over in agony, so that I had to call the doctor again. He suggests nothing else but warmth but I told him we had no coal. So he gave me a special Medical Permit for coal. This was indeed a relief. The doctor must have phoned the Coal Merchant and expressed the immediate need, because shortly after he'd gone the van was here with 5 cwt.

--- Poor Nanny, Peter said. Remember when she caught shingles in the 60s and suffered the pain for the rest of her life? Never grumbled once. Remarkable.

3rd March 1945

My mother is still very ill and cannot walk at all, so I have to do everything possible, even washing and dressing Fan. But in her thoughtfulness she gave me £2 and her book of clothing coupons to buy myself some personal gifts 'for looking after her so well.' Isn't she considerate?

7th March 1945

I am still off work looking after my mother, who is lots better by the way. She is downstairs out of bed now but is lying on the settee with her feet up all day long. This afternoon, mother is having a sleep and some kind lady from over the street has been and taken Fan out for a run in her carriage. The King and Queen are here today – not Rockley Street! – and they are visiting Napier's and have paraded through the streets, according to the BBC at one o'clock.

9th March 1945

I'm getting so terribly excited over your homecoming that I am getting more and more domesticated every day. I went into town and bought an assortment of cooking utensils, such as a meat roasting tin, cake tins all of the same 'enamel-ware' called 'Ovenex'. This morning this damned letter arrived from work saying 'unless you resume work by Monday morning, you will be required to be interviewed by the Matron at our head office on Tuesday next without fail.' Honestly, I was so wild that I couldn't help but lose my temper. My mother got such a fright in case I lost my job that, while I was out this morning, she went to the doctor's secretly and got a 'resume work' note for me and told him she was BETTER, which is far from correct. She is still terribly weak but she did this in case I got into trouble. Now I have to go back to work on Monday morning.

17th March 1945

Remember in a previous letter I said I was becoming very domesticated...well, darling, no longer do I look for clothes for myself, but instead I am more interested in bedding and hardware stores!!!! Probably a few months after you get home, I'll be shop-window gazing at baby shops instead!!!!

--- That's me! chuckled Peter. [He was born in May 1946]

This is Saturday night and my dad is listening to the usual Music Hall programme which is on every Saturday. How I loathe it!! I can't concentrate on my typing while that's going on!

20th March 1945

The weather here is absolutely glorious, very sunny and lovely and warm. The air is like wine. You'll be as surprised as we, darling, to know that Beryl, Auntie Gert's ATS daughter, is getting married in 4 days' time. All Auntie Gert knows is that the man is Major Kenneth Hare-Scott R.A.S.C. (Airborne). Somehow I can't imagine Beryl loving anybody but herself. The wedding is in London apparently.

I went to your mother's on Sunday for tea and they are nicely settled now, but your dad is trying to cement the back-kitchen wall. [They had moved to a house nearer Rockley Street, at 13, Westcote Road, Liverpool 4]. *Jimmy is terribly optimistic in his letters, saying that he'll be home again soon because he thinks the war will end within 6 weeks!!!*

23rd March 1945

My own Beloved Darling,

It was with great curiosity and excitement that I read your letter, dated 13th March, in which you gave an account of your happiness over something 'really wonderful, wonderful, wonderful' that had happened. I have read it over 5 times and I'm still uncertain as to just what it can really mean and all last night I lay awake in bed wondering and wondering....and the only thing that came to mind to make you really happy would be repatriation. I can't wait for the next instalment!

25th March 1945

No news today (from you). This is Sunday, so I'll be waiting for tomorrow with bated breath!!! Beryl, my cousin, should have been married yesterday but it has had to be postponed due to the bridegroom-to-be going off suddenly on ops.

--- Of course they did eventually marry, said Peter, and had a son called Simon, our cousin, with whom I played as a boy.

--- And, I added, by a bizarre coincidence, I ended up teaching *his* children. Now, Mother, here is your final letter!

26th March 1945

My Dearest Darling,

I'm taking a risk sending this because I don't know whether or not you are still there. Darling, I've never in all my life been as excited as I have this morning. My whole life seemed to change when I read your marvellous air letter, telling me that we would be in the Lake District 'A MONTH AFTER OUR ANNIVERSARY' [i.e. May]. *Well, surely you must be leaving India <u>now</u> because I'm told the journey takes 6 weeks!!*

Gosh, I'm so excited I can't think how to fill my time; the waiting for you to get here will be really terrible, the suspense will be worse than all these 3+ years!!

Well, darling, I'll close now. This will probably be my last letter.

Bye for now, and all my love, Phyl. xx

--- Wow! Peter said. How moving!

Mother, meanwhile, was having a quiet weep, slumped against Father's shoulder, so, instead of a tactful comfort break, I decided to move straight to Father's final letters to round off the session.

6th April 1945

I was awfully pleased that you had got my telegram giving you the great news. Tonight one part of my staff gave me a most delightful farewell party. The end consisted of speeches and praises for me. I can hardly believe I was so well liked by my staff and the surrounding friendly tribesmen.

Father, garlanded, at his farewell party.

9th April 1945

Officially today I handed over all my duties to my Assistant. Any moment now I am expecting to receive my 'marching orders'. For the last two days my staff have been giving me parties and making all kinds of speeches praising my work, character, etc.

--- These last three letters are simply headed 'At Sea' with no dates. You were on the HMV Winchester Castle, weren't you?

--- That's right.

Letter 1

I am afraid I cannot give you any more information about where I am for obvious reasons. Every second now brings me nearer and nearer to you. I left Wana on 15th April, actually before my final movement orders had arrived. After much thought I decided to get out of Waziristan and make a temporary home at the Colonel's Office in D.I.Khan because hostile trouble was beginning to boil up and I did not want to find myself besieged in Wana. After staying the night in Jandola I reached D.I.Khan the following afternoon. On the 17th my orders arrived. I was to report to a transit camp at a certain place between 19th and 22nd April. Gosh, there was no time to waste, so that same afternoon I charged across the River Indus and caught the afternoon train. Now I am somewhere at sea!!

Letter 2

I am basking in the sun each day with the object of arriving by your side as sun-tanned as possible. The other day I wrote to my people and told them not to prepare a party or anything of that nature. Phyl, I want nothing else than to see my parents, your parents and then to vanish into the blue with you so that we can love and love and love.

Letter 3

This will in all probability be my last letter to you written during my service overseas. I really do not know just how many letters I have written to you since I left your side on 24th July 1941. I wonder if I will see a difference in you or whether you will see a difference in me. How wonderful it is to realise that the German war is over and <u>WE</u> can live normally again without any fear of further separation.

Your most devoted hubby

Stan xxxxx

--- And now there are the final telegrams from Father:

23rd May 1945

ARRIVED WEDNESDAY   EXPECT HOME SHORTLY

24th May 1945

SAFELY ARRIVED GLASGOW 23RD DARLING HOPE REACH YOU SATURDAY

--- And your second honeymoon took place at the Lodore Hotel, Borrowdale.

--- That's right.

As ever with something having come to an end, there was a general shuffling about waiting for someone to speak.

--- Well, Tim, our boxwallah, I expect all the letters are back where they belong: mine in the wooden box, Mother's in the leather case.

--- They are. Back in your attic.

--- Hang on, Peter said. I thought **you** were the boxwallah, Father, you said so in an earlier letter when I was here.

--- Yes, I know. I just thought it *could* have applied to me, too, briefly, with all the trappings I brought back from India. Anyway, Phyl and I thank you from the bottom of our hearts for allowing us to re-live our buried past. It's been fantastic, hasn't it, chick?

--- Oh, yes.

While they got lunch ready, Peter and I meandered into the garden.

--- I've only heard snippets of these letters, he said, but I presume you found out what you were looking for.

--- I did. His jealousy more than anything else. India changed him drastically. You've read *'A Passage to India'*, haven't you?

--- A long time ago.

--- Well, I'm not making a clever literary link here just for the sake of it, but there **is** a connection. When Adela Quested and Mrs Moore enter the Marabar Caves they come face to face with their own inadequacies: Mrs Moore's hold on conventional religion ('Poor little talkative Christianity', I think she called it) is destroyed, while Adela is sort of spiritually raped.

--- Surely you're not connecting them with Father.

--- In a small way, yes. In his isolation I strongly believe he, too, came face to face with weaknesses in his own character and, because of this, emerged a better, humbler person.

--- Except that his animosity towards Jimmy never went away.

--- No. That seemed to be ingrained.

--- Anyway, he said, making a move back to the house, at least you helped to postpone Mother's dementia.

--- Yes, that's something.

--- I wonder what will happen to them now.

5

Three weeks later my father again collapsed in the bathroom. This time there was no recovery. He was rushed to hospital and died ten days later. He was 82.

My mother's descent into dementia then became so rapid that she was hospitalised for nine years until her death in 2013. She was 94.

They had dissolved into time.

ENVOI

I leave you with one final memory. One afternoon in 2003, when my mother was still living at home albeit with the constant help of a carer, Peter and I carried her in a chair into the garden. By then she was a frightened, mystified and confused shadow (a week earlier, for example, I arrived just in time to prevent her immersing the still plugged-in toaster in a bowl of sudsy water 'to give it a wash') but she was at that stage in dementia when there were still a few vestiges of understanding before the darkness filled in.

Anyway, we were sitting there in the pale spring sunshine trying to keep her cheerful by talking about the past, of Father and Nanny and Jimmy and Fan. I had picked a flower, I remember, either a daffodil or a narcissus, and held it in my right hand quite close to her face to see if she would recognise it, when Peter started talking:

--- Mummy, dearest, do you remember when Tim – this funny feller here whom we called 'the boxwallah' – read out all your letters to Father when he was in India in the war? Did you enjoy that?

What followed shocked me inconsolably. With the voracity of an animal – I'll always remember her hands, now transformed into bird-like claws – she grabbed the flower, this frail old woman, and proceeded to eat it, the yellow petals slowly disappearing into her chomping jaws.

To this day I can't get over it. I don't even know why I mention it or what significance it might have, if any. All I know is that it does.